MULTINATIONALS AS FLAGSHIP FIRMS

Regional Business Networks

Multinationals as Flagship Firms

Regional Business Networks

ALAN M. RUGMAN

and

JOSEPH R. D'CRUZ

OXFORD

UNIVERSITY PRESS

OXFORD
UNIVERSITY PRESS

Great Clarendon Street, Oxford OX2 6DP

Oxford University Press is a department of the University of Oxford.
It furthers the University's objective of excellence in research, scholarship,
and education by publishing worldwide in

Oxford New York

Athens Auckland Bangkok Bogotá Buenos Aires Calcutta
Cape Town Chennai Dar es Salaam Delhi Florence Hong Kong Istanbul
Karachi Kuala Lumpur Madrid Melbourne Mexico City Mumbai
Nairobi Paris São Paulo Singapore Taipei Tokyo Toronto Warsaw
with associated companies in Berlin Ibadan

Oxford is a registered trade mark of Oxford University Press
in the UK and in certain other countries

Published in the United States
by Oxford University Press Inc., New York

British Library Cataloguing in Publication Data

Data available

Library of Congress Cataloging in Publication Data
Rugman, Alan M.
Multinationals as flagship firms: regional business networks/Alan M. Rugman and
Joseph R. D'Cruz.
p. cm.
A collection of 11 papers, the majority previously published between 1991–1998 as
articles in books or journals.
Includes bibliographical references and index.
1. International business enterprises—Management. 2. Corporations—Growth.
I. D'Cruz, Joseph R. II. Title.
HD62.4.R844 2000 658'.049—dc21 99–086516
ISBN 0–19–829562–6

1 3 5 7 9 10 8 6 4 2

Typeset in Minion by
Cambrian Typesetters, Frimley, Surrey
Printed in Great Britain
on acid-free paper by
T.J. International Ltd, Padstow, Cornwall

Preface

The international dimension of business networks has remained relatively unexplored, mainly because international business writers focus on multinational enterprises and network writers ignore international issues. Here we attempt to bridge the literature on networks and multinationals by introducing the new concept of the flagship firm. In each business network strategic leadership is provided by the flagship firm, which is defined as a multinational enterprise. It has other partners: key suppliers; key customers; key competitors; and key partners in the non-business infrastructure.

We developed the concept of the flagship firm in the best traditions of 'action-based' research. We were asked by the chief executive officer of Kodak Canada, Mr Ron Morrison, to help put the issue of international competitiveness on to the national policy agenda in Canada. Over the period 1989–1992 we produced three original research reports on the topic of Canadian competitiveness. In the 1992 report we first published the flagship concept. We are indebted to Mr Morrison and Kodak Canada for their support of our independent academic research.

Subsequently we broadened our work to consider applications of the flagship concept to the telecommunications, chemicals, automotive, and electronics sectors, amongst others, and the book reports on both empirical studies of and field research on the international competitiveness of these sectors. We are indebted to many executives in these sectors for their time and their support of our research.

We are also grateful to the Social Sciences and Humanities Research Council of Canada, which funded research over the period 1992–5 with a strategic research grant in the area of management for global competitiveness. For helpful assistance throughout the project we thank Ms Hilary Buttrick of the Rotman School of Management, University of Toronto and Mrs Denise Edwards of Templeton College, Oxford University.

We are very pleased to acknowledge the excellent research assistance of Anne Anderson on Chapter 11 and Michael Gestrin on Chapter 9, in particular their assistance with executive interviews. We recognize Professor Alain Verbeke as co-author of Chapter 4. Professors Neil Hood and Stephen Young provided valuable help and comments on Chapter 10. Professor John Stopford helped with comments on Chapter 5. We have also received numerous helpful comments from other colleagues and referees of the papers on which these chapters are based, as indicated in the notes.

Alan M. Rugman, Oxford
Joseph R. D'Cruz, Toronto

Acknowledgements

Chapter 2   Joseph D'Cruz and Alan M. Rugman, 'Business Networks for International Competitiveness', *Business Quarterly* 56(4) (Spring 1992): 101–7. Reprinted with permission.

Chapter 3   Joseph D'Cruz and Alan M. Rugman, 'Developing International Competitiveness: The Five Partners Model', *Business Quarterly* 58(2) (Winter 1993): 60–72. Reprinted with permission.

Chapter 4   Alan M. Rugman, Alain Verbeke, and Joseph D'Cruz, 'Internalization and de-Internalization: will business networks replace multinationals?', chap. 4 in Gavin Boyd (ed.), *Competitive and Cooperative Macromanagement: The Challenges of Structural Interdependence* (Aldershot and Brookfield: Edward Elgar, 1995): 107–28. Reprinted with permission of Edward Elgar.

Chapter 5   Alan M. Rugman and Joseph D'Cruz, 'Partners Across Borders: The Five Partners Business Network Model', *International Management* 1(1) (Fall 1996): 15–26. Reprinted with permission.

Chapter 6   Alan M. Rugman and Joseph D'Cruz, 'The Theory of the Flagship Firm'. Reprinted from *European Management Journal* 15(4) (August 1997): 403–12, with permission from Elsevier Science.

Chapter 7   Joseph D'Cruz and Alan M. Rugman, 'Business Network Theory and the Canadian Telecommunications Industry'. Reprinted from *International Business Review* 3 (3) (1994): 275–88, with permission from Elsevier Science.

Chapter 8   Joseph D'Cruz and Alan M. Rugman, 'The Five Partners Model: France Telecom, Alcatel, and the Global Telecommunications Industry'. Reprinted from *European Management Journal* 12(1) (March 1994): 59–66, with permission from Elsevier Science.

Chapter 10   'The Five Partners/Flagship Model and the Scottish Electronics Cluster', pp. 165–84 in Jean-Louis Mucchielli (ed.), *Research in Global Strategic Management Volume 6: Multinational Location Strategy* (Greenwich, Conn.: JAI Press, 1998).

Chapter 12   Part of this in Joseph D'Cruz, 'Business Networks for Global Competitiveness', *Business Quarterly* (1993). Reprinted with permission.

Contents

List of Figures

List of Tables

Abbreviations

AAB	Asea Brown Boveri
ASAB	Avesta Sheffield AB
AutoSTEP	Automotive Standard for the Exchange of Product model data
BCE	Bell Canada Enterprises
CAW	Canadian Auto Workers (union)
CCITT	Comité consultatif international télégraphique et téléphonique
CEO	Chief executive officer
CGE	Compagnie Générale d'Eléctricité
CLOSE	Chrysler Lean Operating Supplier Enterprise (programme)
CNES	Centre National d'Etudes Spatiales
CNET	Centre National d'Etudes des Télécommunications
CRTC	Canadian Radio and Telecommunications Commission
CSGINT	Cadre Supérieur de Gestion de l'Institut National des Télécommunications
CVT	Continuously variable automatic transmission (cars)
DGPT	Direction Générale des Postes et Télécommunications
DGT	Direction Générale des Télécommunications
EC	European Commission
EDI	Electronic data interchange
EGR	Exhaust gas recirculation (cars)
ENSPT	Ecole Nationale Supérieure des Postes et Télécommunications
ENST	Ecole Nationale Supérieure des Télécommunications
ENSTB	Ecole Nationale Supérieure des Télécommunications—Bretagne
ENSPTT	Ecole Nationale Supérieure des Postes, Télécommunications et Télédiffusion
EU	European Union
EVA	Ethylene vinyl acetate
EVAC	Ethylene vinyl acetate chloride
FDI	Foreign direct investment
FMPTS	Federal-Mogul Powertrain Systems
FSA	Firm-specific asset/advantage
FTA	Free Trade Agreement (Canada-USA)
GSM	Groupe Spécial Mobile
IDATE	Institut de l'Audiovisuel et des Télécommunications en Europe
IO	Industrial organization
ITAC	International Trade Advisory Committee
JIT	Just in time
LAN	Local area network
LETI	Laboratoire d'Electronique et de Technologie de l'Informatique
MAI	Multilateral Agreement on Investment

ME	Medium-sized enterprise
MNE	Multinational enterprise
MPTT	Ministère des Postes, Télécommunications et Télédiffusion
NAAMS	North American Automotive Metric Standards
NAFTA	North American Free Trade Agreement
NAM	National account manager
NBI	Non-business infrastructure
OECD	Organisation for Economic Cooperation and Development
OEM	Original equipment manufacturer
PICOS	Purchase input concept optimization system (General Motors)
PNGV	Partnership for next generation vehicle
PTO	Public telecommunications operator
PTS	Professional training system (Ford)
PVAC	Polyethylene vinyl acetate chloride
QC	Quality circle
R&D	Research and development
RONA	Return on net assets
SAGIT	Sectoral Advisory Group on International Trade
SCORE	Supplier cost reduction effort (Chrysler)
SME	Small and medium-sized enterprises
STEP	Standard for the Exchange of Product model data (automotive industry)
TIM	Telecom Italia Mobile
TNC	Transnational corporation
TQM	Total quality management
USCAR	United States Council for Automotive Research

1
Introduction

What this book is about

This book aims to make a contribution to business strategy and international management. The conceptual framework of the flagship/five partners model provides a useful intellectual toolkit to address current managerial issues linking the role of multinational enterprises (MNEs) to issues in business policy and organizational learning. The five partners consist of a flagship firm (usually an MNE), key suppliers, key customers, competitors, and the non-business infrastructure (NBI). This last partner refers to the non-traded service sectors, government, social services, healthcare, cultural industries, and education. The flagship/five partners model serves to integrate much of the new thinking about business networks and the case studies provide insight into the relevance of this approach in North American and European contexts. In addition, we draw comparisons with the Asian experience of similar (but distinctive) business network systems, namely the Japanese vertical *keiretsu*, the Korean *chaebol*, and the Chinese family firms.

Key themes

Business strategy traditionally has focused on rivalry, and business structure on hierarchy. Such thinking is now giving way to the idea that sustainable international competitiveness can best be achieved through co-operative relationships in a business network structure. Long-term collaboration is a promising and increasingly popular mode of international activity.

Over the past forty years, North American and European MNEs have been able to compete effectively in world markets through vertical integration and the exploitation of tightly held resources. In an increasingly borderless world, the traditional approach of the MNE is being challenged. They must now compete against businesses that are co-ordinating and sharing strategies, resources, and competencies in the network structures of the Japanese *keiretsu*, Korean *chaebol*, and Chinese family firms. Traditional western multinationals are responding to the challenge. France Telecom, for example, has organized itself as a business network by partnering with educational institutions, key suppliers, and competitors. But business networks will not make the traditional MNE obsolete.

North American companies are also beginning to realize that long-term competitiveness may not be achieved by going it alone, but rather by competing as a business system. Shorter product-development cycles, rapid technology diffusion, quicker product obsolescence, and the proliferation of quality producers world-wide have forced firms to see that they cannot excel in every aspect of their business system. Those that attempt to do so may succeed in doing nothing well. A more appropriate way of viewing competitive advantage is to discard the market power perspective and adopt one which emphasizes collaboration for mutual advantage. The flagship/five partners model developed in this book does just that. It organizes economic activity through co-operative relationships among five partners in a business network.

These partners are linked together by a common global strategy and purpose. The MNE flagship has the resources and perspective to lead the network and strategically manage its activities. It makes the network competitive by bench-marking network activities and processes to global standards, restructuring the production and service operations to different network partners, and adopting a paradigm of relationship-based co-operation. The partners yield the strategic leadership role to the flagship firm often because it is the network's global strategic purpose that prompted the partners to join. These partners accept the strategic autonomy of the flagship firm, but also assume leadership and responsibility in the execution of the strategies.

Key suppliers are expected to give near or total exclusivity to the flagship firm. In return, they benefit from increased volume and a greater portion of the value added to the product. The flagship firm and its key suppliers essentially work together to design and implement a significant portion of the configuration of the business system. Similarly, relationships with key customers are marked by collaboration and sharing of information and resources. The past practice of effectively competing with customers for a share of the profits was short-sighted. Competitors can enter into more co-operative relationships with the flagship firm through market-sharing arrangements, joint R&D projects, shared training ventures and facilities and supplier development programmes. The non-business infrastructure (NBI) contributes human and technological capital to the business network. The flagship firm provides capital for use by the non-business infrastructure to conduct work in areas deemed mutually beneficial.

Collaboration within the business network allows partners to accelerate organizational learning through access to the resources and expertise of other organizations. The five partners model envisions fostering co-operative relationships among partners as a means of mobilizing each partner's competence in a business system. The long-term competitiveness of the business network and of each firm in the network depends upon mutually beneficial relationships which help each partner become competitive in its chosen activity. Managing in the network demands that managers understand and foster patterns of behaviour and decision making which build trust, relationship stability and longevity, and shared inter-organizational purpose.

The flagship/five partners framework can be contrasted with the dominant strategy paradigm of Michael Porter's 'five forces' model of competitive strategy. Porter developed this in his 1980 book *Competitive Strategy* with its focus on industry-level external economic forces (suppliers, customers, rivalry, substitutes, and new entrants). Our level of analysis is also mainly at industry level but we link to the resource-based view of the firm with our central focus on the behaviour of managerial relationships at firm level, between MNEs, key suppliers, key customers, competitors, and the service sector. We blend industry and firm-level analysis and emphasize the strategic implementation issues of managerial relationships embedded in business networks.

Case studies

The case studies in Part III are designed to provide balance between country/area applications and industry/firm applications. Three major industrial sectors are analysed: the high technology and deregulation issues of the telecommunications sector in Canada and France; the strategic repositioning of the automotive and chemicals sectors in North America after the Canada-USA Free Trade Agreement; and the role of the Scottish electronics sector as an offshore assembly platform for the European Union (EU) with large components of American and Asian foreign direct investment. In these chapters we also make applications of the flagship/five partners model to the service sector, as services dominate the NBI. We have added updates to the case studies published previously, at the end of Chapters 7, 8, and 11.

The case studies are the result of a seven-year process of interactive fieldwork in which the authors, and several key collaborators such as Michael Gestrin and Anne Anderson, have interviewed senior executives, and others, across these sectors. The resulting analysis uses a contribution of intellectual work and conceptual thinking, based upon the practical realities of past, present, and future practices in these sectors. The North American basis for the fieldwork is a special strength of our research, but we demonstrate throughout the text that this flagship framework is also applicable to European and Asian firms. Again, in the end-of-chapter updates we consider some of these wider applications of flagship linkages in Europe and Asia.

These case studies provide a basis for the general interpretations and conclusions of Part IV. Here we draw on our wider work and knowledge of other published articles and books on business networks to assess the significance of the flagship/five partners framework.

Porter's competitive strategy and the flagship model

We will develop a model in this book which demonstrates that the supply chain and business system can operate as an integrated business network. Business competitiveness, in the long run, will be based on competition between business networks in which partners build mutually reinforcing tacit flagship relationships rather than only on price-based, arm's-length relationships.

The five partners flagship model challenges traditional models of competitive strategy, such as Michael Porter's five forces model (Porter 1980), based on arm's-length relationships and bargaining ability based on market power. As such, they emphasize a short-term view with each participant being primarily interested in their own profitability. In today's integrated global economy, however, long-run competitiveness is more a question of entire business systems outperforming each other.

Porter's model of competitive strategy

Perhaps the most influential model of business strategy, and one which is readily applicable in an international context, is that by Michael E. Porter (1980). Porter developed a model of competitive strategy which extends the components of business strategy from a concern with general and environmental factors to a more specific focus on the nature of competition facing a firm.

His model integrates the work of industrial organization theory, where the linkages of structure, conduct, and performance are explored, often in an economic context, with that of business strategy formulation, in which concepts of strategic planning seek to match the internal strength of the company (its firm-specific advantages or capabilities—FSAs) to its external environment. In this approach strategic planning has its roots in the competitive aspects of industrial organization. It fills a gap in the economist's structure–conduct–performance view of the world, in which conduct can be viewed as the economic aspects of a firm's strategy—aspects typically ignored or skimmed over in purely economic analysis but of critical importance in corporate planning.

Porter shows that competition in an industry is influenced by five factors: the rivalry among existing firms, the threat of new entrants, the threat of substitutes, the bargaining power of buyers, and the bargaining power of suppliers. These are illustrated in Figure 1.1.

To some extent, all of these competitive forces reflect structural (environmental) factors facing the firm, and together they determine the attractiveness of the industry and the performance of the firm. However, the firms can influence all of these factors by the appropriate strategy; strategy unlocks the environmental constraints.

Rivalry exists when a competitor sees the opportunity to improve its position. Intense rivalry results from many factors, including numerous or equally balanced competitors, high fixed costs, and high strategic stakes. Since these factors can and do change, companies can attempt to defend or improve their position, for example through strategic moves, such as offering a new service or product development.

The threat of new entrants depends largely on the ability of the industry to erect entry barriers which exclude newcomers. Substitute products can act as a competitive threat by placing a limit on potential returns through price ceilings. Two categories of substitutes deserve the most attention: those that are subject to trends improving their price performance and those that are produced by industries earning high profits.

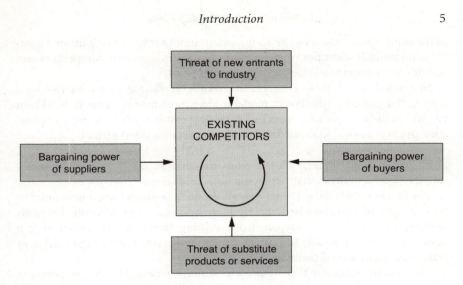

Figure 1.1 Porter's five competitive forces
Source: Adapted from Porter (1980).

Competition can also be influenced by the bargaining power of buyers and suppliers. Purchasers compete by forcing down prices or demanding higher quality or more service. Alternatively, a supplier can use its market power to raise prices or lower quality. Thus a firm's choice of buyer and supplier must be viewed as a major strategic decision. The complexities of this are greater for MNEs, since they often face government purchase and local content requirements, which constrain the strategic choices open to the MNE.

Porter finds that there are several diagnostic components necessary for successful competitive analysis. The firm must be able to define and recognize its future goals, current strategy, assumptions used, and capabilities. Once these elements of competitor analysis are known and understood, there is a platform for the implementation of a global strategy.

Competitor analysis is a process used to develop a profile of the likely strategic changes that a competitor might make in reaction to a firm's strategic moves and general industry conditions. Four components must be examined in competitor analysis: the future goals, current strategy, assumptions, and capabilities of the competitors of an industry.

A knowledge of future goals helps to predict the competitor's response and its degree of satisfaction with its present position. The second component, assumptions, is examined to identify 'blind spots' or biases that affect the way managers in competing firms see their environment. Statements of the competitor's current strategy expose key operating policies in each functional area. Capabilities, the fourth component, determine the competitor's ability to react to strategic moves.

Integration of the four components enables a firm to develop a profile of each of the competitors, which can be an important input for forecasting future industry conditions. It identifies where the firm has advantages over competitors and how it can overcome weaknesses.

In general, all of these concepts are readily applicable in an international context. We can adapt the Porter model to determine how it relates to MNEs. In particular, the international aspect of entry and exit barriers is of great importance and is examined in more detail. These barriers are listed in Table 1.1.

Entry barriers and strategy   Porter finds that *barriers to entry* stem from six sources. Several of these relate to production constraints.

The first barrier is the existence of scale economies which force a newcomer to start up a product line on a large scale if it is to be cost competitive. Potential rivals also experience strong resistance from existing firms, to the extent that a newcomer may not be able to capture a sufficiently large share of the market to realize sufficient scale economies.

The second barrier is that of product differentiation. This forces potential entrants to overcome product loyalties and brand names. It may involve considerable expense, for example in large advertising and R&D expenditures.

Third, there are capital requirements which entail large up-front expenditures to enter a new market.

Switching costs, the fourth barrier, are one-time costs involved in switching from one supplier to another or breaking down the long-term relationship between existing rival firms and their suppliers. Such costs can be reduced if the entrant can find cost or performance improvements over existing suppliers, but this is a difficult task.

Access to distribution channels acts as the fifth barrier. The newcomer must gain acceptance in marketing channels, which can require a large amount of time and effort.

A sixth barrier exists in the form of government regulations. These interact with the other barriers and serve to limit entry into certain industries by imposing requirements such as mandatory licensing to host firms, export quotas, or provisions to purchase from local suppliers.

Table 1.1 Porter's entry and exit barriers

Entry barriers	Exit barriers
Scale economies	Specialized assets—difficult to liquidate
Product differentiation	Fixed costs—difficult to terminate
Capital requirements	Strategic costs
Switching (supplier) costs	Information barriers
Distribution channels	Manager's emotions
Government regulation	Government and social expectations

Source: Adapted from Porter (1980).

In addition, fear of retaliation from existing rivals is a powerful entry barrier. Such a threat is signalled by factors such as the existence of a large powerful firm with a history of retaliation by devices such as price wars or predatory pricing. Whatever their form, these barriers change with time. Their intensity is influenced by the strategy that the firm chooses to follow.

Porter develops three generic strategies that an established firm can follow to protect its market position. These are: cost leadership, involving strict cost control; product differentiation based on brand names; and focus, which is the creation of a 'unique' product or area of sale, that is, the creation of a market niche. There is clearly some degree of interaction amongst these strategies, but each strategy alone, although involving different skills, resources, and risks, provides some degree of protection against the structural environment of the five competitive forces. Of course, there are also risks involved in these strategies. For example, a cost-leadership approach can be undercut by a newcomer with low-cost learning. Similarly, product differentiation narrows differences in product lines and leads to the risk of imitation. Finally, competitors may be able to hit upon submarkets in the chosen niche, thus destroying the focus of the MNE.

The extent to which international competition can erode profitability depends on several factors, some on the demand side and some on the supply side. There are several major reasons for demand-side erosions of profitability, stemming from demographic changes, changes in tastes, or changes in consumer incomes. On the supply side there may be technological substitution and other changes affecting performance. From this it is clear that it is vitally important for the MNE to develop a planning system which allows it to assess and respond to changes in information affecting its FSAs and strategy.

Exit barriers and strategy   Despite the existence of falling profits, there are important factors which keep firms producing in an industry. These are termed *exit barriers* and result from six sources.

The first one is the presence of specialized assets, especially for large, capital-intensive firms in the steel, heavy engineering, or mineral resource industries. These are difficult to place elsewhere and lower the liquidation value of a plant or business.

A second factor reducing liquidation value is the fixed costs associated with slowing down and stopping production. These include labour settlements and payments for pension funds and are complicated by low employee productivity.

Third, strategic exit barriers may inhibit the firm from divesting, as the unprofitable business may still be important to the success of the overall company. Exiting may hurt the company's image and endanger its access to capital markets.

Fourth, information barriers can make it difficult for management to obtain accurate data to assess performance and exercise the judgement to exit.

The fifth exit barrier is somewhat more intangible. It is the reluctance of management to leave a business, as a result of subjective emotions and pride, the fear of having 'nowhere to go', and the personal identification of managers with certain projects.

Finally, governments and society often impose exit barriers, for reasons such as the wish to minimize the adverse employment effects of a plant closing down.

Given these structural barriers, Porter finds that there are four strategies that can be followed when an industry is in decline. The first one is a leadership strategy which involves taking advantage of a declining industry to earn high profits. Second, a niche can be developed by identifying a segment of a declining industry that will maintain stable demand and profits. Harvesting is the third strategy. It involves the optimization of cash flows by such tactics as reducing the number of distribution channels used. Finally, there is always the option of quick divestment by selling early, when uncertainty about the future is greatest. The choice of any strategy depends ultimately on the capabilities of the firm in its environment.

The flagship model

Porter's strategy model argues that positioning the firm to maximize its own bargaining power and to minimize that of others is a critical element to competitive success. We argue that this is too simplistic in today's global business environment.

In order to develop our flagship model we studied existing successful forms of networked organizations such as the Japanese vertical *keiretsu* (not to be confused with the horizontal *keiretsu*), including those associated with Sony, Matsushita, and Toyota, as well as overseas Chinese family firms and the Korean *chaebol*. The key to such organizations' success is their adoption of strategies that are mutually reinforcing within a business system. These foster a collective long-term outlook between the partners, rather than the corporate individualism found in traditional models. We based the five partners/flagship model on this alternative concept.

The key players in the five partners model   The rationale underpinning our model is that the parties will calculate the costs and benefits they expect across an indefinite stream of transactions rather than on one transaction at a time. This encourages the sharing of market intelligence and intellectual property without recourse to formal contracts to protect the self-interest of each party.

As Figure 1.2 shows, the business system consists of a 'flagship' firm that provides leadership to a vertically integrated chain of businesses with which it has established key relationships. This business system competes as a whole with others to serve the same end markets. The relationships are shown by arrows that demonstrate the interfirm co-operation. Double-headed arrows which cross organizational boundaries show the key partners in the business system; arrows which stop at organisational boundaries demonstrate traditional arm's-length relationships. The role of each of the five partners is described below.

The flagship firm   The MNE or flagship firm lies at the hub of the five partners model. The flagship has the vision and resources to lead the network in a successful

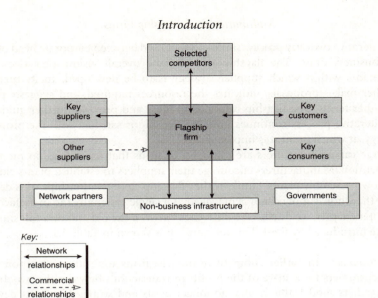

Figure 1.2 The flagship model

global strategy. It defines the products and markets in which its network partners will operate, selects the courses of action they will use to develop necessary competencies, and largely determines their capital investment programmes.

The key role for the chief executive officer (CEO) and senior team in the flagship firm is to provide strategic leadership. In particular, they need to develop a vision for the network, communicate it to the network partners, ratify strategies, and mobilize resources to implement strategy.

The relationship is asymmetric in that the four other network partners have no reciprocal influence over the flagship's strategy. They must relinquish overall strategic leadership of the network. In return they gain increased sales volumes, access to advanced technology, and participation in the brand image of the flagship.

Key suppliers The network model recognizes that suppliers perform some functions more effectively than the flagship. International benchmarking rather than competitive tendering is used to manage input costs. Key supplier status is accorded to suppliers whose inputs are critical to the development of competitive advantage. These key suppliers (to be distinguished from other suppliers) are selected to enter a close relationship with the flagship firm in which strategies, information, resources, and responsibility for the success of the network are shared. Other suppliers are kept at normal commercial arm's-length relationship. A significant proportion (sometimes all) of the key suppliers' production is dedicated to the flagship firm.

Strategy formulation in the five partners model closely involves key suppliers in an iterative two-way process similar to that used between corporate head offices and business units. The flagship provides the overall vision, objectives, and constraints within which supplier strategy is to be developed. In its turn the supplier makes proposals, indicates the resources required, and suggests prices and other terms. The flagship responds to these and provides further guidance. This iterative process continues until the flagship is satisfied with the proposed strategy, at which point it is implemented.

Large car manufacturers are examples of firms that use a flagship model of competition. Manufacturers encourage their suppliers to establish plants close to their own assembly plants. Similarly they develop close relationships with dealers while the whole supply chain is managed as a single system by the manufacturer. In a later chapter, we discuss the difference between the old and new full supplier service introduced by Ford. This relationship is shown in Table 3.1.

Key customers   In earlier competitive models, firms were in competition with their customers for a share of the profits in transactions between the two. In the five partners model, this rivalry no longer exists and so flagship firms develop relationships with customers that involve the sharing of resources and information. A key customer is committed to the network and follows the guidance of the flagship firm with regard to the products and services it purchases.

The non-business infrastructure   Modern flagships also develop partnerships with universities, trade unions, research institutes, and government bodies to give the network access to intellectual property, human capital, and technology. These institutions are in effect suppliers of intangible inputs to the network and so the flagship will exercise significant influence over the work they carry out (by prescribing areas of research for university partners, for example).

Such collaboration is markedly different from past practice when multinationals usually viewed governments with suspicion and governments took the lead in developing national industrial strategy. Within the flagship framework, flagship firms may assume leadership in a country's industrial strategy development.

As shown in Chapter 8, on France Telecom, the company aimed to develop a telecommunications system using the leading-edge fibre optic and digitalization technologies. It therefore required its suppliers and distributors to develop capabilities in these areas and as a result a network of government-funded telecommunications research centres grew up. Additionally France Telecom directed the country's telecommunications training institutes to change their curricula so that they would provide a work-force with the right skills for the future.

Key competitors   Flagships compete with each other. Under certain circumstances, however, usually where economic risk is greater than could be borne by either party alone, flagships develop limited alliances with direct competitors. The authors cite as an example of such collaboration a market-sharing agreement concluded by Glaxo with several US pharmaceutical companies to share development of the market for over-the-counter drugs. Other forms of collaboration between competitors are joint research, consortia to bid for large projects, and agreements on technical standards for the industry. Under such agreements, the relationship of the flagship with competitors is collaborative but not asymmetric, like its links with its network partners.

Examples of the flagship model

We can use the example of Benetton, the Italian clothing firm, to show how strategy and structure are interdependent. The company has succeeded in textile manufacturing in Europe when most competitors shifted their production operations abroad.

Founded in 1965, Benetton has over 4,000 stores world-wide and operates its business via a co-operative network. Linked to the network are 350–400 subcontractors, who produce almost exclusively for Benetton, and some 80 independent agents. Benetton delivers to a chain of investor-owner shops.

The company subcontracts roughly 95 per cent of its manufacturing, distribution, and sales activities. Raw material purchase, cutting, and dyeing are retained in-house. Benetton also centralizes technical research, production planning, and product development. As Benetton is the largest wool purchaser in the world the company enjoys significant economies in central buying.

As shown in Figure 3.2 of Chapter 3, Benetton provides its subcontractors with production planning, raw materials in exact production quantities, materials requirement planning, quality control, technical assistance, and financial aid for leasing and buying equipment. The subcontractors in exclusive supply relationships enjoy a guaranteed market and high level of capacity utilization.

Benetton also encourages its managers to become involved in the subcontracting system through ownership of subcontractors or directorships in subcontract firms. The company buys equity positions in subcontract firms to retain flexibility and low costs. Hundreds of small subcontracting firms managed by entrepreneur-owners in a low-skill, labour-intensive industry deliver significant cost saving and process improvements that cannot be achieved in a large plant with multiple layers of management.

The company's agents manage the shops system and are encouraged to be shop owners themselves. Agents are allocated an exclusive sales territory and assist the shops in this territory to find investors, train managers, select the garment mix, and control their finances. The agents act as shop owners and investors are linked to the marketplace through interaction with customers in their own shops and the shops in their territories.

The partners in Benetton's network recognize that co-operative relationships facilitate stability and that the long-term perspective reduces the risk of opportunism (such as subcontractors raising prices in tight capacity situations) in the outsourced activities. Benetton is organized to reward co-operation and relationship building and the company's structure has been created to capitalize on the benefits of long-term relationships.

A related example is Marks and Spencer, which introduced its highly innovative and continuously successful relationship with direct suppliers in the 1920s and 1930s. One of the problems facing Marks and Spencer today is that these were not key supplier relationships as they were squeezed by the flagship to reduce costs.

Another example is IKEA, which restructured the traditional Scandinavian furniture value chain in the 1960s by means of two new flagship-type arrangements. The traditional and new business systems are shown in Figure 3.3 of Chapter 3.

In less than fifty years IKEA grew from a small, private, Swedish furniture retailer to a multinational business with 140 stores in 30 countries with annual sales in 1997 of $US6 billion. This internationalization process was remarkable in that IKEA kept to the basic philosophy of its founder, Ingvar Kamprad, throughout its global expansion. Today it remains a private company.

Kamprad was a creative maverick in the furniture business. He redesigned the business system in the furniture industry by introducing knock-down kits that customers could take away from the store and assemble themselves. This saved on delivery and changed the image of the furniture store from the traditional frosty 'showroom' to a more 'fun' place with children's playpens, nurseries, and cafés such as are found in IKEA stores. IKEA built on the fast-growing, informal, suburban culture by providing lots of parking spaces and making a trip to IKEA an entertainment for the family.

This Scandinavian image of relaxed, informal, yet efficient service was extended to Switzerland in 1973, Munich in 1974, to ten more stores across Germany by 1980 and then throughout the rest of Europe, with entry to Britain in 1987. It opened in Australia in 1975 and Canada in 1976. Expansion to the United States started in 1985, through the Canadian IKEA operation. IKEA expanded into Eastern Europe in the early 1990s and into Shanghai, China in 1998.

IKEA also brought innovation to the logistics of furniture production. It set up groups of key suppliers to produce components at low cost. These subcontractors made money by obtaining large-volume orders for standardized components from IKEA.

IKEA kept tight control over product design and quality to maintain the IKEA brand name and distinctive identity of its furniture. IKEA was able to expand rapidly because it did not have to establish its own expensive manufacturing facilities around Europe, but it retained centralized control over its subcontractors.

IKEA's marketing strategy has been to build on the Swedish home-base stereotype of clean and efficient service. Its furniture is well designed, modern, functional, durable, of high quality, and is price competitive. Its image and brand name are well established and it has survived against several imitators. IKEA has moved from its Scandinavian base to being a strong regional player in Europe, and is now competing successfully in the global arena.

IKEA is a successful multinational business because it has introduced a highly differentiated product into a traditional industry and has now built up a globally recognized brand name for high-quality, inexpensive, and attractive furniture. It has combined the generic strategies of differentiation, low cost, and niching and has outsourced both production and delivery components of the value chain.

A final example is The Gap, a US-based clothing flagship, which has developed an effective supply network in Asia, based on three themes: high quality, low cost, and quick response to changes in demand. Its key suppliers in Asia have been required to build facilities and networks that are simultaneously optimized on all three dimensions. In contrast, the networks of many of its competitors, such as the larger department stores, are optimized on only one or two of the three. The network of The Gap is clearly the more competitive.

In more general terms, the flagship model is another way of describing the rapidly growing alternatives that managers face in defining the boundary line of their organizations and the degree of management control they wish to retain. Alliances, joint ventures, outsourcing, partnering are all related issues of organizational boundaries and control, as are ideas of 'value streams' and 'lean enterprises' or 'value constellations'.

Conclusions

In this introductory chapter we have outlined the major focus of this book, on the flagship model and its managerial implications. We have summarized the flagship model and discussed the five partners in the modern business network. We have contrasted the five partners/flagship model with Porter's five forces model. We have also provided a few examples of the existence of flagship-type managerial relationships in some well-known business systems, especially in the retail services sector. In the following chapters of Parts I and II we shall develop the flagship model across increasing levels of depth, and then turn to a discussion in Part III of flagship relationships in the telecommunications, automobile, chemicals, and other sectors.

PART I
The Concept of the Flagship Firm

2

The Flagship Firm and the Five Partners Business Network

Introduction

The business sector must play a leading role in the drive towards competitiveness. Indeed business leaders must provide the leadership that governments cannot in meeting the new challenges of competitiveness. Alterations to government regulations, policies, and fiscal measures are all necessary preconditions for improving a nation's ability to compete, but by themselves these adjustments will be far from sufficient.

This chapter shows how business leaders can actively nurture competitiveness. It covers a neglected area—the development and employment of international business networks. After describing business networks, we will show why they are crucial to the development of competitive advantage in global industries. Next, we will specify the important elements of an effective network, including the role of government as part of the non-business infrastructure. Finally, we will outline strategies for advancing the effectiveness of business networks in a Canadian context.

This chapter is a summary of the new conceptual framework for business networks developed in more detail in our study, *New Compacts for Canadian Competitiveness* (D'Cruz and Rugman 1992*b*). That study contains an updated scorecard on Canada's international competitiveness, extensive discussion of the role of government and other parts of the non-business infrastructure, an action agenda for the leaders of the clusters, and a set of specific recommendations. Here we explain the core framework of the larger study and focus on the role that managers can play in improving Canada's international competitiveness.

What is a 'business network'?

The term business network has entered the vocabulary of competitive strategy, along with terms such as strategic alliance and joint venture. Yet there is considerable confusion about the meaning of these terms. Let us define business networks within the context of strategic clusters.

To put it simply, a strategic cluster is defined as a group of firms within a small geographic region, all of which participate in the same industry or a closely related group of industries. Each cluster includes a flagship firm (or a small number of firms), which plays a dominant role in exports from the cluster, as well as a number of other firms that participate in business dealings with the flagship firms. The flagship firms compete globally, so their strategies and internal organizations need to reach the benchmark of international standards. In *Fast Forward: Improving Canada's International Competitiveness*,[1] we described, in depth, the ten major strategic clusters in Canada.

A business network is the web of strategic relationships that tie the members of a cluster together. It is important to distinguish network linkages from two other relationships: transactions between firms in a market and internal transactions within individual firms. Market transactions cover the buying and selling of goods and services; they are governed by the terms of contracts or by commercial practice and legal requirements. Intrafirm transactions are conducted by means of organizational structures and policies.

Network linkages are achieved through the harmonization of the strategies of the firms within a cluster. In other words, firms within a network agree to align and harmonize their competitive strategies for mutual advantage. Thus, network linkages involve some of the characteristics of both market transactions and intrafirm structures and processes. If this appears perplexing, it is; business networks are difficult, troublesome relationships that require a high level of sophistication on the part of management. Yet, for many types of global competition, business networks are essential for survival.

By networking, firms can make use of resources owned by others. While some of these external resources are tangible and can be bought when needed, others are based on the skills and relationships of the people in the firms concerned, and are therefore hard to acquire through market transactions. The global competition for Canada's key industries has become so demanding and so complex that few Canadian firms possess the resources essential for long-term success. Even the world's largest multinationals are finding that they cannot rely solely on internal resources. For this reason Asea, Sweden's largest electrical products manufacturer, merged with Brown Boveri, one of the largest firms in Switzerland (ABB). Similarly, IBM is forging network links with other multinationals. The leading firms in Canada's major strategic clusters need to forge comparable networks to develop their strategic advantage.

Building an effective network

Canada's flagship firms are now locked in competition with European, Asian, and American multinational enterprises, many of which already use networks to gain competitive advantage. How should a Canadian firm develop similar networks? Responsibility for forging the basic structure of the networks within a strategic

---

[1] Rugman and D'Cruz (1991). The clusters are: (1) The Western Canadian Forest Products Cluster; (2) The Alberta Energy Cluster; (3) The Prairie Farming Cluster; (4) The Eastern Canadian Forest Products Cluster; (5) The Base Metal Mining Cluster; (6) The Southwest Ontario Automotive Cluster; (7) The Southern Ontario Advanced Manufacturing Cluster; (8) The Toronto Financial Services Cluster; (9) The Montreal Aerospace/Advanced Transportation Cluster; (10) The Atlantic Fisheries Cluster.

cluster must lie with the flagship firm. Only it has the necessary influence to effect change. Choices must be made concerning what activities should take place inside the flagship firm and what should be left to network partners. These are key decisions for forging a modern global strategy. Suppliers, customers, competitors, and the NBI must all be included in an effective network. We shall discuss each in full.

Suppliers

The structure of an effective network for suppliers as displayed in normal arm's-length commercial relationship is shown in Figure 2.1 as solid arrows that do not cross organizational boundaries. Network linkages, which involve the development of closer relations, are shown as dotted arrows that go beyond organizational boundaries.

Two apparently contradictory trends have changed supplier relations dramatically. First, many businesses have adopted programmes to decrease the number of suppliers they deal with. Following the example of the Japanese, Ford has dramatically reduced the number of its component suppliers; for a few components, it has adopted a single source policy. Previously, Ford management had feared that single source suppliers would develop substantial market power—and use it to Ford's disadvantage. To overcome such fears, Ford has developed sophisticated means for managing its suppliers. It has recognized that special efforts must be made in order to align the strategies of Ford and its suppliers in a manner that minimizes conflicts of long-term interests.

The second trend has been a general increase in the supplier's share of value added when it becomes a network partner. Whereas suppliers were previously

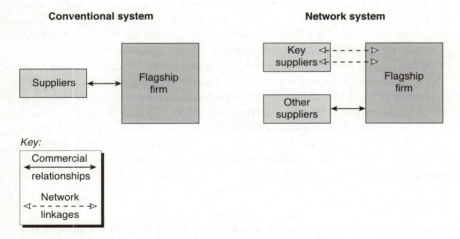

Figure 2.1 Major multinationals are making fundamental changes to their supplier systems

held responsible for only manufacturing and assembly tasks, now network partners are also being asked to develop new materials and components to perform
industrial engineering functions for their customers, and, in some cases, to
assume liability for warranties. However, an increase in the share of value added
in the business system does not necessarily result in increased profits. On the
contrary, profitability (measured by returns on sales) can actually decline because
many of the newer activities are more risky, in large part because they are more
fixed-cost intensive. It is therefore equally in the supplier's interest to participate
actively in the processes of strategic alignment with the flagship firm.

Customers

Forging network linkages with customers involves changing the focus of the relationship from one in which the emphasis is on trying to get the best from individual transactions, to one in which the goal is to optimize the long-term
prosperity of both parties. Canadian firms need to shift from arm's-length relationships toward the dotted arrows, that is, to commit to closer relations.

The new network linkages between business leaders and customers are
depicted in Figure 2.2. Such linkages are changing the shape of distribution
systems, particularly across international borders.

In the conventional structure the flagship firm and its customers maintain an
arm's-length relationship, as shown in the top half of Figure 2.2. With this
approach, there is little direct contact between the firm and the actual consumers
of its products. Instead, the firm deals from a distance with distributors, whom
they regard as their immediate customers. Our view is that these arm's-length linkages should be maintained for many customers, but that new relationships are
required for key customers. In Figure 2.2, a direct link has been developed between
the flagship firm and its most important customers in segments 1 and 2, while
traditional relations were kept up with some distributors to serve the firm's less
important customers. As a third alternative, network linkages could be developed
with key distributors to better serve other customers in segments 2, 3, and *n*.

Achieving the full benefit of networking with customers requires much more
than the improvement of communication channels and procedures; it necessitates
alignment of strategies. This requires the divulgence of sensitive information,
which makes many companies nervous. They fear that the disclosure of their
strategies might allow the customer to develop powerful market advantages.
Certainly, discussing details of the firm's strategies with every customer would not
be sensible. Indeed, the selection of customers to include within the primary
network of the firm is itself a major strategic decision.

Competitors

Network linkages with customers, as described above, are substantially different
from those with competitors. Anything other than arm's-length relationships with
competitors is usually avoided in the United States because of Combines/Antitrust

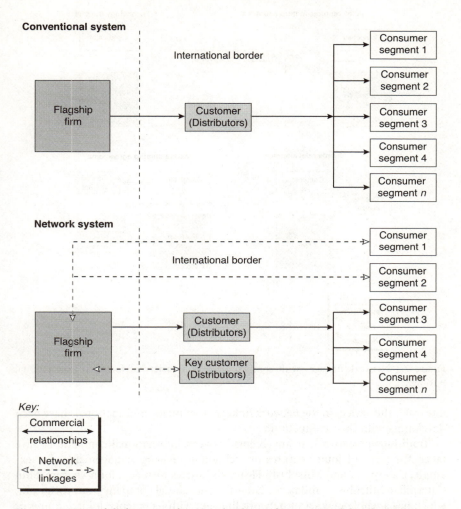

Figure 2.2 Network linkages are changing the shape of international distribution systems

legislation, and, even in Canada, close relations are looked on with suspicion. Recently, Canada's competition policy has been reinterpreted to consider Canada's global competitors, but the law, and its administration, is still in an evolutionary stage, lagging behind global reality.

When it comes to international trade, network linkages between competitors are fairly common. They can take the form of joint ventures in third countries, agreements to market one another's products, technology-sharing arrangements, and combination efforts to develop the capabilities of a supplier base. Figure 2.3

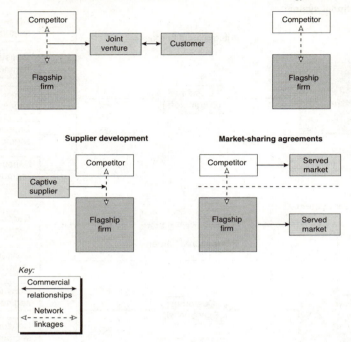

Figure 2.3 Network linkages with competitors take a variety of forms in international business

illustrates the variety in the network linkages that major multinationals have been developing with their competitors.

Traditionally, network arrangements between international competitors have taken the form of joint ventures or technology-sharing arrangements. For example, Caterpillar and Mitsubishi Heavy Industries formed a joint venture, Shin Caterpillar-Mitsubishi. Today, the latter is a substantial company in its own right, which has a whole new set of network linkages with its parents. Joint ventures of this nature have become the preferred entry strategy of western companies going into Japan.

Another common form of traditional network linkage between competitors has been to share technology. For instance, Hymount, a major chemical producer, has licensed its polypropylene technology to competitors in many parts o6
f the world, to the extent that these systems for manufacturing now hold the dominant market share in that field. Similarly, technology licensing has been a successful strategy for Union Carbide in its polyethylene manufacturing process.

The newer forms of network linkages between competitors are more varied and more subtle than the traditional forms. Instead of relying on the establishment of jointly owned but separate business entities or on elaborate structures based on painfully negotiated contractual arrangements, the new ventures achieve integration through the day-to-day interaction of managers from both parties who are working together toward the achievement of mutual goals.

Sometimes these ventures take the form of back-to-back market-sharing arrangements. A Japanese company might agree to sell the products of a European firm in Japan in return for the European firm agreeing to sell Japanese products in Europe. Successfully implementing such arrangements has proved much more difficult than their originators imagined. The deals make sense at the strategic level to those involved in striking the partnerships. However, the sales forces may have little interest in implementing the deal, and can usually find many plausible reasons for dragging their feet, thus scuttling any chance of success.

An interesting variation is Ford's network arrangement with Mazda. In addition to owning a significant minority interest in Mazda (25 per cent), Ford has an umbrella structure for specific joint-venture deals with Mazda. Although each deal is treated as an entity that is separately negotiated and managed, the umbrella arrangement provides an indication of the good faith of both parties and sets out a framework for their negotiations. The initial deal was negotiated at a time when Mazda was in serious financial difficulty, and has survived the changed circumstance of the two firms.

The history of network linkages between multinationals holds an important lesson for multinationals based in Canada. Frequently, the first attempt at such a relationship fails to meet the expectations of the firms involved. The popular business press contains many stories about failures of initial network linkages, all of which seem to feature how disappointed each party is with the other. However, firms that persist in developing second and third network linkages usually find that they can avoid the mistakes they made the first time around; subsequent linkages are more robust. Curiously, linkages that do work are those that tend to rely less on formal mechanisms, such as contracts and joint management structures, and more on informal arrangements based on mutual trust. The truly adept firms apparently come to prefer network linkages to all other forms of international expansion; they certainly use this arrangement more often.

The non-business infrastructure

The role of the non-business sector is also important in improving Canada's international competitiveness. By non-business sector we mean, in particular, the non-traded service sectors which employ well over half of the 70 per cent of Canadians working in services. These include education, health, social services, and cultural industries—which, along with transportation, were the five sectors exempted from the Free Trade Agreement—and government at all levels.

There is a widespread misconception in Canada that because these service sectors do not engage in international trade, they are not pertinent to competitiveness issues. Nothing could be further from the truth. They have a vital role to play because the quality and costs of the services they provide directly influence the ability of the exporting sector to remain internationally competitive.[2] Their performance affects the quality and costs of business firms that compete globally. These non-traded sectors are, in fact, indirect participants in world trade. Effective linkages between business firms and the non-business infrastructure are a critical component of competitiveness. As illustrated in Figure 2.4, similar types of network linkages should be developed between flagship firms and the institutions in the mainly service-based NBI. A few links already exist between flagship firms and non-business organizations such as universities, community colleges, research institutes, and government departments. However, these links must be reformed to surpass the traditional arm's-length connections that are common today.

It should be noted that Figure 2.4 differentiates governments from the other institutions in the infrastructure. This separation was done deliberately to emphasize the differences between the two types of institution. Building links with governments should follow, not precede, the creation of a network structure with the rest of the infrastructure. If governments are brought into the process too

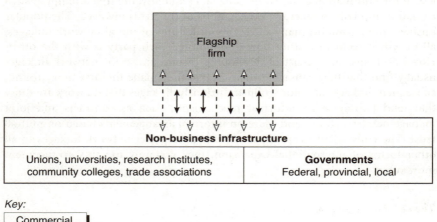

Figure 2.4 Flagship firms must be leaders in developing network linkages with institutions in the non-business infrastructure

---

[2] This point is developed in more detail in Rugman and D'Cruz (1990).

early, their agendas will tend to deflect attention from competitiveness issues. Governments do have a role to play, but they are not likely to be in the vanguard of a drive toward competitiveness.

Most network arrangements with non-business organizations will be of a project nature. For example, a flagship firm may develop a scheme with a community college to provide specialized courses tailored to the particular needs of the firm and the industry. Employees of the flagship firm are encouraged to take these courses as part of the upgrading of their personal skills. Tuition fees may be partly or fully subsidized, and classes may be conducted during work hours and even on company premises. The firm benefits because professional educators tailor the content of their courses to the particular needs of the industry. The community college does not have to advertise or promote the courses so it benefits as well. In return for a guaranteed class size, it can lower the fee per student. Most important, the long-term character of the link encourages both parties to work for the interest of each other.

Network linkages change the frequency, intensity, and honesty of the dialogue between the firm and the non-business institution. As the alliance assumes true strategic dimensions, the institution can begin making adjustments to its programme structure, including capital commitments, with greater confidence. The firm can then consider implementing technological changes that require major improvements in the skills base of the work-force. Obviously, these plans must include workers outside the firm. People who work for the suppliers of the network must also participate in the upgrading of skills.

The role of small business

A final point to note is the role of small firms in the business network strategy. Some small firms will be an integral part of the business networks described above; that is, they are suppliers, customers, or competitors of the flagships firms. Their relationships with the flagship firms are critical both to their own success and to that of the entire cluster. The more managers and workers in these small businesses develop a global perspective, the better. Other small businesses will be in the service sector component of the non-business infrastructure. These are local firms such as doughnut shops, barber's shops, and dry-cleaning establishments that, on the surface, appear to have absolutely no international component to their businesses. However, their costs have an impact on the competitiveness of the clusters, since they are suppliers to these firms.

Another group of small firms to consider consists of those that operate internationally by exporting their products. These businesses are most certainly selling into niches in a foreign market. In the case of such small-business exports, network linkages with the cluster will be just as important as but quite different from the linkages described above. The small business that exports on its own is responsible for gathering all its own export market intelligence, foreign exchange information, customer profiles, and so on. These small businesses can be helped by government officials in federal and provincial trade offices, as well as by experts familiar with foreign markets. They are beneficiaries of the expertise developed by the suppliers of the cluster, and may also benefit from the development of the non-business infrastructure as described next.

In terms of the relative importance of small-business exports, while there are thousands of such exporters their share of Canada's exports is quite small. In contrast, the 50 largest Canadian exporting firms account for over 70 per cent of Canada's exports. This is why our focus on competitiveness has been devoted to the nature of the global competition facing larger firms.

The five partners framework

The final framework for the structure of effective networks across Canada appears in Figure 2.5.

At first glance Figure 2.5 may appear to be rather complex and forbidding. In fact, it is just the aggregate of the four components of the network relationships developed sequentially. While not a simple diagram it does provide a powerful statement about the need for a network to be developed with the flagship firm, in four areas as follows:

(a) suppliers;
(b) customers;

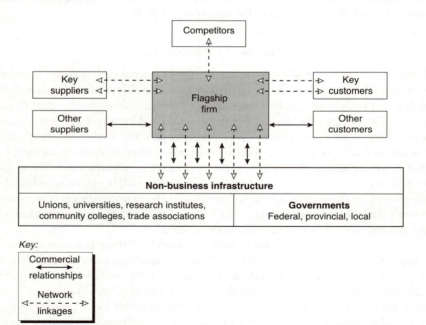

Figure 2.5 The flagship/five partners business network

(c) competitors; and

(d) the non-business infrastructure.

Within Figure 2.5 we demonstrate the traditional arm's-length relationships by solid arrows and the more desirable network linkages by dotted arrows. As explained in earlier discussion of the four components, moving towards network linkages will not be easy, but it is feasible. Canada can and must develop more network linkages in order to compete globally. In the next section we consider how, in practice, Canada's leading clusters can achieve the new relationships demonstrated in Figure 2.5.

Reshaping the flagship firm

The network strategies described above require a radical new vision for the flagship firm itself. It needs to formulate and implement new global strategies in concert with other members of the cluster. To succeed, its own strategy must be first rate, with a constant ability to manage change internally as the external environment becomes ever more challenging. The lesson of history dictates that changes in strategy must be accompanied by appropriate adjustments to organizational structure and process. What has been discussed so far are changes in the external relationships of the flagship firm. Major internal changes will also have to be made in order for the new strategies to work. The flagship firm will be sharing strategy with its partners in the cluster; new thinking is required.

First, adopting network strategies will lead to major changes in the scope of activities conducted within the flagship firm itself. Functions that can be performed more effectively or efficiently by others should be transferred to network partners. Just a few examples will illustrate the types of changes that should take place in this realignment of strategies:

- Shifting labour-intensive tasks to suppliers by integrating them into production components rather than final-assembly operations.
- Eliminating incoming inspection and quality-control procedures by helping suppliers adopt total-quality systems of their own that meet the needs of the flagship firm's quality system.
- Outsourcing all activities peripheral to the core business of the firm. Examples include everything from snow-cleaning to medical services for employees.
- Mobilizing the non-business infrastructure to provide services such as training, research and development, and certification of standards.
- Encouraging key customers to develop strategic alignment with the flagship firm by taking responsibility for some aspects of distribution and sales.

The overall impact of adopting a network approach means that the scope of activities of the flagship firm will shrink over time as the cluster network develops.

A range of activities can be transferred to network partners. The scope of activities conducted within the network firms shrinks as a consequence of the success of the cluster in sharing strategies. What remains will represent the core competences of the flagship firm: strategic management; nurturing of the major technologies from which distinctive competences are based; capital- and knowledge-intensive operations; and maintenance of the network itself.

Second, adopting network strategies will have profound implications for the internal structure and management processes of the flagship firm. The senior managers of the new organization will be required to make four major changes to implement this model. These will need:

(a) to replace the traditional 'command and control' organizational structures that are in place in the majority of Canadian businesses with new structures that are supportive of upgrading and continuous enhancement of all aspects of competitiveness;

(b) to empower front-line workers to take initiatives in the day-to-day aspects of upgrading the competitive capabilities of the firm;

(c) to redesign the role of middle managers in the firm; their antiquated concepts and privileges will be the most difficult hurdle to overcome before the new organizational forms can be implemented; and

(d) to foster the new mindset and attitude toward workers that management must adopt for the new compacts to work.

The role of chief executive officers in creating effective networks

Like most complex business strategies, building a network is best accomplished one step at a time rather than in a few sweeping moves. Thus, rather than invest much effort in an elaborate strategic plan complete with details of the many steps needed to implement an effective network strategy, flagship firms should instead undertake many small initiatives on a variety of fronts, building network linkages with suppliers, customers, and competitors wherever appropriate.

The overall vision of the complete network has to come from the CEO of the flagship firm, as does the initial impetus toward networking as the central element of the firm's strategy. The detailed strategies and specific projects should be developed largely through bottom-up initiatives by members of the senior management team.

Creating an organizational climate within the firm that is supportive of experimentation is crucial for developing networks. This requires a tolerance of the failures of many of the initial efforts and a determination to proceed with networking as a basic objective of the business strategy for the flagship firm despite occasional setbacks. Successful network linkages, no matter now minor, need to be celebrated to provide others with the incentive to experiment.

As the number of small successes increases, a stage will come when the pace of development of the network can be increased substantially. At this point, a number of role models of successful linkages will be available, and the management team will have learned how to build linkages that suit the nature of their firm and the international competitive environment of the industry. But to start the process of change leadership is required. The CEOs of Canada's ten clusters leaders—the flagship firms—must provide this leadership. Today, Canada has no cluster with these fully developed network linkages. It is time to start building them.

3

Corporate Strategy and the Flagship Firm

Introduction

Multinationals with a global scope must forge co-operative relationships with their partners in their business system. In the 1990s, long-run competitiveness in global industries is less a matter of rivalry between firms and more a question of competition between business systems. Thus, what is critical for General Motors is much less its rivalry with Ford and Chrysler and much more its ability to outperform the business systems of Toyota and Nissan, the networks that support Mercedes and Volvo, and the emerging business system that Hyundai is forging. Instead of developing and using market power to gain competitive advantage over them, these firms must learn to collaborate in co-operative relationships aimed at enhancing their mutual competitiveness.

The five partners model

The five partners model is a form of organizing economic activity through co-operative relationships among five partners in a business network (D'Cruz 1993). These partners consist of a leading partner, called the flagship firm, key suppliers, key customers, competitors, and the non-business infrastructure. This last partner encompasses the non-traded service sectors of government, education, health-care, social services, and cultural industries. Figure 3.1 provides a summary of the relationships of an effective business network.

The flagship firm is typically a multinational corporation that has the perspective and resources to lead the network in the crafting and successful execution of a global strategy. It is the flagship firm that provides strategic direction and purpose to the network by orchestrating the relationships among the partners. Specifically, it is the global perspective and scope of the flagship firm that enables it to guide the network to attainment of international competitiveness. The flagship firm leads the network in a co-operative model of relationship-based competitiveness through: benchmarking network activities to global standards; restructuring the production of products and services to different network partners; and adopting a new approach (for Canada) to relationships and competition.

The four partners with the flagship firm yield strategic leadership of the network to the flagship, but assume leadership in the execution and operationalizing of the strategies. Key suppliers differ from other suppliers in that they enter

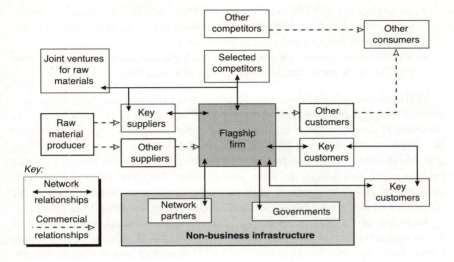

Figure 3.1 The flagship firm and the five partners business system

into a close relationship with the flagship firm, sharing strategies, information, resources, and responsibility for the success of the network. Typically, a significant part of the production of key suppliers is dedicated to the flagship firm; in some cases, this may amount to near or total exclusivity.

Key customers also will develop relationships with the flagship firm that entail close co-operation and sharing of resources and information. As part of its commitment to the network, a key customer follows the guidance of the flagship firm in regard to the product/service it purchases. For example, a key customer's choice of vendors for telecommunications may be shaped by the leadership of a flagship firm. In their choices of markets and segments, key customers are expected similarly to fall into line with the direction set by the flagship.

Flagships compete with flagships

Flagship firms continue to compete with other flagships. The four leading Japanese automakers—Toyota, Nissan, Mazda, and Mitsubishi—compete aggressively with each other for sales and market share. At the same time, where their interests come together, they are equally likely to collaborate. Such collaborative relationships between flagships are becoming increasingly common. Examples of these new relationships include:

- *Market-sharing agreements.* Glaxo has concluded agreements with several US pharmaceutical firms to share development of the market for over-the-counter drugs.

- *Technology transfer and development arrangements.* ICI concluded an agreement with a Japanese competitor to build a plant in Japan to manufacture a replacement for ozone-depleting fluorocarbons.
- *Supplier-development programmes.* The Japanese steel companies work together to develop overseas suppliers of raw materials.

Collaboration in a business network allows competitors to accelerate organizational learning through accessing the expertise and resources of other firms. As multinationals acknowledge the importance of balancing their capabilities within the Triad—North America, Western Europe, and Asia-Pacific—they are finding that collaborative relationships with competitors are the most effective way to make up the deficiencies in their global scope. Network relationships with competitors allow companies to gain such advantages as economies of scale and scope, as well as less tangible aspects associated with interorganizational learning.

Inclusion of the NBI as an explicit partner in the production and trade of goods and services is a vital part of the business network form of organization. Components of this infrastructure such as universities and trade schools are indispensable as providers of human capital and technological resources. Flagship firm can also negotiate with other non-business organizations such as research institutions and government laboratories to provide capital for specific projects or to provide equipment, facilities, and institutional arrangements. The flagship will provide strategic direction and will mobilize capital and other resource requirements (for example physical space, human resources) for the NBI.

The traditional multidivisional multinational enterprise model is not good enough

The five partners network model described above differs substantially from the traditional multidivisional model of the MNE, which was pioneered by Alfred Sloan at General Motors in the 1920s and 1930s. The MNE model was improved and refined over the years, and became predominant in North America during the 1980s. The principal characteristics of Sloan's model included:

(a) substantial vertical integration of the production of goods and services within the MNE;
(b) replacement of market transactions by the internal co-ordination and deployment of resources;
(c) a heavy reliance on central control and ownership;
(d) expansion of the size and role of the corporate head office function; and
(e) development of large bodies of specialized staff in areas such as human resources, training, and information technology.

While the role of the MNE is not decreasing in importance, its traditional organizational approach is becoming increasingly outdated. The Triad economies have become interdependent and integrated as a result of the elimination and dissipation of barriers in communications, transportation, and technology. This borderless world and its new technologies have made global competition an everyday reality, making it difficult for companies to maintain dominance or competitive advantage by relying on barriers to entry to protect them. Many North American firms are discovering that the traditional organizational structure has become a hindrance to the development and maintenance of competitiveness.

The Japanese *keiretsu*, Korean *chaebol*, and overseas Chinese family enterprises in countries such as Indonesia and Taiwan, for example, are network forms of organization which recognize the importance of co-operative and close relationships as a means of developing and maintaining competitive advantage. The principal deficiencies of the traditional multidivisional form as it has evolved in North America are that it is costly, cumbersome when it comes to developing processes to improve product and service quality, and slow in bringing new technology to market.

The Japanese adopted management techniques from the USA such as Total Quality Management (TQM) during the 1960s and perfected them. These, and other Japanese techniques such as Quality Circles (QC), were later adopted in North America during the 1980s, proving that these processes have global applicability and are not culture-bound. Similarly, the organizational approach based on collaboration and sharing is one that can and should be replicated in North America, and particularly in Canada. However, it is insufficient to try and promote these co-operative processes within the regimented constraints of the traditional structures of the MNE.

The new model in action

The following examples, both of European firms, illustrate how structure and strategy are interdependent. In particular, they show how co-operation with network partners is integral to successful strategy implementation; and how restructuring the locus of 'production' in the business system can become the principal means for achieving competitive advantage.

Benetton

Benetton, with over 4,000 stores and several billion dollars in sales, uses a co-operative network-like structure as its way of doing business (see Figure 3.2). Through a network of 350–400 subcontractors who produce almost exclusively for Benetton, and approximately 80 independent agents, Benetton delivers its products to a chain of investor-owner stores.

Benetton subcontracts close to 95 per cent of its manufacturing, distribution, and sales activities, keeping only raw material purchases and cutting and dyeing in-house. These activities are retained in-house to provide a measure of central control. As the largest wool purchaser in the world, the company reaps significant economies in central buying. Cutting and dyeing require expensive and

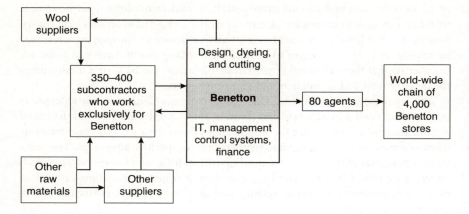

Figure 3.2 The Benetton global network of co-operative relationships

sophisticated technology processes using CAD/CAM and chemicals, respectively. Benetton also centralizes technical research, production planning, and product development.

Benetton provides the following services to its subcontractors: production planning, raw materials in exact production quantities, materials requirement planning, quality control technical assistance, technical documents, and financial aid for leasing and buying equipment. The subcontractors, in exclusive supply relationships to Benetton, enjoy a guaranteed market and a high level of capacity utilization.

Benetton encourages its managers to become involved in the subcontracting system through ownership of subcontractors or directorships in subcontractor firms. The company also buys equity positions in subcontracting firms. This method of organizing subcontracting allows flexibility and low costs. The efforts of hundreds of small subcontracting firms managed by entrepreneur-owners in this low-skill, labour-intensive industry results in significant cost savings and process improvements that cannot be achieved in a large plant with multiple layers of management and the separation of line and staff functions.

The company's agents manage the stores system and, in fact, are encouraged to be store owners themselves. The agents get an exclusive sales territory and assist the stores in their territory in finding investors, training managers, collecting orders, selecting the garment mix, and controlling the financial aspects of the store. The agents, as store owners and investors, are linked to the marketplace through interaction with customers in their own stores and the stores in their territories.

The partners in Benetton's network recognize that trust and co-operation facilitate relationship stability and long-term association. This longevity reduces the risk of opportunism in the outsourced activities in Benetton's business system.

Opportunism, such as subcontractors raising prices in tight capacity situations, is counter-productive because it harms co-operation and reduces trust. Benetton is organized to reward co-operation and relationship building; and the company's structure has been created to capitalize on the benefits of long-term relationships.

IKEA

IKEA has invented a way of doing business in the furniture industry that has literally redesigned the business system (see Figure 3.3). For one thing, IKEA makes the consumer an active partner in the system. The consumer transports the product home and does the final assembly, eliminating two of the most cumbersome aspects of the traditional furniture business. IKEA's stores are a combination of gallery and warehouse. Products are displayed in rooms that are fully furnished, allowing the consumer to visualize how they look in a home setting. Products are stored in flat cartons which the consumer picks up and takes home right away, the ultimate in convenience and speed. IKEA will even hire out automobile roof racks! This form of furniture retailer eliminates many of the costs associated with traditional approaches, allowing lower prices for the consumer.

Other cost savings are found in the supply system. IKEA has developed a global network of low-cost, high-quality suppliers, who work exclusively or largely for IKEA and receive orders for large volumes of standardized components which are designed and engineered by IKEA. In return for co-operating with the IKEA system, suppliers receive technical and engineering support, assistance in securing finances, management training and development, and a host of specialized

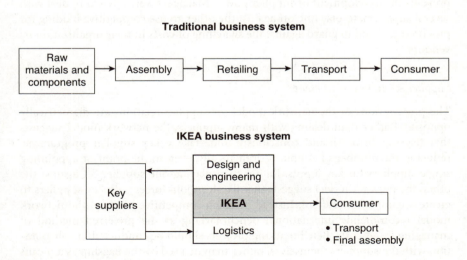

Figure 3.3 The redesigned IKEA business system

services designed to integrate them into the IKEA way of doing business. Suppliers ship components to one of 15 IKEA logistics centres where they are assembled into cardboard cartons complete with instructions for final assembly. The entire IKEA network, from checkout terminals in their stores to these logistics centres and beyond to the suppliers, is linked through a computer system that is one of the most sophisticated in the world.

Managing the flagship firm

The strategic issues for managers in flagship firms are distinctly different from those that face the network partners. It is vitally important that each understands and appreciates the role of the other; it is, of course, equally important that they all play their own role properly. The key role for the CEO and senior executive team of the flagship firm is best described as *industrial statesmanship*. Their concerns are as much for the welfare of the network as a whole as for the flagship itself. This being so, they have to:

- develop a compelling vision for the network;
- communicate that vision to the network partners clearly;
- ratify and provide legitimacy for the strategies that are proposed for the execution of the vision;
- mobilize the deployment of resources for the implementation of strategy.

The distinguishing characteristic of the network form of business is the shift from competitive to co-operative behaviour in dealing with network partners. Take, for example, supplier relations. The traditional multidivisional model encourages managers to structure relations with suppliers in a manner that prevents the development of supplier power. Managers were advised to deal with several suppliers, to play one off against the other, to use competitive bidding for procurement, and to guard against the switching of costs in their organization by vendors.

Supplier relations are different

The prescriptions of the network model for supplier relations are diametrically opposite. Rather than dealing with many suppliers, the network model suggests that flagship firms should consciously undertake a key supplier programme, reducing the number of suppliers dramatically, even to the point of appointing single suppliers for key inputs. Rather than playing one supplier off against the other, the network model suggests that flagships join forces with key suppliers to create a competitive system. Instead of using competitive bidding, the network model recommends international benchmarking as the preferred method of managing input costs. Benchmarking projects should be conducted in collaboration with the suppliers themselves, rather than be used by the flagship as a means of adversarial monitoring of their performance. Finally, rather than avoiding the development of switching costs, the network model encourages them in the recognition that suppliers may frequently be able to perform some functions more effectively than the flagship.

The role of key suppliers in the crafting of strategy for the network is critical, and requires a two-way process not unlike the top-down, bottom-up process between corporate and business units in a large multidivisional corporation. In the top-down process, the flagship provides the supplier with the overall vision for the direction of the network and the supply relationship, the objectives and constraints within which supplier strategy is to be developed, and general guidelines for the strategy-development process. In the bottom-up process, the supplier proposes specific strategies to achieve the objectives, indicates the resources that will be required to execute these strategies, and proposes prices and other terms. The flagship responds to the supplier's proposals, indicating where improvements are necessary and providing further guidance and direction for the refinement of the strategy. This iterative process continues until the flagship is satisfied with the proposed strategy; at that stage, the strategy is ratified and the focus shifts to implementation.

Not every supplier can be treated in this manner; only those suppliers whose inputs are critical to the development of competitive advantage for the network should be accorded status as key suppliers. Others should continue to be treated at arm's length, using conventional supplier-management practices.

Ford's reorganization of its auto parts supply system is a good example of the changes that are taking place as the network form of organization is adopted. Originally, Ford, along with the other North American automakers, kept its suppliers at arm's length, using a competitive bidding system to discipline prices. Ford has now adopted a system whereby it appoints a small group of key suppliers for each major subsystem of an automotive platform. Some of the more significant changes in the system are detailed in Table 3.1.

Collaboration with customers

Equally important changes have to be made in dealing with customers. Under the previous system, the firm, in effect, was in a competitive relationship with its customers for a share of the profits in transactions between the two. This competition showed itself in the prices customers paid for the firm's products and services and in the terms of trade between the two. Wherever customers were able to develop market power, they were likely to use it to exercise downward pressure on prices and impose unfavourable terms of trade on the firm. Consequently, under the old system, firms tended to guard against the development of market power by their customers. For example, firms would keep to themselves information that could be used by customers to enhance their market power.

In the new network form of organization, the flagship firm makes conscious choices about which customers are considered key customers and deals with these in a very different manner than that which it uses for dealing with the rest of its

Table 3.1 Ford's supplier relationships

	Old system	Full service supplier
Design	Done by Ford engineers and handed over to suppliers for execution	Complete design responsibility shifted to suppliers
Tooling	Owned by Ford and loaned to suppliers, who returned it after use	Owned by suppliers
Pricing	Competitive bidding by several suppliers	Negotiated between Ford and the key supplier based on annual cost-reduction targets
Process engineering	Done by Ford engineers at the assembly plants	Key suppliers responsible for developing assembly methods for their components
Raw materials	Purchased in bulk by Ford and assigned to suppliers	Purchased by suppliers, with Ford involvement for some items
Scheduling	Suppliers informed by Ford about changes on an *ad hoc* basis	Suppliers provided with an electronic window into Ford's master scheduling system
Invoicing	Paper system, with careful checking by Ford of every detail	EDI system, with suppliers providing paper details only on an exceptions basis
Warranty	Ford's responsibility	Supplier's responsibility

Source: Authors' interviews.

customers. Central to this relationship is the theme of collaboration with customers—sharing information and analysis of the competitive environment freely, developing joint strategies to enhance the prosperity of the customer while conferring competitive advantage to the firm, and developing a high level of integration of operations between the firm and these key customers. As in relations with key suppliers, the flagship firm will have a leading role in the strategy-development process for the customer in this relationship. Vision and strategic direction will come from the flagship, but this does not preclude the customer from playing an active role in converting that vision to strategies and in the implementation process.

The Signature Service programme of Stentor is a good example of this form of relationship. Stentor is an alliance created by Bell Canada and eight other telecommunications companies. Its aim is to provide seamless telecommunications service throughout Canada. Its Signature Service programme is directed at the

300 largest users of telecommunications in the country. For each customer, a Signature Service team is established which develops a blueprint for the customer, specifying the services that the Stentor partners will provide. In their advanced form, these blueprints enunciate telecommunications strategies for these customers and define service standards the telecommunications companies will maintain in providing them.

They also describe the approaches that will be used to help the customer contain its costs of telecommunications. This is where the long-term collaborative aspects of Signature Service come into focus. Most of the cost-containment strategies for the customer involve some loss of revenue for the telecommunications companies. On the other hand, if the telecommunications companies are unwilling to accept these losses, they risk losing the customer's long-distance business to competitors. Thus, there is a sense of mutual interdependence between Stentor and its key customers. Stentor has to be able to demonstrate that it can provide these customers with a competitive package of telecommunications services, while at the same time the customers have to indicate some loyalty to the Stentor partners.

Corporations, not governments, set national industrial strategy

Finally, the relationship between the flagship firm and governments is quite different. The traditional approach of large multinationals tends to keep governments at arm's length and regard them with suspicion. The phrase, 'the best government is the least government', captures the spirit of this attitude well. Further, governments have attempted to exercise a leadership role in developing national industrial strategy, and have tried to elicit the co-operation of business through a variety of incentive schemes and regulatory measures. In the new network arrangements, these approaches are reversed. Flagship firms tend to seek close co-operative relationships with government; moreover, the flagship firm must assume the leadership role in the industrial-strategy development process. The recent problems that the government of Quebec has encountered in implementing its new industrial strategy would have been avoided had they allowed Quebec's flagship firms to lead the strategy-development process. Instead, many Canadian provincial governments, in their haste to appear to be doing something to address the economic problems that their provinces face, cling to an old-fashioned notion that this is a process that can be led by politicians and bureaucrats.

Re-engineering the flagship firm

At the same time, there are a number of issues about managing the flagship itself that require senior management attention. The transfer of operational responsibilities to network partners should be used to bring about a re-engineering of the flagship firm along the following lines.

Downsizing For Canadian flagships, downsizing is perhaps the most critical aspect of re-engineering themselves. Having developed during the era when size itself was often equated to importance, these firms now find themselves with too many people for the new roles they are assuming. Excessive numbers are particularly problematic in staff and support functions such as public relations, employee benefits, and various co-ordination functions. These functions cannot be effectively downsized merely by across-the-board proportionate reductions in employee numbers. Neither is it useful to reduce numbers without significant changes to workload. Instead, what is needed is a rigorous questioning about what parts of these functions actually need to be done in the new organization and what parts can be eliminated. Naturally, current incumbents cannot be expected to make such judgements objectively. Therefore, flagships will need to employ outside consultants or a special internal task force to re-engineer staff and support functions.

Delayering Associated with downsizing is the elimination of layers of middle management. To manage the complexities of a network style of doing business, new flagships should have no more than two layers of management between the CEO and the front line. Three issues need to be tackled for successful delayering. First, a fundamental change has to be made in the status and authority of persons in the front line of the flagship firm, those in direct contact with network partners. It has to be clear to all that these individuals are regarded as highly skilled professionals, who are able to speak authoritatively about the flagship's strategies and policies, and who are authorized to commit the firm where appropriate and to take initiative without having to refer each situation to senior management for approval. In other words, the front-line personnel have to be treated as managers, not functionaries. Second, delayering provides the flagship with the opportunity to get rid of managers who lack the skills for operating in the new system of doing business in a network. Ironically, many managers whose skill sets were well suited to the old environment will be found to be unsuitable for the new. Thus, past performance in middle management is not a good indicator of suitability for the new organization, and may even be a contra-indication. Finally, delayering has to be accompanied by a radical restructuring of the organization. It is wrong to eliminate some middle management positions and merely shift the workload to the survivors. Instead, the CEO should use delayering as an opportunity for the organization to undertake a substantial rethinking of its structure and working arrangements.

Reducing fixed assets As a consequence of the changes discussed above, flagship firms are likely to find themselves with a surplus of fixed assets, particularly head office space, central laboratories, and training facilities. With the transfer of functions to network partners, there is also likely to be surplus space in production facilities. Apart from the financial benefits of asset disposal, the sale of fixed assets will have an important symbolic value.

Using the five partners model to manage a network partner

The role of a network partner is significantly different to that of the flagship. Consequently, the managerial implications for network partners are also different, for the following reasons:

- Network partners have very limited strategic autonomy. They have to operate within the constraints that the flagship delineates for the network as a whole. For example, network partners have little or no choice when it comes to the product/markets they will serve. Other important decisions, such as the choice of architecture for their information technology platforms, are either pre-determined or made within confines that have been shaped by the flagship.
- Within its assigned domain, the network partner is expected to become more effective and efficient than the flagship; in fact, it is principally because of the partner's effectiveness and efficiency that flagships choose to hand over operational responsibility to it.
- A paramount value of the culture that the network partner is expected to display is loyalty to the network. Employees must possess and be seen to possess fidelity to the flagship. It is not unusual for them to be expected to use the flagship's products (Ford suppliers invariably are expected to drive Ford cars), to display flagship emblems and insignia in their office and workwear, and to protect the confidentiality of company data.

Keeping effective contact with the outside competitive environment is a major strategic issue for network partners. Key suppliers may be faced with the problem of selling the bulk of their output only to the flagship. Precluded from dealing with other customers, these suppliers lose valuable feedback about their market-place. They may have only a vague notion about market prices, sketchy information about product developments by their competitors, and a poor realization of the thrusts of technology development in their industry.

Similarly, key customers may be precluded from dealing with the flagship's rivals. IBM discovered that its exclusive retail dealers had a poor understanding of the prices and performance of the clones and were ineffective in developing approaches to contend with competition from clones. Notwithstanding these shortcomings, the network does offer significant benefit to the partners. Association with a successful flagship brings with it the assurance of substantial sales volumes, access to a global intelligence system, exposure to leading-edge technology, and participation in management systems that are usually far beyond the reach of most partners on their own. Further, if the flagship is demanding of its network partners, they are likely to enhance their own competitiveness.

Prescriptions for network partners

To play their role effectively, network partners should keep the following prescriptions in mind.

- *Strive to become and remain the lowest-cost producer.* It is almost impossible to overemphasize this point. Not only must the network partner perform its functions at a lower cost than the flagship could perform them, but also the partner must strive to become a lower-cost producer than partners of competing flagships. To do this well, the partner should: keep overhead and co-ordination costs to a minimum, in particular by avoiding duplication of activity with the flagship; invest in process technology that reduces costs; and develop a cost-conscious culture in all parts of its operation.
- *Meet and exceed the quality expectations of the flagship.* Cost competitiveness should not be attained through compromise of quality standards. In the network form of organization, many of the operational aspects of the business belong in the network partners. It is here that quality management is most needed. Consequently, the network partners have the primary responsibility for developing and operating the systems for management of quality.
- *Enhance capabilities for delivering product and service innovations quickly.* One of the major reasons why the traditional larger organizations have experienced declining competitiveness is the slow pace of bringing innovation to market. Consequently, a major expectation when converting to a network form of organization is that the new system will perform better in this regard. Hence, the network partner will be expected to outperform the internal organization that it replaced, in terms of the speed and effectiveness it achieves in its assigned role in bringing new products to market. By avoiding committees, lengthy bureaucratic reviews, and complex organizational arrangements for managing innovation, the network partner can ensure that it is not a bottleneck in the system of bringing new products and services to market.

The key aspects of the prescriptions for network partners can be summed up in three words: *cheaper, better,* and *faster.* All aspects of network partners' operations will be enhanced if they attempt to follow these prescriptions with a framework of co-operative behaviour established by the flagship firms in their network.

PART II

Multinational Enterprise Theory and the Flagship Firm

4

Internalization and Deinternalization: Will Business Networks Replace Multinationals?

The internalization decision of a multinational enterprise (MNE) needs to take into account concepts of business policy and competitive strategy. From the modern theory of the MNE, that is, the theory of internalization, it is recognized that proprietary firm-specific advantages yield potential economic profits when exploited on a world-wide basis. Yet the MNE can find these potential profits dissipated by the internal governance costs of its organizational structure and the difficulty of timing and sustaining its foreign direct investment (FDI) activities. This leads to deinternalization when the benefits of internalization are outweighed by its costs. The form and type of deinternalization usually occurs within a business network of the type discussed in this chapter. The movement from internalization to business network requires analysis of parent–subsidiary relationships and the governance costs of running an MNE as compared with managing relationships in a business network.

The first part of this chapter examines the relevance of internalization theory for analysis of the strategic decisions of the MNE, especially FDI decisions. Particular attention will be devoted to the choice of entry mode to penetrate foreign markets. In addition, it will be demonstrated that internalization theory can be extended to deal with the different perspectives of complex parent and affiliate relationships and the nature of governance costs associated with different institutional arrangements, through which FDI decisions are made.

This work is an extension of Rugman (1980a, 1981, 1982, and 1986). Rugman has synthesized much of the literature on the theory of the MNE, reviewed here, into the theory of internalization, originally developed by Buckley and Casson (1976). The theory of internalization explains the organizational process by which imperfect markets are internalized by private companies up to the point where the costs of internalization equal its benefits. In this framework, for example, proprietary know-how can be turned into firm-specific competitive advantage on occasions when the market would fail to develop such know-how due to the public goods nature of knowledge. It is shown here that internalization theory constitutes the core theory of the MNE.

From a strategic perspective it can be shown that four conditions need to be fulfilled before an MNE will engage in FDI. These are essentially strategic investment criteria.

First, in spite of the perceived riskiness and 'additional costs' of operating abroad, the MNE must be able to develop production activities that will be competitive in the short or long term compared to the domestic operations of host-country companies. For a basic analysis, see Rugman, Lecraw, and Booth (1985), especially Chapter 5. Second, the net benefits associated with FDI must be higher than they would be in the case of foreign market penetration through exports, licensing, or joint-venture activity. Third, one or more optimal locations must be identified for the foreign investment. Fourth, the management of the MNE must be able to decide upon the optimal timing for execution of the investment project.

Here a theoretical framework is developed which will allow MNE managers to determine when to make a particular FDI decision, based upon judgements regarding the four conditions stated above. The governance costs of managing the organizational structures of MNEs are considered, since these costs offset the perceived benefits of internalization. The literature on the theory of the MNE has focused mainly on the benefits of internalization while ignoring the costs of this type of activity. Consequently assessment of the firm's decision about FDI is likely to be biased, unless the managerial/governance costs of internalization are considered. This work helps to broaden our understanding of strategic investment decisions when the net benefits of internalization may be so limited that alternative structures, such as business networks, need to be considered.

Internalization theory and multinational enterprises' strategic investment decisions

Hymer (1976) was the first scholar to improve on the traditional international trade theory framework, that is, the Heckscher–Ohlin–Samuelson, or HOS, paradigm. In his 1960 dissertation (finally published in 1976) Hymer developed an explanation of the functioning of the MNE which emphasized international production rather than international trade. The HOS paradigm does not explain why companies located in one country are able to transfer intangible assets, such as technological know-how, to other countries, while maintaining property rights and direct control over production activities in these other countries. Such real direct investment contrasts sharply with portfolio investment, where no direct control is exerted by the investors: see Rugman (1987) and Rugman and Yeung (1989) on this issue.

It was apparent to Hymer that FDI decisions could not be explained by differences in financial rates of return in the different countries involved. This is consistent with an interpretation that strategic FDI decisions cannot be compared with portfolio investments. Hymer attempted to explain how MNEs were able to compete with domestic companies in host countries (the first condition for FDI). In his view, competitiveness resulted from the monopolistic advantages of MNEs. Hence, FDI would occur primarily in imperfect markets.

This view was elaborated further by Kindleberger (1969), who identified imperfections in markets for finished products and for production factors, together with scale economies and government regulations of output and entry. Caves (1971) investigated why certain MNEs were able to engage successfully in horizontal integration on an international scale. Caves argued, in accordance with Hymer and Kindleberger, that the MNE's ability to achieve product differentiation is the main reason for such investments.

It can be observed that the early work of these three pioneers focused on the first condition for FDI. Unfortunately, this economics-based framework was characterized by an absence of managerial considerations and a neglect of the implications of governance costs for the efficiency aspects of FDI decisions. In short, the Hymer–Kindleberger–Caves approach developed the first condition for internalization of FDI, but it ignored other reasons, as well as the costs of internalization. Both of these issues have been explored in more recent work.

Benefits of internalization

The concept of appropriability implies that individuals and organizations, which possess a unique body of know-how, will attempt to avoid dissipation of this know-how to third parties: see Magee (1977, 1981). First, the costs required to generate technological know-how can only be recaptured through a stream of benefits flowing to the MNE in the long run. Second, technological know-how can become a public good. Once such know-how is dissipated its use by third parties cannot be prevented by the initial owner, whose ability to singularly exploit it is then severely affected, with a reduction in private benefits. Hence, this problem of appropriability explains strategic FDI decisions by MNEs. Internalization is preferred to other entry modes to keep the firm's unique know-how proprietary, a point also recognized by Ethier (1986).

Different prescriptions for managers can be drawn from this analysis. Foreign direct investment should be preferred to other entry modes when: (a) the reputation or brand name of the firm is considered important by consumers, so that the MNE must engage in direct quality control; (b) after-sales service is important, and cannot be assigned to a domestic firm in a host country through a licensing agreement; (c) complementarities exist among the different products, so that production within the MNE is the most efficient way of operating; (d) products are new and differentiated, leading to an information asymmetry between the buyer and seller, such that internalization through vertical integration may generate large benefits; (e) diversification of product lines creates learning effects and spreads risks.

Magee's approach therefore mainly deals with the second condition for MNE activity. The benefits of the MNE's know-how can only be fully appropriated through FDI. This framework demonstrates the highly complex nature of strategic investment decisions in MNEs. Careful assessment of the risks of dissipation of the firm's proprietary knowledge is a key component in the investment process.

Buckley and Casson (1976) and Casson (1979) also investigated the issue of control over an MNE's know-how as a major generator of internalization decisions. In their view, imperfections in markets for intermediate outputs are the main rationale for internalization. Such imperfections include: (a) difficulties in developing long-term contracts for specific types of intermediate outputs; (b) the absence of possibilities for price discrimination; (c) the danger of opportunistic behaviour by a contracting party where there is a bilateral concentration of market power; (d) the existence of an 'information asymmetry' between suppliers and buyers, leading the latter to offer an insufficient price for a particular good; (e) government regulation such as import tariffs and international differences in tax systems. These five elements have a substantial impact on technological know-how and scarce raw materials, often found in limited geographical areas. The creation of an internal market can eliminate problems caused by these market imperfections.

Buckley and Casson recognized that there are, however, governance costs associated with internalization. These include: communication costs among production facilities that are dispersed geographically; administrative and capital costs; and potential political costs (such as when discriminatory measures are taken in favour of domestically owned firms). The costs and benefits of internalization need to be carefully evaluated, and will depend on firm, industry, host country, and regional characteristics. This clear statement of the second condition for MNE activity has been the basis for further work on the theory of the MNE summarized in Buckley and Casson (1985).

The eclectic approach

Dunning's (1979, 1981) eclectic paradigm explains why MNEs make particular FDI decisions, based on an integrated analysis of the first three conditions for strategic investment. First, the MNE must be competitive with local producers because it possesses ownership advantages, that is, proprietary intangible assets such as patented technology, management know-how, etc. Second, FDI must be preferred to contracts with local producers and licensing agreements, when the MNE's core know-how can be protected only through internalization. Third, the best geographical location is typically chosen as the result of careful analysis of different sets of relevant costs, such as costs of production, quality control, transportation, etc. Dunning also recognized that the location element as a major determinant of FDI may differ from one industry to another. In a similar vein, corporate perceptions of environmental factors, such as government regulation of MNE activity, and political stability, are considered important. The key idea developed by Dunning in his eclectic model is the possibility of strong interaction among ownership advantages, internalization advantages, and the identification of an optimal geographic location in the FDI process.

In contrast to the Hymer–Kindleberger–Caves approach discussed earlier Dunning has also devoted some attention to managerial issues related to the FDI process. In this context the distinction between the structural and transactional advantages of MNEs is essential: see Dunning and Rugman (1985). The former result from the ownership of distinctive assets which give the MNE a competitive edge in the market, but which are unrelated to the multinational character of the firm. This type of advantage would include scale economies and the use of proprietary assets. Transactional advantages reflect the comparatively greater efficiency of the foreign investment process in MNEs than in uninational firms.

The greater efficiency of MNEs results from four elements. First, a larger set of investment opportunities are available to the MNEs. Second, they have better access to (and processing of) information on the inputs (cost elements) and outputs (benefits) of particular investment decisions. Third, the possibility of risk reduction through international diversification exists: see Rugman (1979). Fourth, the possibility of exploiting international differences in market imperfections is present (for example pricing of factors of production). The implications of these four elements for strategy are of major importance, as they help the strategic positioning of the MNE in comparison to domestic companies in host countries.

The optimal timing of strategic investment decisions

Buckley and Casson (1980) have also conducted an analysis of the optimal timing for FDI decisions (the fourth condition for FDI). They assume that exports, licensing, and FDI are alternatives characterized by a particular mix of fixed and variable costs. Fixed costs would be highest for FDI and lowest for exports, whereas the opposite situation would be characteristic of variable costs. In cases where each entry mode would constitute an efficient means to serve foreign markets, exports, licensing, and FDI will be chosen in a sequential fashion. If the foreign market is large or if one of the modes is inefficient, such sequences may not be observed. Furthermore, if an MNE already has production facilities abroad and fixed costs to manufacture a new product are low (a case of incremental investment), then FDI may occur immediately. A slightly different model of the timing issue was developed by Giddy and Rugman and is summarized in Rugman (1981).

Furthermore, according to Rugman (1981), the choice of timing (as well as of location) constitutes merely a part of the decision to internalize. This means that the third and fourth conditions for FDI are interrelated. Rugman (1986) has demonstrated that the specification of additional parameters, such as entry and exit barriers, the risk of dissipation of technological know-how, and the level of tariff and non-tariff barriers, determines when a switch occurs among modes of entry. Hill and Chan Kim (1988) have also designed a model aimed at identifying changes in the choice of entry modes in a dynamic perspective. Most MNEs now use modern strategic management techniques which indeed determine these switching points.

In Rugman's view, the investment process in MNEs is characterized by the increasing importance of firm-specific strategic management considerations.

These are replacing traditional financial or portfolio capital elements, especially under the pressures of multinational global competition. This is consistent with the findings of a substantial body of empirical studies on multinational finance, summarized in Eiteman and Stonehill (1989).

Transaction costs and organizational structure

Williamson (1981, 1985) and Teece (1982, 1986) view the existence of an efficient organizational structure capable of implementing investment decisions as a major explanatory element in the growth of MNEs in world trade and investment. An example of such an organizational structure is the so-called multidivisional structure (M-form).

An M-form would reduce governance costs associated with the functioning of MNEs as compared to a unitary, or functional, structure (U-form). The main reason is that corporate management would be able to devote most of its time to strategic management decisions, including investment decisions. Conversely, management at the divisional level would be concerned mainly with operational decisions and the achievement of profitability for their respective divisions. This view of the functioning of larger corporations is in accordance with the framework developed by Simon (1957) and empirical research by Chandler (1962).

The investment process in unitary or functionally organized MNEs would be less efficient. A functional structure could stimulate opportunistic behaviour by functional managers, even at the corporate level. Furthermore, it would be more difficult to separate strategic decisions such as capital budgeting and operational decisions. Finally, effective control and sanction systems aimed at monitoring the outcomes of the investment process would be much more complex.

Related to such organizational aspects are problems associated with the transfer of technology abroad, such as the problem of 'disclosure' and the problem of 'team organization'. Disclosure concerns the so-called fundamental paradox, a refinement of the public goods externality as described by Arrow (1971). The value of information, in this case technological know-how, is not known by its potential buyer until it has been disclosed, but through such disclosure the buyer acquires the information at no cost. Team organization implies that technological know-how in a firm is often spread among a number of individuals, each of whom masters only part of this know-how. In such a case a technology transfer contract is excluded. If technological know-how needs to be transferred on a continuous basis, FDI will occur.

In terms of the multinational investment process, Williamson's main contribution is his emphasis on the importance of organizational elements as a major determining factor in strategic investment decisions. His work confirms that the financial, or portfolio, aspects of foreign investment projects are secondary to the issue of control. Teece (1982, 1983, and 1993) has expanded Williamson's analysis by developing a contingency theory which explains the choice of FDI as the preferred entry mode, taking into account governance costs. He distinguished between investments generating vertical integration and those generating horizontal integration.

Vertical integration occurs wherever the presence of specific assets leads to strong mutual interdependence between two economic agents and when opportunistic behaviour by one party creates high costs for the other. Vertical integration thus eliminates high contractual costs (especially control costs related to the enforcement of contracts). Horizontal integration occurs if two conditions are fulfilled. First, the organization must have assets which are not entirely 'used', such as technological know-how in the form of a patent or brand name. Second, the direct investment abroad must lead to higher net benefits than there would be in the case of exports or a licensing agreement.

Teece's work demonstrates that the multinational investment process cannot be reduced by a simple process of choice among different investment projects. The choice of an optimal mode of entry for each individual project considered is, in itself, a decision problem which, at least from a conceptual perspective, needs to occur prior to the choice among FDI projects. Thus the strategic nature of the FDI decision will govern and constrain the investment decision of MNEs.

Internalization theory and parent–subsidiary relationships

It has been argued in the previous section that the main contribution of internalization theory to the multinational investment process is related to its focus on (a) the choice of entry mode to penetrate foreign markets and (b) the necessity to control proprietary know-how. The main weakness of the theory, except for the Williamson–Teece approach, is the assumption that the MNE's 'administrative heritage' in investment decisions will not affect the investment process.

Yet the issue of administrative heritage is critical. It is especially critical for on-going foreign investment decisions (as opposed to the initial choice of FDI as an entry mode by a firm). Exports, licensing, FDI, and joint ventures as modes of entry simply cannot be compared without taking into account the administrative and organizational characteristics of the firm involved. In fact, the governance costs associated with FDI will depend largely upon the efficiency of the MNE's organizational structure. This explains why firms facing similar environmental conditions and having similar characteristics in terms of proprietary assets may still choose a different entry mode. For example, firms that do not have an organizational structure allowing the separation of strategic and operational decisions may prefer not to engage in FDI because of the costs of operating a large hierarchy. According to Williamson (1985), the early availability of the M-form in US corporations provided them with an internal management capability which only became available about a decade later to non-US corporations. This would explain Tsurumi's (1977) observation that FDI by US firms increased rapidly after 1953, while FDI by non-US MNEs only became prevalent in the 1960s.

Moreover, even when leaving aside the issue of choice of entry mode, we should recognize that the outcomes of the investment process itself will be strongly influenced by the firm's administrative heritage. In particular, the structure of parent–subsidiary interactions may substantially affect the outcomes of the investment process.

In other words, the main decision problem in the multinational investment process is not the 'objective' evaluation of the costs and benefits associated with particular internalization decisions. Rather, it is the design of a decision process which allows an objective assessment of (a) the costs and benefits associated with the different entry modes for each project and (b) the relative net benefits associated with the optimal entry mode for all projects under consideration.

The next section develops a simple framework to illustrate these points. It should be emphasized that this framework is designed for top management, the strategic planners responsible for the FDI decision. Once the strategic decisions about FDI, or other modes, are made then a centralized finance function is normal. However, at a strategic level, the decision making can be centralized or decentralized. It depends upon the optimal method of exploiting the proprietary assets of the MNE.

A framework for the strategic investment process

Using a transaction cost perspective, a conceptual framework can be developed which allows us to determine whether or not the strategic investment process in an MNE can be considered efficient. Only if this is the case can objective assessments be made of the costs and benefits of specific investment projects. This model constitutes an extension of internalization theory since it specifies the conditions to be fulfilled by the investment process in an MNE in order to guarantee optimal resource allocation decisions.

There are four generic types of the investment to be distinguished, as represented in Figure 4.1.

The vertical axis of Figure 4.1 measures the degree of centralization of the strategic investment process. This process includes the design, evaluation, and choice of investment projects. It can be either centralized or decentralized. In the former case, all investment activities are executed at the corporate management level. The latter case reflects the execution of specific activities in the investment process by different levels in the hierarchy of the MNE, including the level of subsidiary management.

The centralization of the strategic investment process at the corporate management level will lead to severe problems of 'bounded rationality'. The information-processing capabilities of a decentralized decision structure are, however, much lower than those of a centralized system, as demonstrated by Simon (1961) and Aguilar (1979). This issue is especially important when the MNE is faced with a rapidly changing and complex environment.

The horizontal axis deals with the transaction cost concept of 'opportunism'. It

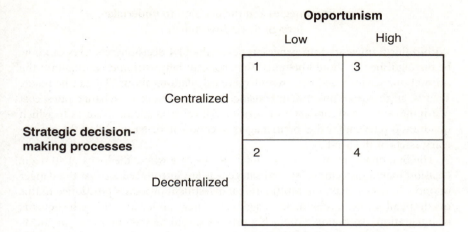

Figure 4.1 Strategic decision processes and opportunism

captures the presence or absence of safeguards in the structural and cultural context of the organization. Such safeguards are necessary to protect the investment process against the impact of local rationality, that is, subgoal pursuit. For an overview of the research on the choice between structural (formal) and cultural (informal) co-ordination and control systems in MNEs, see Baliga and Jaeger (1984).

The issue of safeguards in the investment process reflects the existence of control costs in a hierarchical mode of organization. The main reason for this problem of control is that managers of the different subsidiaries (in the case of a decentralized system) and even the functional managers at the corporate level have weak incentives to maximize the total output of the global organization.

In the case of a decentralized system aiming at the achievement of high national responsiveness, subsidiary managers' knowledge of the expected costs and benefits of particular investment projects is superior to that of corporate managers. The reasons for this include the information asymmetry between subsidiary managers and corporate managers concerning the market characteristics of the foreign environment and the geographic distance between corporate headquarters and the host-country environment. These factors make it difficult for corporate headquarters to exert direct control on subsidiary managers. Especially in cases where such projects will affect the functioning and the profitability of other subsidiaries it is difficult to design appropriate incentives to eliminate the problem of opportunism: see Hennart (1986). Then, through cultural safeguards such as extensive socialization and training, the goals of subsidiary managers can be made consistent with the goals of corporate management.

Generic strategies and the decision to undertake
foreign direct investment

Within this framework four generic types of the FDI decision processes can now be distinguished. It should be noted that, conceptually, within each quadrant the normal financially based net present value calculations about FDI can be made. That is, all the usual investment considerations about taxes, exchange rates, cost of capital, etc., are secondary to the prior critical strategic decision as to which quadrant is relevant for the top managers to choose in order to exploit the proprietary assets of the MNE.

The first quadrant of Figure 4.1 refers to the case where the locus of strategic decision making is centralized and safeguards are introduced against the danger of opportunistic behaviour. Multinational investment processes positioned in this quadrant allow the development of a global strategy aimed at reaping the benefits of integration. An example of such a process would be the one found in an M-form. Hout, Porter, and Rudden (1982) have argued in favour of such centralization of strategic decision making, which allows the integration of a firm's strategies across several domestic markets.

Unfortunately, multinational investment often requires some degree of national responsiveness. In this case realistic investment projects may well have to be initiated at the subsidiary (host country) level. The second quadrant reflects the fact that only 'induced' investment projects are being generated, that is, projects which are in accordance with the MNE's dominating concept of a strategy and which fit into the firm's existing product-market domain. In this case, an optimal balance can be found between the requirements of integration and national responsiveness in the investment process. It should be recognized, however, that the decentralization of strategic investment activities toward the subsidiary level may initiate problems of fragmentation if structural and cultural safeguards are not carefully designed.

The issue of cultural safeguards in quadrant two is especially important if regional or world product mandates have been assigned: see Rugman (1983), D'Cruz (1986), and Rugman and Douglas (1986). In this case, resource allocation decisions taken at the corporate level result from an extensive strategic confrontation between the views of subsidiary managers and those of corporate level managers. Elements such as the reputation of subsidiary managers and their ability to initiate commitment at the corporate level become of prime importance. Ghertman (1981, 1988) has investigated the role of 'go-betweens' in investment and divestment decisions of MNEs. Go-betweens include both outsiders, such as consultants, and insiders, such as managers, who understand the divergence between parent and subsidiary views on investment projects.

The occurrence of conflicts between the different levels of management in MNEs has been observed by several authors, such as Doz and Prahalad (1981, 1984, 1987), Globerman (1986), etc. Corporate management should be careful to avoid the introduction of false safeguards in the investment process. These would include short-run profitability requirements of new investment projects, leading to a neglect of valuable long-run investment opportunities by subsidiary managers.

The third and fourth quadrants of Figure 4.1 are characteristic of processes where opportunistic behaviour strongly influences investment decisions. An example of the former (quadrant three) is the U-form whereby functional managers at the highest level of the MNE attempt to generate investment decisions in favour of their own functional units. The latter (quadrant four) includes cases where subsidiary managers actually dominate the company and no central co-ordination at all is being performed by the corporate headquarters.

The conclusion of this analysis is that only the investment processes in the second quadrant are efficient. In an environment of global competition, each MNE needs to be responsive to the needs of both integration and national responsiveness. Indeed, it is only in the case of efficient safeguards against opportunistic behaviour that objective assessments can be made of the costs and benefits of different entry modes. Only then can the net benefits of the different investment projects under consideration be found. The basis for such efficient strategic investment decisions by MNEs is the theory of internalization. Neglect of this analytical tool will lead to inefficient investment behaviour by MNEs.

From this analysis it is apparent that neither the conventional centralized, hierarchical, M-form structure of the MNE (in quadrant one) nor the U-form (in quadrant three) is really suitable for efficient strategic FDI decision making. Instead, the managers of an MNE need to cope with a decentralized structure which incorporates critical elements of national responsiveness. Only a few MNEs are good at doing this: see the analysis of ABB by Bartlett and Ghoshal (1993), building upon their concept of the 'transnational solution', Bartlett and Ghoshal (1989). In terms of this analysis the transnational solution is in quadrant two. Given the tremendous difficulty facing MNEs in adopting the decentralized and non-opportunistic transnational solution of quadrant two it is necessary to consider alternative methods of organization. One of these of great relevance today is a new type of business network, discussed in the next section.

The five partners business network model

The five partners model of a business network organizes economic exchange among partner organizations through co-operative, non-equity relationships. It has been developed by D'Cruz and Rugman (1992*a*, 1992*b*, 1993, 1994). Specifically, the partners include: a leading 'flagship firm' which is a multinational corporation; key suppliers; key customers; selected competitors; and the non-business infrastructure (NBI): see Figure 4.2.

The NBI comprises government, the non-traded service sectors, educational institutions, social services, trade unions, trade associations, and non-profit cultural organizations. The business network's governance structure depends upon (a) asymmetric control of the network's strategic purpose by the flagship

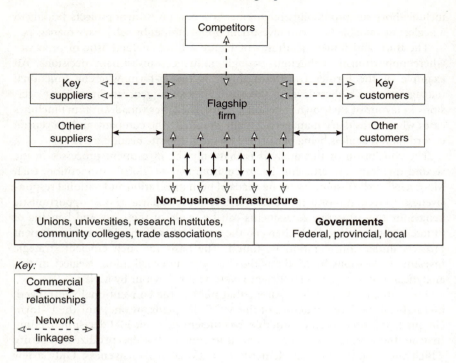

Figure 4.2 The five partners business network

firm and (b) a structuring of aspects of the partners' business systems (value chains) to create a network business system.

The flagship firm's resources and global perspective enable it to develop global strategies which can capitalize on the capabilities and knowledge of all partners. Because partners may compete in business systems not related to that of the business network, it should be emphasized that the flagship firm's asymmetric strategic control extends only to those aspects of its partners' business systems committed to the network. Through adoption of a paradigm of co-operation predicated on long-term association, the business network benefits from the development of trust among network partners. The trust that is developed within the co-operative context of network relationships decreases the need to establish elaborate internal MNE structures and systems to guard against opportunism. That is, relationship stability and longevity coupled with shared interorganizational purpose (of the business network) help to decrease inefficiencies similar to those found in traditional MNE M-form governance structures built around the protection of firm-specific assets (FSAs).

The business network's structure of co-operative relationships reduces the number of asset-specific investments for any given partner. Organizations which choose to participate in a business network realize that the demands of global markets may preclude any given firm from having the capability to be competitive in every aspect of its current business. The rapid pace of technology change, product obsolescence, and market growth places heavy burdens on companies if they wish to remain competitive.

Many corporations now understand that they are competing against global business systems as opposed to within broadly defined industry groupings. Restructuring and outsourcing those activities in which the partner has no core competence (Prahalad and Hamel 1990) lessens investments in 'non-core' assets and, particularly, those in which the partner has less knowledge. Consequently, the likelihood of investment in assets which quickly become 'non-performing' is decreased. When partners focus on investment in core assets and the exploitation of their core capabilities they are better able to follow, predict, and adapt to market changes which affect their operations. If all network partners assume similar approaches, then the boundaries of the business network can shift more easily to accommodate changes in the global market. The network's business system, therefore, benefits from the permeability of its boundaries and its shared strategic purpose.

The five partners business network developed here has many of the attributes of a Japanese interfirm network, *keiretsu* system. However, the major difference is that our business network does not have a major bank or a general trading company as a partner, whereas these are deeply involved in the *keiretsu*. For a discussion of the complexities of the Japanese enterprise system, of which vertical (and horizontal) groupings in *keiretsu* are but one form, see Fruin (1992).

Strategy and the business network's five partners

The strategic direction and purpose of the business network is led by an MNE which has the resources and industry perspective to develop and co-ordinate the execution of global business strategies. This flagship firm's experience in international markets is vital for the business network's determination of which markets to serve and what products/services to produce. Essentially, the flagship firm's strategic hand guides its partners towards a vision of global competitiveness for the network as a whole.

The business network's global strategies will draw from the MNE's experience in market entry, whether it be through international trade, licensing, joint venture, or FDI (Rugman 1981). However, the execution of strategies will differ from past practice because the MNE will not depend on internalization as the sole means by which to protect FSAs and gain competitive advantage. As shown earlier, typically internalization meant vertical and/or horizontal integration in order to monitor, meter, and regulate the use of its proprietary knowledge (Rugman 1981). Instead of depending on internalization to protect its knowledge-based FSAs, the flagship firm focuses on sharing knowledge among network partners in order to facilitate interorganizational learning. This business network strategy reflects the difficulty of gaining competitive advantage via protecting knowledge through internalization (a) in an environment where ease of communication negates protection from national borders, language differences, physical geography, etc. and (b) in markets characterized by rapid change and innovation (for example, leading to product obsolescence).

The business network as a governance structure operationalizes the thesis of Kogut and Zander (1992, 1993) that knowledge sharing is a determining factor of organizational form and boundary. Specifically, they argue that the boundaries of a firm, and by extension a network of firms, are defined by how well current capabilities (or a recombination of them) generate knowledge. We argue that the business network structure facilitates knowledge generation and interorganizational learning. In particular, we propose that strategic asymmetry assists the development of a 'common language' by which partners can communicate. It follows, therefore, that intranetwork learning and knowledge generation are important processes which enable the business network to be flexible and responsive to changes in the external market environment. We argue that this responsiveness outweighs concerns over losing FSAs and in fact obviates the need to protect them through internalization.

The flagship firm's asymmetric strategic leadership is manifested in the following important areas:

(1) Adopting and promulgating a long-term, relationship-based, co-operation paradigm for network activities.
(2) Relocating and restructuring the loci of production and service provision for value-added activities through the network.
(3) Benchmarking and measuring network partners' activities and processes to global standards of competitiveness.
(4) Encouraging the development of a 'common language' to facilitate knowledge generation and intranetwork learning.

It is evident that network partners determine that strategic leadership by a flagship firm offers rewards that could not otherwise be obtained. As with all partners who voluntarily join the business network, key suppliers expect that participation in the network will be beneficial to them. These suppliers should receive increased order volumes when the flagship firm undertakes a supplier reduction programme as it converts to a network procurement style. Moreover, the key suppliers can expect to enter multi-year supply contracts. The reduction of risk which accompanies open-ended, multi-year contracts (Fama 1980) is enhanced by risk sharing with the flagship firm related to technology and capital expenditures. The second significant benefit of network participation for key suppliers is capturing a higher proportion of value-added activities deintegrated from the flagship firm. Third, through benchmarking to the global standards required by the network, the key suppliers' processes, technologies, and systems will reflect standards of competitiveness which may ensure its continued survival and pros-perity. Moreover, if a key supplier owns other businesses outside the network, it may be able to transfer knowledge and learning garnered from network partici-pation to these operations.

Key customers yield to the strategic leadership of the flagship firm for several reasons. First, there may be structural and contractual obligations which tie the key customer to the flagship firm. Automobile manufacturers and their dealers are an example of this type of relationship. Second, there may be strategic reasons which compel the key customer to follow the expertise of the flagship firm. Typically, this scenario will be encountered when the network's business system organizes economic activity more efficiently, at a lower cost, or with better tech-nological capability than can the key customer. If these activities are integral to the key customer's operations, then it may be willing to cede a measure of control to the flagship firm. While it may seem counterintuitive to follow such a strategy, the logic flows from the inability of the key customer to 'maintain' these activities due to the pace of change in the operational environment. For example, if telecom-munications services are integral to a brokerage firm's operations, it may wish to engage the expert services of a third party contractor to oversee its telecommuni-cations needs. This type of arrangement is fairly common and often takes the form of an on-site contract worker or mini-department at the key customer's premises. Therefore, the leap to ceding strategic control to the flagship firm is not so high as might be thought. Beyond being a market for the flagship firm, key customers serve as a market-feedback mechanism for the business network as a whole.

The business network model explicitly incorporates the NBI into its partner-ing relationships. Moreover, it departs from traditional approaches, which tend to view that infrastructure as frictional bodies, rather than integral members of economic production. Relationships with the NBI focus on those aspects of the partner's organization which contribute to the strategic purpose of the network. Research ties between the flagship firm and educational institutions are an obvi-ous example of mutually beneficial relationships. The flagship firm, and poten-tially other network partners, mobilize financial resources to assist the NBI's efforts. In return, the NBI will agree to pursue activities that exploit resources and competencies in a manner beneficial to the network's purpose. Also, the NBI part-ners may provide other non-financial resources like facilities, equipment, human resources, or other institutional arrangements.

One of the most important roles for NBI partners, and particularly govern-ment and educational institutions, is to provide a forum for co-operative exchange—a non-adversarial venue where organizations can foster relation-ships. Ouchi (1984, 29) makes this point in his research on Japanese trade asso-ciations, government ministry 'discussion councils', and public–private economic institutes: these bodies 'in the end, serve the sole purpose of creating a setting in which competitors can arrange non-adversarial relationships for the common good. It is these institutions that are the loci of social memory'. We argue that government and other NBI organizations can fulfil this role in the context of business networks. To date, North American business has ignored these non-market forums for exchange and has limited its participation in such bodies. The result is that proficiency in contributing to and accessing commonly built pools of knowledge is limited; and that interorganizational partnering remains unsophisticated. However, business network relationships predicated on long-term association will eventually create loci of social/economic memory which network partners can access.

Relationships with selected competitors comprise the fifth element of the business network partnerships. The perspective brought to this shared relationship differs from past interorganizational relationships. Because business network partners understand that internalization may fail to structurally position the firm for competitiveness, they are willing to engage in more open-ended relationships based on knowledge sharing, not knowledge protection. Such firms organize their structures to change with the market. The form of relationship, on the surface, appears to be traditional: joint ventures, supplier development, market-sharing arrangements, technology transfers, etc. However, the method of implementation, through managerial interaction and joint working teams, rather than static contractual arrangements, is devised to encourage co-operation and knowledge development. Obviously, such relationships generate benefits associated with economies of scope and scale, but such advantages are insufficiently compelling to bind organizations together. Selected competitors commit to a business network because they (a) understand the learning benefits of the co-operative relationships and the guiding strategic purpose and (b) wish to 'restructure' their firm boundaries, capabilities, and culture to meet the demands of the global competitive environment.

Deinternalization of the multinational enterprise

The implication of this new analysis of business networks is that such a structure can be a substitute for internalization outside core processes by the MNE. Thus, a well-functioning five partners business network will be consistent with selective deinternalization. An illustration of this is depicted in Figure 4.3.

In Figure 4.3 the five partners business network will shrink the size of the MNE as the need for internalization is retained only for the core activities of the MNE, the central shaded area. A surrounding grey area indicates activities previously internalized by the MNE which can now be undertaken by its partners in the business network. The grey area represents activities that are newly peripheral to the MNE, but these offer considerable value added to the business network as a whole. The grey area activities are now undertaken by independent companies (that is, there is no equity control of them by the MNE) although, as discussed earlier, the partners have developed long-term relationships with the MNE and there is considerable interdependence between them and the MNE.

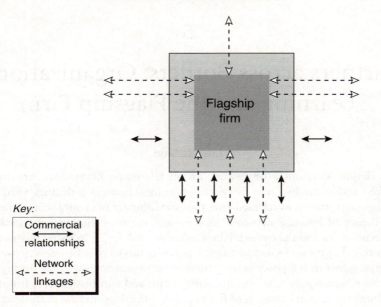

Figure 4.3 Multinational enterprise deinternalization in a business network

While this chapter has its focus on the theory of business networks and the internalization/deinternalization decision of the MNE it is apparent that these ideas need to be tested by further research on the existence of such business networks, and the trends towards deinternalization by MNEs. This is undertaken in Part III of this book.

5

Partners across Borders: Organizational Learning and the Flagship Firm

Introduction

This chapter develops a framework for an alternative governance structure to markets and hierarchies. The five partners business network is distinguished by its strategic asymmetry, which facilitates the establishment of credible commitments. The theory of business networks incorporates the contributions of transaction cost economics and the embeddedness of economic action in social relations.

In this chapter we introduce the five partners model of a 'business network'. A business network is a governance structure for organizing exchange through co-operative, non-equity relationships among firms and non-business organizations. The business network consists of five partners—the flagship firm as the lead partner, key suppliers, key customers, selected competitors with which strategic partnerships have been formed, and the non-business infrastructure (NBI) (which includes government). This latter set of mainly service-related sectors is viewed explicitly as a partner and its inclusion is new to the literature on business networks. The flagship firm is a multinational enterprise that competes globally and sets international benchmarks for the entire business network.

As the primary theme of this chapter, we propose that the business network, as we define it, can ameliorate the costs inherent in opportunism in markets and asset specificity in hierarchies. Further, we believe that such a network of interfirm linkages is most effective when there is asymmetric control by the flagship firm over the strategic direction of the network. We argue that asymmetry in regard to a narrowed strategic agenda for the network as a whole has important implications for the level of trust, stability, and knowledge development in the network. The concept of asymmetric strategic control by the flagship firm is a distinguishing feature of our business network. This asymmetry need not be characteristic of the whole of the relationship with each partner. In other words, any given partner of the flagship firm may compete in other, non-related industries. Therefore, those aspects of the partners' businesses that are not pertinent to the business

We are pleased to acknowledge extensive research assistance by Michael K. Scott, Research Associate at the Centre for International Business, University of Toronto. We received helpful comments on previous drafts from Alain Verbeke, Steve Tallman, Donald Lessard, John Stopford, Eleanor Westney, and Gunnar Hedlund, and from participants in seminars at the Sloan School of Management, MIT, the University of Hawaii, UCLA, Brandeis University, and the University of Toronto. A previous version was presented at the annual meetings of the Academy of Management in Dallas in August 1994. Financial support was provided by the Social Sciences and Humanities Research Council of Canada.

system of the network will be operated separately by the partner and without influence from the flagship firm. The asymmetry in the relationship between flagship firm and partner reflects the strategic leadership of the flagship in those aspects of the partner's business system which are germane to the network's strategic intent (Hamel and Prahalad 1989).

As a secondary theme of this chapter, we argue that the five partners governance structure can establish credible commitments (Williamson 1985) and efficiently transmit knowledge and know-how. We build upon related work by Kogut and Zander (1993) and develop a model where social relations are embedded in the five partners framework (through a common understanding, code, or language) to facilitate its effective strategic management.

This chapter draws upon the work on networks in the field of strategic management by Ouchi (1980) and Jarillo (1988) and on strategic clusters by Porter (1990). It also draws upon the transaction cost work of Williamson (1975, 1985), especially the concept of opportunism and its applications to the theory of the multinational enterprise (e.g. Rugman 1981), and upon the concepts of relational contracting (Ring and Van de Ven 1992) and embeddedness (Granovetter 1985).

The concept of the business network

In this section, we describe the nature and structure of the business network and advance a rationale for structuring relationships among the five partners. Of particular importance is the leadership role of the flagship firm.

At the core of the business network is a flagship firm.[1] This is a large multinational enterprise (MNE) which has a global perspective on its industry or industries and the resources and capabilities for crafting and executing global business strategies. The MNE's choice of entry mode, whether by international trade, foreign direct investment (FDI), licensing, or joint venture is a major component of these strategies (Rugman 1981). Figure 5.1 shows the five partners and the key elements of a business network.

In the past, the multinational enterprise would 'internalize' ownership of a set of core competencies or firm-specific advantages to gain a competitive advantage over its global rivals. Internalization often meant vertical or horizontal integration, or both, so as to monitor, meter, and regulate the use of its proprietary knowledge (Rugman 1981). This view of internalization, so as to reduce the transaction costs of the public goods nature of knowledge, is readily linked to the tacit

---

[1] A flagship firm is a multinational enterprise and is different from Jarillo's (1988) 'hub' firm. He uses the term to refer to the hierarchical leader of a 'strategic' network, whereas we use it to refer to asymmetric strategic leadership of a 'business' network by a flagship firm in areas agreed upon with network partners. It is also different from the firm at the centre of Harrigan's 'spider's webs' (Harrigan 1988) and from her 'focal business unit' in a vertically integrated network (Harrigan 1985). Neither of Harrigan's firms is a multinational enterprise with network partners operating across borders, as is the case of our flagship firms.

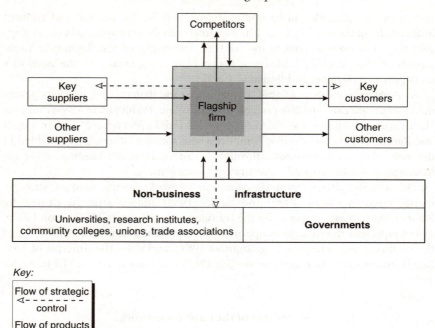

Figure 5.1 Elements of a business network

know-how focus of the resource-based view of strategic management, as summarized by Wernerfelt (1984) and Conner (1991), amongst others.

What is now occurring in large firms, however, is a great deal of deintegration of business system activities (Blois 1990). Increased flexibility and responsiveness to the market are important catalysts for vertically integrated firms to deintegrate value-added activities to their network partners. Moreover, advances in communications technology, such as electronic data interchange (EDI) and shared software development interfaces, have increased the feasibility of outsourcing important activities. A good example of the extent of outsourcing can be found in Lorenzoni and Baden-Fuller's (1993) description of Nintendo.

In the business network, the flagship firm must provide strategic leadership and direction to its partners. Essential to the functioning of the business network is the willingness of these partners to agree that the flagship firm is the lead partner in crafting strategies for the network as a whole. Because the flagship firm is an MNE accustomed to designing global strategies, the strategic purpose of the business network is best driven by the flagship firm's global perspective and benchmarks. Otherwise, it is unlikely that a coherent and globally oriented focus can be created through negotiation among the partner firms and the NBI. Given that the network partners may be large firms (or government), it is reasonable to assume they may compete in industries not related to the network's business system. In these businesses, the partners will operate independently and will not take strategic direction from the flagship firm. Still, in regard to their participation in the network's business system, presumably the partners have decided that it is in their best interests to follow the strategic leadership of the flagship firm. This would suggest, therefore, that there is substantial benefit to be gained from participation in the business network.

In exchange for giving up autonomy in strategic decision making for the network as a whole, the flagship firm's partners expect and receive a series of rewards.[2] Let us examine the role of *key suppliers* in this light. First, flagship firms will adopt some form of a supplier reduction programme when switching to a network-style approach to procurement. Thus the chosen supplier benefits through the increased volume and multi-year supply contracts that accompany participation in the network. Tier one suppliers to the North American automobile manufacturers are a good example of this network preference for adopting key suppliers. The suppliers' business risk can be significantly reduced, partly because of the reduced uncertainty that accompanies multi-year, open-ended contracts (Fama 1980) and partly because the flagship firm assumes some risks related to technology and capital expenditures. In terms of the reduction of risk for the automobile suppliers, it is still debatable whether the automobile manufacturers assume a reasonable level of capital or technological risk in their dealings with their key suppliers.[3] This is especially pertinent to key automobile suppliers who must make large investments in assets specific to fulfilling the supply contract, and who must necessarily be concerned with the stability of the multi-year contract. Second, network suppliers will capture a greater share of the value added in the business network, primarily through transfer of value-added activities previously performed by the flagship firm.

A similar pattern, with a few significant differences, emerges with respect to the *key customers* who become part of the business network. Network relations with customers have distinctive aspects, since customers need not be final consumers. Customers in a business network are best regarded as part of the production process, that is, intermediaries between the flagship firm and final consumers. Examples are agents and distributors. Strategy development in the relationship requires that the flagship firm understand the customer's customer. Thus market segmentation and targeting begin with strategic analysis of the final markets that the intermediate customer serves, and choices made in this regard inform and

---

[2] Perhaps the key challenge for the flagship firm is its ability to increase trust among the partners in the business network. Following Williamson (1975), opportunism is a major transaction cost facing any business network, so the flagship firm's ability to build trust and co-operative behaviour, to the benefit of all partners, becomes a critical issue. Jarillo (1988) makes a similar point for his 'hub' firms.

[3] A thorough review of the advantages and disadvantages of the more collaborative buyer–supplier relationship can be found in a paper by Lyons, Krachenberg, and Henke (1990).

guide all subsequent strategic decisions. Final customers are usually too numerous to be organized, and when this occurs they are not included as partners in our model.

Flagship firms need to forge longer-term relationships with the *non-business infrastructure* (NBI) in the community: universities, research institutes, community colleges, trade unions, trade associations; and, most important, the various levels of government. These potential relationships are related to the principal strategy or strategies of the business network and focus on mobilizing the resources of the NBI to make the network as a whole more competitive. Here, too, the relationship between the flagship firm and the NBI will be asymmetric. The flagship firm will provide the vision and leadership for strategic decision making (as it applies to the pertinent area of resource allocation and competency exploitation) and will mobilize financial resources for specific projects. The non-business network partner will contribute the non-financial resources—facilities and equipment, human resources, institutional arrangements—and will assume responsibility for implementation of the projects.

In terms of the role of the NBI, Ouchi's (1984) view of Japanese trade associations, public–private economic institutes, and government ministry 'discussion councils' can be extended to the North American economies. He says (1984, 29) that these bodies 'in the end, serve the sole purpose of creating a setting in which competitors can arrange nonadversarial relationships for the common good. It is these institutions that are the loci of social memory. Each actor participates in many such institutions and thus knows that the future memory of his or her current behavior will be stored, remembered and justly rewarded or punished.'

Conversely, North American business interests typically characterize government as a source of friction whose presence and effect in the marketplace need to be minimized at all costs. If government is to be considered a contributing partner in a business network relationship, then an approach more akin to Ouchi's description needs to be adopted. Indeed, the bureaucracies of government and other quasi-government bodies in North America also offer (a) a forum for co-operative exchange of ideas and (b) an institutionalized locus of memory. The onus of blame for the historically ineffectual relationship between business and government may just as easily rest with business. The convenient 'government as interference' perspective does little to contribute to a co-operative environment. Further, the business community may continue to do itself a disservice by ignoring government as a repository of memory and as a facilitator of exchange.

The final distinctive feature of business networks is partnering relationships with *selected key competitors*. A range of relationships between competitors characterizes business networks engaged in global competition—for example, joint ventures in third countries, technology transfers, supplier development, and market-sharing arrangements. These partnerships differ from formal strategic alliances since they need to rely on joint working teams to elaborate and implement the network's strategic purpose rather than depend upon formal contracts. There are both tangible and intangible benefits to this approach. The former come from traditional economic factors, such as economies of scale and scope. The latter are related to the cumulative nature of the competitive advantages that accrue from technology.[4] The network relationship with selected key competitors covers much of the same ground as the literature on strategic alliances.

Industry structure, clusters, and competitive dynamics

In this section, we review relevant literature on the clustering and localization of industry so as to demonstrate that business networks (partnerships across borders) should not be confused with Porter's (1990) strategic clusters nor with industrial districts (on which there is a large body of literature). Rather, our treatment of business networks is differentiated by: (a) its focus on international, interindustry relationships, as opposed to nation-bound intraindustry clusters; and (b) its view that networks can be designed to achieve an ongoing strategic purpose, as opposed to evolving haphazardly through 'historical contingency'.

Research into the theory of networks encompasses a wide range of academic disciplines, including economics, sociology, and management. As so much of the discussion about networks must necessarily address personal relationships, ties, and interorganizational relationships, it is not expected that the camps of industrial organization (IO) economics and strategic management emphasize different aspects of network formation.[5] The IO view says that industry structure determines competitive strategy, whereas the strategic management perspective is that industry structure is determined by competitive dynamics. It is important for both perspectives to be considered here in our discussion of the business network form of organization.

Many other writers discuss network forms of organization, leading to a great deal of ambiguity in the field. Networks can be separate and distinct forms of organization like the 'networks' of Powell (1990) and the 'hybrids' of Williamson (1991). 'Strategic linkages', that is, getting access to other firms' strategic capabilities by creating linkages or pooling resources, are discussed by Richardson (1972) and Porter and Fuller (1986). Nohria and Garcia-Pont (1991) suggest that the

---

[4] After this chapter was drafted, John Stopford passed on to Alan Rugman in November 1993 an unpublished paper, 'Creating a Strategic Centre to Manage a Web of Partners' by G. Lorenzoni and Charles Baden-Fuller, University of Bath, June 1993. Their strategic networks framework is closely related to our business network in that they use the terms 'central firm' or 'strategic centre' instead of 'flagship firm'. As we do with the asymmetry that we propose, Lorenzoni and Baden-Fuller indicate that their strategic network should be led by a central firm in an asymmetric manner, although they do not explicitly use the term 'asymmetry'. The partners in the network include suppliers, customers, and competitors but not the non-business infrastructure that we include in our model. Lorenzoni and Baden-Fuller also envisage a strategic network that is not geographically bound and that operates internationally. Lorenzoni and Baden-Fuller also discuss the importance of outsourcing and de-integration but not in terms of why a business network is an alternative to a hierarchy or a strategic cluster. They also mention trust and co-operation and the importance of interorganizational learning. As industry examples of their strategic networks, they list the business activities of Apple, Sun, Nintendo, and Benetton.

[5] Some of these ideas are derived from private communication and discussion with Steve Tallman of the University of Utah.

'strategic imperative' is sufficient to organize activity not in the market or hierarchy. The omission of transaction-cost-related arguments in most of this work is noteworthy. Again, papers in Nohria and Eccles (1992) explore the sociology of the organizational processes of networks but few of them do so from an international perspective. The narrow focus of this work has been compounded by the national 'home base' diamond of Porter (1990). This sampling of the recent extensive literature on networks makes it important to understand where global business network theory stands in relation to industry-level analysis of competitive advantage and, particularly, the work of Porter.

The business network developed above is fundamentally different from Porter's strategic cluster but his characterization of clusters is essential to an understanding of the nature of business networks. According to Porter, competitive industries in a nation will not be evenly distributed in the economy, but rather will consist of groups of industries that are closely linked to each other through vertical and horizontal linkages. These groups are termed by Porter, strategic clusters of industries. As is well known, Porter's work has always emphasized industry-level determinants of competitive advantage (Porter 1980, 1985, 1990). In Porter's (1990) work on the competitive advantage of nations, related and supporting industries in the 'home-base' diamond of competitive advantage interact with industry rivals, industry-level demand conditions, and the natural and human resource conditions. Porter's strategic clusters are industry clusters. The organizational relationships of relevance would be intraindustry ones, rather than the interindustry ones of concern to us in our analysis of business networks. In Porter (1990) the case studies reported, and the empirical tests of the 16 strategic clusters, are all at industry level. The unit of analysis for Porter's (1990) strategic clusters is the same industry level as in Porter (1980), not firm level or business unit level. Some scholars have criticized Porter's industrial organization view of strategy as a form of 'environmental determinism' and a framework where 'industry structure . . . is the primary determinant of the competitive rules of the game, and thus of firm strategy' (Bartlett and Ghoshal 1991, 8).

One aspect of strategic clustering is particularly relevant to our analysis. Such clusters tend to develop within geographic regions. Thus particular areas of a country will tend to sustain the development of specific clusters that will not be found in other regions. Furthermore, Porter's use of a 'home base' diamond of competitive advantage means that his clusters are nation bound, that is, all the partners come from a local region (such as small-scale ceramic tile makers or textile makers in Italy) with strong family ties and historical collaboration. Business networks, in contrast, are not geographically bound and include partnerships across national borders.

The localization of economic activity and the benefits of clustered industry have received extensive treatment by scholars other than Porter. Krugman's (1991) work on economic geography states that the location of economic activity is greatly influenced by 'historical contingency', namely, social, cultural, and political forces. Enright (1993a, 20) characterizes this same theme by saying that

'Economic development is an intensely path dependent process. It cannot be divorced from history ... The skills and capabilities that firms develop are often rooted in local history.' This statement is supported by the clustered industries so prevalent in Italy. In his discussion of the Emilia-Rogmana region, Brusco (1982) also provides localization explanations for the economic success of the region. Prominent in his determinations are social/political/cultural factors that can be traced back through the economic development of the region. These factors, for example, include the cultural orientation towards work, a long and proud history of artisanry, and the structural power of trade unions.

In terms of the localization of economic activity, Enright (1993*a*) highlights the advantages of local rivalry, demanding customers, skill development, etc.—the advantages of clustered activity characterized by Porter (1990). Enright also argues that these advantages are dynamic and more dependent on the informa-tion flow among individuals and organizations than on a particular geographic space. In fact, Enright appears to agree with Kogut and Zander's (1992) thesis about knowledge sharing being a determinative factor of organizational form and boundary. He proposes (1993*a*, 19) that information flow 'ultimately determines the geographic scope of competitive advantage and the economic identity of regions'.

The reasons for network development across borders are not simple. It seems that a productive approach to try to answer some of these questions is to examine 'intentional networks' like our business network. This approach has the advantage of not viewing a network simply as a patchwork of strategic alliances and joint ventures. It looks at the network as a totality and a system that is created to accom-plish a strategic purpose or purposes. From this perspective, it may be easier to discern the advantages and drawbacks of a network organization.[6]

Transaction costs and business networks

In this section of the chapter, we briefly review the literature on the organization of economic activity in markets and hierarchies which is relevant to our discus-sion of business networks. We proceed by discussing the limitations inherent in the size and bureaucracy of the traditional hierarchical firm. This discussion suggests that the environment of continual and rapid change in global markets

---

[6] Another unresolved theoretical issue relevant to the emerging theory of business networks and strategic clusters is the extent to which a new V-form organizational structure is emerging (where V stands for a business network 'virtual' corporation). There have been references to this type of struc-ture in the popular business press (*Business Week* 1993) but no significant analytical development on a par with the M-form of Williamson (1975). To date, the term 'virtual' corporation has been used to describe quite different situations. In some cases it refers to short-term, project-related linkages (for example, Hollywood film making); in others, it describes more lasting relationships to address numer-ous strategic objectives. Both uses of the term, however, depend upon accessing the resources and expertise of others. Conceptually, many of the external linkages discussed here, which need to be devel-oped for a business network to be successful, can be thought of as a V-form organizational structure. But our V-form is asymmetrical, with the strategy of the flagship firm being that of the network and with the partners more responsible for its operational success.

has new implications for the efficiency of the hierarchy as a governance structure relative to business networks.

Williamson's framework (1975) for transaction cost analysis has become the mainstream explanation in economics and management for determining whether particular activities or transaction should take place through market mechanisms or be conducted within a firm (hierarchy). The hierarchy is the preferred mediating mechanism when some form of market failure occurs or is anticipated, or, in other words, when there are significant transaction costs to doing business through market mechanisms.

The transaction cost approach has been extended to explain the existence of the MNE through the development of internalization theory (Buckley and Casson 1976). The MNE is organized to capture those aspects of its firm-specific advantages (FSAs) that cannot be protected in market transaction because of the substantial transaction costs involved, particularly those costs related to uncertainty and opportunism (Rugman 1981, 1986). The MNE replaces market mechanisms with internal governance mechanisms—organizational structures, systems, and processes that ensure that its intangible proprietary assets are not dissipated. These governance mechanisms, however, are themselves not without cost (Williamson 1975, 1985). Both tangible and intangible costs are involved. The tangible costs are those related to the people and the communications infrastructure required to operate the governance apparatus. Intangible costs arise because individuals and subgroups within the firm may pursue objectives other than those of the firm itself, using guile and opportunism to further their own ends by turning the governance machinery to their own uses (Allison 1971).

Williamson's work is particularly useful in explaining the emergence of large-scale enterprises (like MNEs) that exceed the conventional scale efficiency levels of their industry. Still, the limitations inherent in the transaction-cost-economics approach are being recognized in the literature on business networks. These oft-repeated criticisms include: (a) the focus on single transactions as the unit of analysis, an approach that ignores considerations of how repeated transactions and governance structures could be related in a more dynamic manner; (b) the assumption that economic actors are motivated only by efficiency, an approach that ignores governance structures that may be created or prolonged past their 'efficiency' contribution, for reasons other than efficiency; (c) the assumption that these 'atomistic actors' will behave opportunistically to further efficiency goals, an approach that ignores governance structures, the design and evolution of which have been influenced by trusting and co-operative behaviour.

Business networks arise as forms of organizing economic activity outside hierarchies and markets. There are two key reasons from a transaction costs perspective. First, using the governance systems of large firms is costly because hierarchies often require elaborate formal structures, complex systems and procedures, and onerous reporting requirements to meet stakeholder concerns as well as organizational control. An example is the M-form, regarded by Williamson (1975) as a general case of hierarchical control.[7] In other words, the transaction costs of using the hierarchy to integrate complex value chains are substantial. This leads to the development of a network of subsidiaries (Bartlett and Ghoshal 1989), or to the type of business network outlined earlier in this chapter.

Large hierarchical organizations need internal organizational processes to implement their strategies; but, in turn, these structures are subject to governance costs and entropy. Entropy, the tendency towards disorder or degradation, is not limited to natural systems such as chemical or biological processes. Over time, large artificial constructs and systems also tend towards degradation. An example analogous to bureaucracies (hierarchies) is useful. Energy is put into building a stone wall. The wall is highly structured and ordered. Gradually, internal and external forces cause the wall to fall apart. Unless energy is applied constantly to maintain the wall, the original energy put into building the wall dissipates into the surrounding environment, and the wall becomes disordered.

Many large firms attempt to resist this entropic tendency by keeping the firm highly ordered. Unfortunately, today's competitive market environment increasingly penalizes firms with rigid structures. This rigidity limits interaction, communication, learning, innovation, and the ability to adapt quickly.

The consequence of entropy on organizational structures is that large firms would need to expend energy in creating and maintaining structures and relationships (internal and external). The just-in-time (JIT) inventory systems and lean production techniques of firms in the automobile industry are examples of attempts to circumvent the limitations of the rigidity inherent in bureaucracy. Implicitly, the automobile industry firms are diminishing the impact of this rigidity by tapping the competencies and resources of others and, in so doing, are changing the very structure that limited them in the first place. The new structure is part of a business network, a key point of which is linkages to competencies and resources of others.

It is evident that large firms do experience these limitations of size. They spin off smaller subsidiaries; create new R&D laboratories; empower employees with more responsibility and autonomy; de-layer their organizations; establish alliances and joint ventures; sell off business units to focus on core competencies; and so on. Once the cost of internal development of such competencies and resources is too high in the rapidly changing environments in which firms compete today, then business networks arise. Again, when the cost of staying in a status quo position is too high due to (a) the wasted energy (time, money, human resources) required to maintain the structure and (b) lesser returns (adaptability, innovation) on the energy input, then business networks replace hierarchies.

Second, the market solution can be inadequate as well. Complex value chains

---

[7] Hedlund (1992) states that the N-form organizational structure of collaborative ventures is more representative of international business arrangements than is the Williamson (1975) M-form (multidivisional) structure. We agree and, indeed, would argue that the M-form is now a special case of MNE activity, not the general case.

require investment in proprietary assets that are difficult to protect through market contracting. There is an overwhelming need to build relationships based on trust—relationships that cannot, because of the high degree of uncertainty and risk inherent in the business system, be reduced to formal contractual arrangements (Ouchi 1980).[8] This theory leads to the expectation that business networks will emerge in business systems involving complex value chains.[9] Many contemporary industries exhibit these characteristics (Miles and Snow 1984). An excellent example is the automobile industry. Design, production, and marketing of automobiles require a business system that is capable of efficient and effective organization of an extremely varied set of economic activities. At the same time, the volatility of the regulatory and market environment is extremely high, leading to high risk and uncertainty.

A framework for business networks

Using a simple two-by-two matrix (see Figure 5.2), we demonstrate that markets, hierarchies, strategic clusters, and business networks can be defined by two axes: governance costs and the level of integration of the organization. Further, we explore the need for asymmetry in business networks as a means of reducing the governance costs that may arise due to co-ordination outside the hierarchy.

The vertical axis of the matrix can be operationalized by consideration of transaction costs relevant to the level of integration of the organization. Complex organizational structures with a high level of integration experience opportunism, or asset specificity, or problems of small numbers, or information complexity. A low level of integration is characteristic of organizations with a simpler structure; these have fewer transaction costs.

On the other axis, the 'internal' governance costs of the organization exist in the sense of Coase (1937) and Williamson (1975). The governance costs of organization are greater for business networks than for hierarchies and are also greater for strategic clusters than for markets. The reason is that business networks involve managerial relationships with 'external' partners, that is, there are intra-industry governance costs. In contrast, there are lower governance costs with an 'internal' intrafirm hierarchy. Similarly the governance costs of a market, with its 'invisible hand', are lower than for strategic clusters with the many external relationships that must be managed.

---

[8] It is important to distinguish our concept of a business network from Ouchi's concept of 'clans'. Ouchi (1980) says that a clan will succeed when its informational requirements are satisfied by traditions and when its normative requirements are met by reciprocity, legitimate authority, and a set of common values and beliefs. While these attributes are useful in a business network, they are secondary to the vision generated by the flagship firm's commitment to a successful global strategy. In other words, Ouchi's clan system is a necessary (process-based) condition but not a sufficient condition for the success of a business network.

[9] Ouchi's three modes of organization—markets, bureaucracies, and clans—are transformed into four modes by Jarillo (1988), when he retains bureaucracies and clans but splits Ouchi's 'markets' into classic markets and strategic networks, where the latter reflect co-operative, non-zero-sum relationships as opposed to zero-sum, adversarial relationships for the firm.

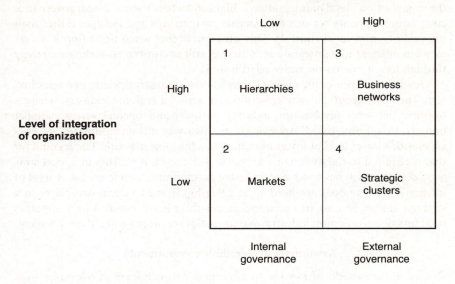

Figure 5.2 Governance costs and integration of organizations

Quadrant 1, in an international context, is the MNE. Here governance costs are low but the level of integration is high, and hierarchies result—a process achieved by internalization. This occurs, for example, when the assets to be protected are intangible brand names, intellectual property, or industrial know-how, or when buyer uncertainty must be overcome. Internalization leads to a firm-specific advantage for the MNE (Rugman 1981). Historically, most MNEs have had a low degree of interaction with other firms and so have a lower degree of governance costs than firms with such relationships.

In quadrant 2, individual firms again have low governance costs (due to the 'invisible hand' of the market) and have a low level of integration, that is, they use the economist's neoclassical market. This occurs when the product or service can be produced efficiently at low scale, where few proprietary assets of an intangible nature are involved, and where other opportunities for economic rents are absent. Often firms in quadrant 2 are small. A particular form of these circumstances occurs when governments impose on large firms costs that do not apply to small firms. A case in point is the Italian textile industry, which 'deintegrated' from about 700 firms in 1951 to more than 9,500 firms in 1976 because the government enacted laws that taxed large firms at a higher rate than small firms, and exempted the smallest firms from onerous reporting requirements (Lorenzoni 1982).

Quadrant 3 describes a business network. It deals with circumstances where the organization's level of integration is high, and where there are high governance costs (since there are reasons for external partnerships and linkages rather than internal organizational control). This situation occurs when firms find it necessary but efficient to deintegrate activities yet still attempt to co-ordinate strategy through long-term, co-operative relationships.

Quadrant 4 captures the case of Porter's (1990) industry-specific strategic clusters. These are geographically close linkages across a regional industry, whereas business networks involve non-industry partners and operate across national borders. In a 'home-based' strategic cluster, two-way intrafirm linkages are possible, with a lower level of integration than in a business network. The asymmetry that is required in the more complex business network is missing in a local strategic cluster, which has fewer non-industry partners and therefore a lower level of integration. There does not need to be a flagship firm as a dominant player in a strategic cluster. Instead, in a strategic cluster, there is a two-way flow to the strategic process, as common industry characteristics are more similar than divergent.

Asymmetry and credible commitments

One of the drawbacks of moving to a business network form of organization is that certain other governance costs, once minimized in the hierarchy, are likely to become meaningful factors. A good example is the potential increase in opportunism. The business network, however, has mechanisms to overcome opportunism. Specifically, we argue that the asymmetry[10] of the business network lessens the impact of such costs by increasing the credible commitments (Williamson 1985) of the five partners. We propose that asymmetry is effective in:

(a) increasing interorganizational trust;
(b) increasing the stability of the network; and
(c) increasing interorganizational learning.

The first organizational benefit of asymmetry is supported by Ring and Van de Ven (1992). They posit that more lasting and high-trust relationships evolve from cumulative transactional experience. They also criticize transaction cost economics for its flawed emphasis on single transactions, not repeated transactions—also noted by Doz and Prahalad (1991). Due to the greater degree of transaction exclusivity in the business network, asymmetry facilitates easier accumulation of transactions and consequently the development of trust. Higher levels of trust lower transaction costs associated with opportunism, monitoring and enforcing agreements, loss of proprietary knowledge, etc.

---

[10]   We are using the concept of asymmetry in a different context than does Harrigan (1988). She explores the role of partner asymmetries (in relative asset size, national origin, and venturing experience) in strategic alliances rather than in our type of business network. She finds that it is the purpose and the need for a co-operative venturing relationship which are most important to decisions regarding the use of strategic alliances. Less important to the survival, duration, and success of a co-operative venture are the traits of the partners and their sponsor–venture relationship.

In terms of the second benefit of asymmetry (increased network stability), we propose that asymmetry facilitates the permanence of shared interorganizational purpose (Luke, Begun, and Pointer 1989) through agreement on a narrower strategic agenda because it reduces dissension associated with competing strategic objectives. The permanence of shared interorganizational purpose thus increases the stability of the network. Borys and Jemison (1989) indicate that the sovereignty of hybrid (network-like organizations) partners is a constant threat to the stability and continuity of the hybrid. We argue that asymmetry facilitates stability by decreasing the sovereignty of partners in regard to those aspects of their businesses that are committed to the strategic purpose of the business network—or, at least, by negating the inclination of partners to protect their sovereignty by means of non-cooperation.

In regard to interorganizational learning, we propose that asymmetry assists the flow of information among the network partners. Because the business network has a flagship firm as its strategic focal point, it has a facilitator/co-ordinator to push the development of a 'common language'. Moreover, the strategic asymmetry obviates the need for the partners to protect their knowledge-based FSAs. Interorganizational learning is addressed in greater depth in a later section of the chapter.

Powell (1990) recognizes the imbalances inherent in interorganizational relationships when one party is dependent upon the resources of another (or others). But this imbalance is used to advantage through the pooling of resources. He supports the idea advanced by Kaneko and Imai (1987) that information relayed in networks is 'thicker' than information received from the market and is freer than information communicated in hierarchies. As we have discussed, Powell admits that networks may increase transaction costs; but he suggests that such costs are bearable due to such benefits as fast access to information, responsiveness to the market, and reduced uncertainty.

In contrast to our arguments for the benefits of asymmetry, Miles and Snow (1984) warn against imbalance in interorganizational relationships. They state that dependence on a core firm (for example in a buyer–supplier relationship) is risky because the dependent firm loses the benefits of market participation. They argue that too much dedication/co-operation could cause the core firm to end up managing its partners' assets, to the extent that the network is converted into a vertically integrated firm. They emphasize the voluntarism of network members (the ability to enter into and withdraw from unfairly structured situations) as an important network component. Their use of the term networks, however, encompasses a wide variety of interorganizational relationships, some of which are quite rudimentary.[11]

---

[11] Similarly, Thorelli's (1986) use of the term network is 'two or more organizations involved in long-term relationships'. As an early writer on networks, Thorelli should be given credit for the view that there is a rich and complex area of economic activity which is not suitably discussed in Williamson's (1975) discrete poles of markets and hierarchies. Quite correctly, Thorelli addresses power, influence, and trust as key topics for inclusion in future network theory research.

The issue of close ties is raised by Perrow (1992) when he discusses small-firm networks and explicitly addresses the issue of dependent versus independent subcontracting. He argues that thick-waisted networks (networks with many producers between suppliers and customers, as opposed to production concentrated in several large firms) are a structural basis for co-operation. The advantages of his multiple-tie network include sector/industry flexibility, stimulation of innovation, and sector-wide problem solving. Porter (1990) cites these factors as benefits of close geographic clustering of firms in an industry. In regard to dependent subcontractors, Perrow uses German industry as an example of many large firms insisting that their subcontractors not become dependent on them because such dependence limits the subcontractors' viability and health.

The opposite argument to that advanced by Perrow can be supported as well. It is open to question whether the aforementioned benefits result from multiple ties or from the nature of those ties. Perrow focuses on the structure but perhaps does not emphasize process enough. If the benefits accrue from the nature of the ties (longevity, trust, co-operation, sharing), then it can be posited that a reduction in the number of ties may not be detrimental.

Opportunism, trust, and governance structures

The relevance of arguments outside the transaction costs school of thinking needs to be explored further to understand business networks. Therefore, we now discuss the issues of trust and social relations as they pertain to the efficiency of governance structures. The literature on these issues, on the whole, supports our belief that interorganizational relationships between autonomous organizations can be efficient, and that the five partners model reduces opportunism. We contend that economic relationships that are embedded in mutually designed and formed social relations, that is five partners relationships, will lead to lasting credible commitments. The following literature review lends support to our contention that the formation of governance structures is closely associated with the presence of trust. Moreover, it illustrates the differing schools of thought on the genesis of governance structures—particularly those that do not subscribe to a pure neoclassical model.

While we argue that trust is an important condition for the successful development of network relations, we do not believe its presence is sufficient to guarantee an effective governance structure. Similarly, tightness of social relations alone is insufficient. Moreover, there is not necessarily a causal relationship between the tightness of social relations and the existence of trust, that is to say, there are examples of long-term, tight social relations that operate in the absence of high levels of trust (for example, unions, organized crime syndicates). Therefore, we argue that it is the strategic interdependence among the business network's partners which is the glue that binds social relations, trust, and the efficiency of the governance structure.

Our understanding of the importance of social relations has been greatly assisted by Granovetter's (1985) thinking. But we extend his thesis by proposing that the structure of social relations need not be serendipitous. Rather, the moulding of the selection procedures and relationship structure within the five partners framework maximizes the efficacy of economic action. Granovetter approaches the organization of economic activity from a sociological perspective.[12] He proposes that economic action is embedded in structures of social relations, and that the analysis of the market/hierarchies question from this perspective generates a different understanding of the organization of economic activity. His key point is that social relations between firms can replicate the efficacy of hierarchies. Granovetter's thesis, therefore, is that efficiency of economic transaction is more dependent on the structure of social relations than on the organizational form in which transactions take place. Specifically, he claims that the reasons for internalizing activity within the hierarchy, such as to avoid opportunism and to create order, are a misplaced and simplistic adherence to the assumptions of the transaction costs approach.

Hill (1990) takes a different tack from those authors whose point of departure in analysis is that opportunism is best kept in check through internalization in the hierarchy and through vertical integration. He is on a similar track to us when he questions whether the risk of opportunism has been overstated, particularly with regard to situations characterized by high asset specificity. Hill argues persuasively that the invisible hand of the market selects economic actors that behave in a co-operative manner[13] or, conversely, penalizes organizations that are opportunistic. Hill's argument illustrates the explanatory limitations of transaction cost theory, specifically its inadequacy in capturing repeated transactions, the market's 'evolutionary selection mechanism', and the emergence of 'complex behavioural repertoires' in relationship-based transactions.

Support for network linkages is enhanced by an examination of those situations where co-operation fails to deal with opportunism, as identified by Hill: (a) when the certainty of outcomes is low; (b) when the reputation of parties to an exchange is difficult to establish; and (c) when the pay-off from short-term opportunistic behaviour exceeds the potential gains (discounted to the present) from future co-operation, which is jeopardized by that opportunism. Business networks with 'rational contracting' (Ring and Van de Ven 1992) explicitly promote co-operation in the above instances. The certainty of outcome and the reputation of parties are known to a much greater extent in such a network. Short-term opportunistic behaviour is curtailed because the health of the relationship and future gains are directly and explicitly linked.

---

[12] Another perspective that can be classified as having a strong sociological contribution is that of Burt (1992). His work on structural holes, however, is not particularly relevant to our treatment of business networks, for its perspective is too micro-oriented in terms of relationships. Our chapter's approach discusses interorganizational relationships from a macro level.

[13] Hakan Hakansson and Jan Johanson (1988) give a broad overview of the use of formal and informal co-operation strategies in international business. They make the point that informal co-operation depends on trust developed through exchange, whereas formal co-operation is often 'negotiated' at a higher management level and often may not lead to real co-operation.

A recent paper by Casson and Cox (1992) uses a two-by-three matrix to explain the move to network forms of organization. They use trust as one axis in their matrix and 'contractual economic principle' as the other. In their framework, low trust leads to markets (with external contracts), M-form firms, or U-firm hierarchies. High trust leads to interfirm networks (external contracts), intrafirm networks (internal contract), and paternalistic firms. We agree that trust is important but is insufficiently causal on its own to warrant an axis in their matrix.

The organic and dynamic nature of business networks has been discussed by Ring and Van de Ven (1992), who view the emergence of relational contracts and governance structures as a dynamic process. In their discussion of the structure of interorganizational relationships, Ring and Van de Ven distinguish between recurrent contracting (short-term, low transaction cost) and relational contracting (long-term, high transaction cost). They argue that the evolution towards more lasting and high-trust relational relationships is a result of cumulative transactional experience and the associated degree of trust developed. We add to this point by arguing that it is the strategic interdependence of the asymmetric business network that facilitates the accumulation of these transactions.

In his study of subcontracting in France's small and medium-sized engineering firms, Lorenz (1988) examines interorganizational trust among project and industry partners. Of interest to us in the modelling of business networks are two of his conclusions:

(1) Promoting trust is costly but lack of trust among 'partners' is more costly. Lorenz found that, without the security of commitment in a long-term partnership, contractors were unwilling to invest in technology because of the volatility in their orders (from the partner). This lack of investment eventually harms the competitiveness of the contractor.

(2) Trust can be created intentionally through the accumulation of transactions, not solely by 'the shared values of community members' (p. 209). Consequently, efforts to build business network partnerships need to recognize the importance of forgoing short-term gains so as to develop lasting relationships based upon trust.

Lorenz's study lends credence to Ring and Van de Ven's (1992) assertion that cumulative transactional experience facilitates trust.

From this thinking, we derive the following three implications:

(1) The emergence of organic organizational process structures in a business network is dependent upon an understanding of why and how interfirm linkages form, evolve, and dissolve.

(2) A successful business network is one where the transaction cost of opportunism is diminished by the simultaneous development of relational contracting process structures that can increase trust amongst the partners involved.

(3) The organizational process of external linkages in business networks

evolves in a dynamic manner and is more complex than the more discrete polar choices of markets or hierarchies.

Interorganizational learning

The previous two sections stressed the importance of credible commitments as a means of decreasing opportunism and the costs associated with mediating its effect. Here, we integrate relevant recent literature on learning, skill development, and 'codifying' knowledge. The intent of this section is to argue that inter-organizational learning is not divorced from efficiency-based reasons for changing governance structures.

One of the fundamental assumptions in regard to communication within and among organizations is that internal communication must be less costly and more efficient than external communication. This assumption is predicated upon the convenient view that large organizations are monolithic in culture, norms, and social values. If this is an extreme or exaggerated assumption, then it may be more prudent to argue that the parts of the monolith are more similar than dissimilar. In either case, it is customarily argued that internal procedures smooth the differences. This reasoning no longer reflects the complexity and diversity of the activities encompassed in a globally competing multinational. It would not be unusual to encounter divisions of a multinational which are more culturally diverse than they are similar (Bower 1993). Moreover, the logic of this observation could be extended to conclude that parts of an MNE may have more in common with external organizations than with internal ones. Therefore, the greater efficacy of intraorganizational communication (that is, within the hierarchy) as compared with interorganizational communication through long-term relationships (a network) is not a certain conclusion.

Kogut and Zander (1992) challenge the pure transaction costs perspective, which reasons that internalization is driven by the need to protect against opportunism. Like Granovetter (1985), they believe that knowledge (and therefore, economic relations) is embedded in the social relationships in the firm. Kogut and Zander argue that the distinguishing *raison d'être* of firms over markets is that firms share and transfer the knowledge of both groups and individuals within an organization better than markets can. The authors believe that the boundaries of the firm, or as we discuss a network of firms, are defined by how well knowledge is generated from current capabilities or from recombining them. Knowledge is organized by 'codifiability' and 'complexity', and by such organization facilitates its sharing as a common language. This sharing is dependent upon an understood code or language within the organization which has been created partially by the social relationships in the firm. Kogut and Zander suggest that using the transaction as the unit of analysis of organizational capability ignores the impact that social relations have on knowledge and capability.

As with Ring and Van de Ven's (1992) theory of relational contracting, Kogut and Zander (1993) lend credence to our belief that learning within the business network can be effected just as it is within the firm. Powell's argument (1990) also supports our approach, for he believes that the process of acquiring knowledge and learning of skills is enhanced through the relational, open-ended features of networks.

Hamel (1991) stresses the importance of interorganizational learning. He argues for analysis of 'the process of knowledge acquisition and skill building' (p. 83) and he emphasizes asymmetries in the skill endowment of firms, leading to efficiency-based reasons for collaboration and interpartner learning. Porter's industry-based, competitive strategy paradigm, with its product-market positioning, has been criticized by Hamel as a focus 'on only the last few hundred yards of what may be a skill-building marathon' (p. 83).

It is evident from the research into knowledge sharing and capability development that organizational learning plays an important role in determining how economic transactions are organized. We believe that the success of the business network is dependent, to a certain extent, on organizational learning. Eventually, it is expected that the network will develop its own shared language or means of organizing and transmitting information. The boundaries of the flagship firm, therefore, are open to change as the business network evolves and 'matures'. For example, if the flagship firm and several research institutes in the non-business infrastructure gradually become more adept at sharing information and resources, then the flagship firm's boundaries, effectively, will have been shifted.

In terms of the five partners model of the business network, this implies that skill development must be a more robust process if effected through intersharing of industry linkages rather than intraindustry linkages. As with cross-functional learning, cross-industry learning is more likely to add to an organization's pool of knowledge than are the diminishing returns from intraindustry sharing of knowledge. Asymmetry thus facilitates interindustry learning among partners by increasing credible commitments and reducing the need to internalize knowledge-based FSAs.

Conclusions

In this chapter, we have developed the five partners model of a business network. This model of organizing exchange through long-term, co-operative relationships is a contribution to the traditional market-hierarchy dyad. We related our new model to the discussion of networks in the management field and improved upon the vague definitions used in much of the literature. We have argued that our business network represents a new form of governance structure; it is not merely a firm with several alliances nor one with just a key-supplier programme. The business network is distinguished by asymmetric strategic leadership by an MNE of the network's five partners. We argued that the asymmetry increases credible commitments and thereby plays a valuable role in increasing interorganizational trust, the stability of the network, and interorganizational learning. In a well-functioning business network, asymmetry reduces the need for contractual exclusivity with suppliers due to the credible commitments it produces.

We have integrated relevant concepts from the mainstream literature on international business, strategic management, economic geography, and sociology. In particular, we have drawn together three key ideas: the costs of opportunism and asset specificity in exchange transactions; the embeddedness of economic action in structures of social relations; and the codification of knowledge in a 'language' to facilitate interorganizational learning. Through the integration of these three ideas, we found that the business network is an effective governance structure that recognizes the realities of economic exchange and social relations in an imperfect world.

For an understanding of business networks, it is important that social relations be considered explicitly in the formation of governance structures, and not simply be dismissed as 'frictional matters'. It is becoming apparent that skill development and continuous learning will play key roles in economic competitiveness into the foreseeable future. The changing shape of the MNE through deintegration suggests, therefore, that interorganizational learning must be better understood. The economic competitiveness of firms is becoming less a matter of exploiting advantages of sheer size and market power, and more one of capitalizing on business network flexibility and adaptability. These latter traits, when combined with competitiveness in leading technologies, can be a potent means of achieving overall firm competitiveness.

New governance structures have significant implications for the role of management, especially in the global context of an MNE's operations. These implications have been discussed by Rugman and D'Cruz (1991) and D'Cruz and Rugman (1992a) in their treatment of strategic clusters and business networks in a Canadian context. Senior managers working for the flagship firm of a business network need to broaden the scope of their strategic thinking. They must understand how each of the partners contributes to the international competitiveness of the business network as a whole. Moreover, they must broaden their perspective of control and competition to include sharing and co-operation. In terms of public policy, the development of business networks presents challenges to the role of government, particularly in regard to anti-trust and competition policy. Second, government and business need to determine whose role it is to lead the industrial strategy process. This chapter makes clear our belief that MNEs must assume this responsibility. In terms of further research, the authors are studying the telecommunications industry in Canada; see D'Cruz and Rugman (1994a).

In the future, we will need to devote even more attention to the growing importance of business networks and their new interindustry organizational linkages. We can gain new insight into corporate strategy by expanding the international management perspective from internalization theory and transaction costs to a consideration of the role of business networks as an organizational form that plays an important role in globalization and that creates 'partners across borders'.

6

The Theory of the Flagship Firm

Multinational Enterprise Strategy

Today the competitive strategies of MNEs are determined by a complex web of factors at regional, country, industry, firm, business unit, and organizational task level. To cut through this dense jungle of potential cognitive and motivational factors affecting managerial decision making in MNEs it will be useful to build upon a recent synthesis of work on the theory of the MNE and its interactions with key partners. This is the 'five partners' or 'flagship' model of business networks, as developed by D'Cruz and Rugman (1992b, 1993). The five partners model has been applied to analysis of the Canadian telecommunications industry by D'Cruz and Rugman (1994a) and to the European telecommunications industry by D'Cruz and Rugman (1994b). It has been applied to the Canadian chemicals industry by D'Cruz, Gestrin, and Rugman (1995). The five partners model emphasizes co-operative behaviour in network relationships and it can be contrasted with the five forces model of Porter (1980), which emphasizes rivalry and entry barriers as mechanisms to exercise market power and achieve competitive advantage.

The linkage of the D'Cruz and Rugman (1992b, 1993) five partners model to earlier work on the theory of the MNE comes through the role of the MNE as a 'flagship firm' at the hub of the five partners model. The MNE is competing globally and it provides strategic leadership to partners such as key suppliers, key customers, and the non-business infrastructure (NBI). The rationale for the MNE is explained by transaction cost economics and internalization theory, as first developed by Buckley and Casson (1976). They demonstrated that economic activity takes place by MNEs when the benefits of internalization outweigh its costs and that this usually occurs under conditions when there are market imperfections in the pricing of intangible knowledge. This work was further refined by Casson (1979) and in essays collected in Buckley and Casson (1985). It was expanded into the 'eclectic paradigm' of international business by Dunning (1979, 1981). Internalization theory has been extended and applied in a North American context by Rugman (1980a, 1981, 1986).

The relationship between the modern theory of the MNE and the flagship model, with its implication for some deinternalization (when successful network relationships are developed) has been discussed by Rugman, D'Cruz, and Verbeke (1995). They argue that the internalization decision for an MNE takes into account concepts of business policy and competitive strategy and that proprietary firm specific advantages (FSAs) yield potential economic profits when exploited on a world-wide basis. Yet the MNE finds these potential profits dissipated by internal governance costs of its organizational structure and the difficulty of timing and sustaining its FDI activities. This leads to deinternalization when the benefits of internalization are outweighed by its costs. Deinternalization usually occurs within a business network when successful partnerships are found, as in the flagship model. The movement from internalization to business network requires analysis of parent–subsidiary relationships and the governance costs of running an MNE as compared with managing relationships in a business network.

Recently internalization theory has been linked to the resource-based theory of the firm by Kogut and Zander (1992, 1993), and others, who argue that issues of organizational learning complicate, and may even undermine, the argument for internalization. To help reconcile the basic thrust of internalization theory with the need for explicit consideration of organizational relationships, it is useful to consider the network relationships captured within the flagship model.

The flagship model

Business networks are becoming increasingly common in industries where internationalization and globalization are advanced. In a business network a set of companies interact and co-operate with each other from the manufacture of basic raw materials to final consumption.

Conventional business relationships are characterized by arm's-length competition between firms as they buy and sell. Such relationships, which are the basis of Michael Porter's (1980) five forces model of competitive advantage, are based, to a large extent, on the development and exercise of market power. They tend to foster a short-term orientation among participants, with each participant being concerned primarily with its own profitability.

The D'Cruz and Rugman flagship model is based on the development of collaborative relationships among major players in a business system. Its focus is on strategies that are mutually reinforcing. By their very nature, such relationships tend to foster and depend upon a collective long-term orientation among the parties concerned. Hence, they form an important facilitating mechanism for the development of long-term competitiveness.

There are two key features of such a system: one, the presence of a flagship firm that pulls the network together and provides leadership for the strategic management of the network as a whole; and two, the existence of firms that have established key relationships with that flagship. These relationships are illustrated in Figure 6.1 by black arrows that cross organizational boundaries, symbolizing the nature of interfirm collaboration that characterizes them. Conventional arm's-length relationships are shown as dotted arrows that stop at organizational boundaries.

The five partners business network consists of a group of firms and non-business institutions competing globally and linked together through close interfirm organizational linkages (D'Cruz and Rugman, 1992b). There are five partners in

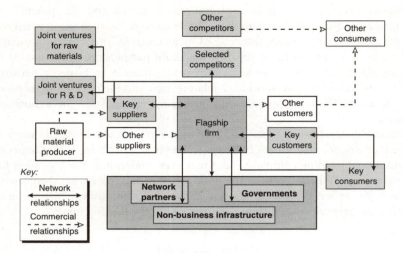

Figure 6.1 The flagship firm and its business network

the business network: the flagship firm (which is an MNE), key suppliers, key customers, competitors, and the NBI. The latter partner includes the service-related sectors, educational and training institutions, the various levels of government, and other organizations such as trade associations, non-governmental organizations, and unions. The strategic management aspects of this flagship model are now developed in detail.

The theory of the flagship firm

The flagship firm is an entity that provides strategic leadership and direction for a vertically integrated chain of businesses that operate as a co-ordinated system or network, frequently in competition with similar networks that address the same end markets. As the central co-ordinating authority in its network, the flagship firm establishes relationships with its key suppliers and key customers and ensures that they operate to implement a strategy for the network that is formulated by the flagship. We have called this relationship *strategic asymmetry* (D'Cruz and Rugman, 1994*a*). This is meant to imply that the flagship exercises control over the strategy of its network partners, while they have no reciprocal influence over the flagship's strategy. It determines and sets limits to the products and/or markets in which its network partners will be allowed to operate, it chooses the courses of action they will adopt to develop competencies in these fields of endeavour, and it directs their capital investment programmes. In return, network, partners are given membership in the flagship's network, which usually carries with it the prospects of significant sales volumes, access to advanced technology, and participation in the benefits of the brand image of the flagship.

In addition to such relationships with suppliers and customers in a vertical chain, modern flagships have also established similar alliances with organizations in the NBI—universities, unions, research institutes, and government bodies. The key feature of these links to the NBI is that they are designed to enhance the access of the rest of the network to intellectual property and human capital. In that sense, these institutions are really suppliers of intangible inputs to the vertical chain. Consequently, it should be expected that the nature of these relationships will resemble those devoted to tangible inputs. Thus, the flagship will tend to exercise significant influence and control over the strategy of these non-business partners as it relates to their membership in the network. For example, the flagship will prescribe the areas for research inquiry of its university partners, set the terms of reference for human capital development projects with unions, and provide leadership for business–government initiatives aimed at enhancing the competitiveness of the networks.

Finally, some flagship firms have established limited alliances with direct competitors. These include joint ventures for development of raw material projects or the manufacture of specialized inputs; in both cases, the minimum economic scale of the undertaking is usually larger than would be justified by the requirements of either partner on its own. Other forms of collaboration with competitors are joint efforts for R&D of a precompetitive nature, membership in consortia to bid for large projects, and agreements on technical standards for the industry. While the flagship's relations with its competitors do not share the strategic asymmetry feature of its links with other network partners, it has another characteristic in common.

A fundamental feature of these relationships is their focus on collaborative rather than competitive behaviour. Thus, in transactions based on a network alliance relationship, the parties are motivated to work closely with each other to further the aims of the network, which they regard as compatible with their own welfare. This can be contrasted with the competitive behaviour described in the five forces model by Porter (1980). The latter model encourages firms to behave in competition with their suppliers and customers for a share of the profits in transactions with each other. It focuses on the development and exercise of a market power in business systems, with managerial attention devoted to optimizing results on a transaction-by-transaction basis—a short-run orientation. On the other hand, the network mode of collaboration requires that both parties to a relationship apply the calculus of the benefits they hope to obtain and the costs they will incur across an indefinite stream of transactions rather than on one transaction at a time. It encourages the sharing of market intelligence and intellectual property without recourse to formal contracting to protect the self-interest of either party. In sum, these relationships are collaborative and long term in orientation.

The large automakers are often cited as examples of firms that have adopted the flagship mode of operations. Thus Chrysler, for example, has developed close collaborative relationships with its key suppliers, who are often encouraged to establish their own plants close to its assembly plants. These relationships are of a collaborative nature, with both sides operating on the assumption that they will continue indefinitely. This facilitates the making of highly specialized capital investments by both parties to optimize their joint operations. Similarly, Chrysler develops close long-term relationships with its dealers, who operate as an integral part of the overall system which is directed by the automaker. The entire chain— suppliers, automaker, dealers—is managed as a single system whose strategic direction comes almost exclusively from the automaker who functions as its flagship. The amount and nature of co-ordination necessary for effective functioning of this system can best be appreciated by considering what occurs when a new platform is created. Decisions about positioning and timing, for example, are the exclusive preserve of the automaker. The introduction of a new platform also involves adoption of new process technology. On the other hand, there are a myriad of operational issues that are the responsibility of the network partners, who are frequently required to make considerable investments in new equipment and training.

As a second example, let us examine the role of France Telecom as the flagship of that country's principal telecommunications system (D'Cruz and Rugman, 1994*b*). Its strategic role is to provide the vision and direction for the technological choices and associated commercial initiatives for the system. Thus, France Telecom determined to develop a system that was at the leading edge in such technologies as fibre optics and digitalization. It required its suppliers and distributors to devote resources to developing their own capabilities in these areas. Equally important, it provided strategic leadership to a network of government-funded research centres on telecommunications to co-ordinate the development of technology in these areas. It also directed the country's training institutions in telecommunications to make appropriate changes to their curricula to ensure availability of a work-force skilled in these technologies. What has emerged is an advanced telecommunications system with a highly centralized process for strategic decision making coupled with decentralized operational capability. The key features of a flagship network—strategic asymmetry and collaborative relationships—are abundantly evident.

Some of the better known flagship networks are those that have been created by the Japanese. Known as *vertical keiretsu*, these networks have succeeded in building formidable global competitive positions in such diverse fields as consumer electronics (Sony, Matsushita), automobiles (Toyota, Nissan) and computers (NEC, Toshiba). It should be mentioned that the strategies and structures of a *vertical keiretsu* are significantly different from the traditional Japanese *keiretsu*, which is a family of broadly diversified companies with a bank/trading company at its centre. For dimensions of Japanese business networks see Fruin (1992), Gerlach (1992), and Westney (1995).

The structure of the flagship firm

Having described the flagship firm and provided some examples, let us now turn to the central question of this chapter—the theoretical rationale for its existence.

To do so, we need to establish certain assumptions about the management structure of the typical flagship firm. Treating it as a single, unitary actor is unsatisfactory. First, this assumption inhibits development of theory about the behaviour of the flagship firm towards its network partners because it requires a constellation of follow-on assumptions about: its objective function regarding profit maximization or shareholder value maximization; the unity of purpose at various levels of the firm; the dominance of economic/financial rationality in decision making.

Second, it introduces a subtle bias in the nature of hypotheses that will be developed for empirical research about business systems led by flagship firms. Hypotheses about a unitary actor naturally tend to be based on expected regularities in its behaviour towards its network partners, given certain conditions. Take the probability of opportunistic behaviour in post-contract transactions. A unitary actor will be hypothesized to have either a non-zero probability or one that is not significantly different from zero but not both. Researchers in the transaction costs tradition are likely to be biased toward the former while those with a resource-based view may not since they regard the firm's reputation as a key resource that managers value and protect. Chandler (1962) initiated a scholarly tradition of inquiry that firmly established the multiple actor assumption, while Mintzberg (1979) legitimated the assumption that even a single actor may work with multiple conflicting objectives.

The structure we propose involves desegregating the flagship firm into three components. These components are based on the function that is being performed by the component, and will generally map closely to specific individuals and organizational positions.

Strategy functions

Strategy functions involve articulation of the goals and objectives of the network as a whole as well as the flagship firm itself, the formulation or ratification of the principal courses of action to be undertaken to achieve those goals, and the allocation of resources for their implementation. Readers familiar with the strategy literature will quickly recognize the similarity of this definition to those used to define strategy itself (Chandler 1962). However, it should be recognized that a flagship firm exercises domain over its entire network and not just over its own organization. This posits that it has a substantial or almost complete measure of control over the strategy of its network partners who, in turn, have given up their strategic autonomy in exchange for the putative benefits of belonging to the network.

Management functions

Management functions involve guiding and directing the work of others in the flagship firm and its network partners to achieve the objectives established by the strategy function. The commonly held view in the organizational behaviour and strategy literatures is that this includes activities such as planning, decision making (Glueck 1976), organizing, staffing, leading, and controlling (Koontz and O'Donnell 1972), but not the strategy functions described above. Here too it is useful to focus on the distinctive aspects of management in a flagship firm—the domain of its management function extends beyond the boundaries of its own organization and includes a substantial measure of control over the work of its network partners.

Operational functions

Operational functions include all the other work performed by employees of the flagship firm, but they do not include any work that is done by employees of the network partners.

The preference for vertical integration

There is a substantial body of theoretical work devoted to vertical integration in chains of production processes where the output of one process becomes a significant input into the next process. In the discussion that follows, we will generalize the propositions of this work beyond the supply of raw materials and the distribution of final consumption goods to include also vertical relationships involving the production of service inputs (engineering services, transportation, systems integration, etc.) and ancillary products and services associated with final consumption (warehousing, after-sales service, etc.).

Three schools of thought have had major influence in this area. The central concern of these theorists has been the choice of mode—vertical integration, spot market transactions, or long-term contracts. Under what conditions is one mode more likely to be preferred over the others? Which mode is more likely to remain stable as conditions change? And which is likely to induce firms to make investments that will contribute to the overall capacity and efficiency of the system as a whole and its various components? Each school provides a different perspective on the conditions and reasons why markets fail to operate satisfactorily and firms are driven to choose vertical integration.

Traditional industrial organization theory

Traditional industrial organization theory was primarily concerned with the behaviour of firms in oligopolistic and near-monopolistic markets—the so-called small numbers condition—and the related ability of incumbents to extract rents. Vertical integration (backward) is preferred when a firm anticipates that its suppliers have or can develop the potential to monopolize the market for an important input; similarly, forward vertical integration is a defence against foreclosure of markets for the firm's outputs or a pre-emptive attempt to gain the benefits of foreclosure for the firm itself.

Transaction cost/internalization theory

The literature on *transaction costs* shifted the focus of attention to the nature of assets involved in vertical integration and to difficulties associated with long-term contracts. It argues that when investments are required in assets that are specific to the vertical relationship, the problem of *ex post* opportunistic behaviour by the partner is difficult to deal with and causes firms to prefer vertical integration to dealing on the spot market or through long-term contracts. The latter option has the additional problem of costs/difficulties related to writing, monitoring, and enforcing contingent contracts. These 'contracting hazards' discourage firms from dependence on long-term contracts when it is feared that adjustment of contract terms to changes in market conditions will be difficult to make or hard to enforce.

If we extend this concept to MNEs, we see that *internalization theory* explains their preference for the FDI mode for international expansion as a function of their need to protect property rights, particularly those of a less tangible nature. Similarly, the theory suggests that MNEs will undertake vertical integration abroad whenever there is a need to protect firm-specific assets (FSAs) such as know-how or a brand name.

Resource-based theory

Resource-based theory encourages us to regard the firm as a bundle of hard-to-replicate *sticky* resources, with particular attention to managerial capability or similar less tangible resources. This theory suggests that firms will prefer vertical integration when it has surplus managerial and other resources that it anticipates being able to deploy more effectively in the vertical chain than would independent suppliers or customers. These arguments are particularly powerful when transactions in the vertical system involve a significant element of intangibles that are hard to price and monitor.

Failures of vertical integration

Given such powerful arguments favouring the vertical integration mode when conditions which frequently lead to market failure exist or are anticipated, why have so many large firms chosen to move away from this solution and adopt the flagship form? There are two classes of explanation, which we will deal with separately below. The first are explanations based on the capture of rent in vertically integrated firms; this involves the appropriation by individuals and groups in the firm of some of the rents that accrue to the firm by virtue of its ownership of resources that are scarce or difficult to replicate. The second set of difficulties relate to failures of the management systems that have been developed within large firms.

Rent capture

A major motivation for avoiding vertical integration is to circumvent rent capture by employees in an upstream or downstream unit who are members of the union, particularly but not exclusively when the same union represents employees of the focal unit. Should this union attempt to negotiate wages and employment terms that capture a portion of the rents, management may respond by establishing network relationships with upstream or downstream firms that are not unionized or which have less onerous union contracts. It is common for suppliers in the automotive industry to experience lower wage costs than their customers, partly because they are regarded as having fewer opportunities to earn rents. Sometimes this is achieved by establishing operations in low-wage locations. Similarly, firms engaged in the distribution of computer products pay lower wages than their flagship suppliers. In both cases, flagship firms are able to circumvent rent capture by employees in the upstream and downstream parts of their business system when they use network partners for these functions. The alternative of paying lower wages in vertically integrated divisions is usually not available, because of a form of conscious parallelism practised by many unions whereby they resist such differentiation.

Note that inflexibilities in personnel practices in large firms can lead to similar outcomes in the absence of unions. For example, many large firms adopt highly structured systems for pay and grade levels and operate a form of seniority system where the employee's length of service is a determinant of wages. The tendency of these firms to apply such schemes uniformly across all vertically integrated divisions can impose a high wage structure on upstream and downstream divisions.

Rent capture by employees in management positions can also raise costs in a vertically integrated firm. In addition to salaries and benefits, rent capture may take the form of management perquisites that are costly. For example, managers in upstream and downstream units may be entitled to similar office space and administrative staff support as their colleagues in the focal division, thus raising the costs of their units above those in firms in the upstream or downstream industry. A common response to these problems has been for large firms to spin off upstream and downstream activities into separate companies with which they then establish a network relationship.

Management failure

It is our contention that the second major set of reasons have to do with managerial failures in the vertically integrated mode. To explain the causes of such failure of vertical integration, we need to establish the characteristics of the organizational structure and processes used by large, vertically integrated firms. The fundamental organizational form that underlies most structures for the management of vertically integrated firms is the multidivisional or M-form arrangement (Williamson 1985). The basic characteristics of this form that are of interest here are multi-tier levels of management, the profit centre concept, and divisional autonomy.

Management roles and functions are specialized by level in this form. Corporate management has stewardship of the overall direction of the firm, including appointment of divisional managers and establishing the rules of engagement between divisions. Divisional general management is responsible for planning and implementing strategies for the division. Functional management in the division reports to the divisional manager and holds responsibility for running a particular function.

The profit centre concept is that each division is treated as a quasi-firm within the firm; it is given responsibility for managing the affairs of the division to achieve profit performance targets that are negotiated with corporate management.

Divisional autonomy defines the scope of authority of divisional management and their responsibility for producing results. Despite prescriptions by organizational theorists about the need to make areas of responsibility co-extensive with the scope of divisional authority, in practice corporate management may choose to ignore this principle for pragmatic reasons.

Reasons for failure

Why do vertically integrated firms sometimes fail to perform as effectively as less integrated rivals?

Internal rivalry among general managers   Corporate systems for the management of divisions in the M-form firm have a built-in bias toward enhancing rivalry among division general managers. Three systems in particular tend to create internal rivalry. First, financial performance measurement systems based on the profit centre principle of treating the division as a quasi-firm place emphasis on overall results calculated by measures such as Return on Net Assets (RONA) and contribution to shareholder value. The message to the divisional general manager is: 'Run your division as if it were an independent firm whose shareholder is the corporation.' Since overall financial results of divisions are easily compared with each other, the incentives for rivalry between upstream and downstream divisions are strong, and the incentives for co-operative behaviour almost non-existent. In effect, financial systems of this nature internalize the competitive aspects of the Porter five forces model described above.

Second, the reward and punishment system for divisional managers is similarly biased toward enhancing rivalry. Since they have overall responsibility for running their divisions, both the formal and informal reward systems are focused on outcomes measured by the financial performance measurement systems mentioned above. Good performance is rewarded through bonuses, management perquisites, and formal recognition. Poor performance is punished ultimately by removal of the divisional general manager from that position. A close and frequently reinforced linkage between divisional financial performance and the self-interest of the general manager encourages rivalry between managers of divisions; many corporate managers believe that such rivalry is healthy because it provides incentives to divisional managers to strive to improve the financial performance. However, when applied to divisions in a vertical system, such rivalry also provides disincentives for co-operative behaviour.

Promotion is a special form of reward in large firms. Divisional general managers compete with each other for opportunities for promotion to positions in the corporate office. Since the number of positions available usually gets smaller toward the top of the hierarchy, there is a natural tendency for division managers to regard each other as rivals for promotion. Performance in their current job is frequently a major criterion for promotion; hence the incentive for rivalry with a view to enhancing one's promotion prospects.

Asymmetry of power among divisional managers Corporate directives regarding terms and conditions for interdivisional transactions can have a significant impact on a division's ability to achieve its performance targets. For example, transfer pricing policies, accounting conventions, and even such relatively trivial matters as the scheduling of maintenance shutdowns can all be the subject of corporate directives that impact on divisional performance. The formal and informal power of divisional managers to influence such directives can vary considerably because of a number of factors.

Perhaps most important is the historical position of the division itself. Divisions that formed the main base from which the vertically integrated firm grew are likely to wield considerable power. Senior corporate managers may have worked their way up through the division, personal relations between division and corporate managers may be deep and of long duration, and the belief may persist that the prosperity of the firm as a whole is intimately connected to the prosperity of the division. This can be particularly true when the acquisitions or internal development of the other components of the vertical system were originally sponsored by the division with a view to enhancing its own profitability.

The power of a division general manager can also be enhanced by the capital intensity of the division, particularly when this is driven by economies of scale in its technology. When the division's assets account for a large proportion of the firm's total assets, its general manager tends to acquire special status in the minds of corporate managers. The divisional imperative of operating capital-intensive assets at high capacity utilization rates can easily be reinterpreted as corporate policy. Corporate directives may then be issued to other divisions to support efforts to achieve these high capacity utilization rates, even when they may not be in the interest of these divisions. For example, upstream divisions may be discouraged from seeking new customers when its outputs are needed by the downstream division.

Similarly, managers of a division that is seen as the custodian or repository of the technology base of the firm can wield considerable influence with a corporate office which regards the firm's technology as a core asset. Divisions which hold proprietary technology or which contain research facilities used for generating new technology can come to have a preferential status in corporate offices leading to influence that goes beyond matters strictly related to technology.

Failures of transfer pricing   Policies about setting prices for transfers between vertically integrated divisions are essential for the functioning of performance measurement in a decentralized firm. The preferred theoretical solution is to use some form of market price because that provides the most accurate signals about the performance of both upstream and downstream operations. However, market prices, even when they are readily available, may fail to capture a number of additional considerations that must be addressed. First, market prices may need to be modified to take account of location benefits, product modifications which improve operations in either the upstream or downstream division, investments in learning that are specific to the relationship, or capacity that has been dedicated to the vertical relationship and which would otherwise lie idle. Readers familiar with Williamson's (1985) classification of asset specificity will recognize that these characteristics have been derived from his scheme. In the absence of market price data that closely reflect such conditions, corporate management may have to establish rules for transfer pricing that depart from strict reliance on data from the market. Three classes of such departures need to be recognized. Each is prone to a particular type of failure.

First, corporate management may apply the 'best alternative' rule—specifying that the selling division be allowed to charge the best price it could obtain outside the firm for similar transactions or that the buying division should only pay the same price as it can negotiate with an outside supplier or both. In any case, such policies are vulnerable to opportunistic behaviour from one side or the other. Either division may seek offers from third parties that comply with corporate rules but which are based on tacit understandings that are kept secret from others in the firm. For example, the upstream division may make tacit commitments to outside customers about the level of technical support that will be offered in the future or indicate a willingness to take back unused product at full price. Conversely, the downstream division may entice an outside supplier with forecasts of future requirements that are substantially in excess of its plans. In general, tacit aspects of supply contracts with third parties may be particularly difficult for the internal partner to detect. Should the corporate office be called upon to arbitrate, it is likely to experience even greater difficulty in making judgements about whether or not there are tacit aspects to the offer from the outside party, and may be forced to make its determination on the basis of the explicit features of the arrangement.

An alternative arrangement is some sort of cost-plus pricing formula which sets transfer prices at the costs of the upstream division plus some agreed-upon formula for profit. Apart from vitiating the firm's performance control system with respect to the upstream division, cost-plus formulae create incentives for several kinds of dysfunctional behaviour in both divisions. An upstream division that is treated as a cost centre by the corporate office may seek ways of keeping its costs below budget targets by underspending on maintenance or process development. Downstream divisions may underinvest in market opportunities that are made inaccessible by a high-cost upstream supplier to which it is tied by corporate edict.

The third class of solution is to use corporate staff to analyse the transfer-pricing issue and recommend a price or pricing formula which corporate management then imposes by edict. This approach suffers from disadvantages associated with inadequate expertise in corporate staff (lack of deep knowledge about the industry, inadequate market contacts, scarcity of tacit knowledge). Assuming that these problems can be overcome by, for example, promoting an expert from one of the divisions to the corporate staff, there remains the problem of acceptance by divisional management of solutions which they have not played a part in developing. Variations of this approach which involve corporate officials or staff serving as facilitators for negotiations between divisions about transfer prices merely arrive at the same outcome through a different mechanism and do not deal with its fundamental weaknesses.

A case study of the flagship model

The flagship model has been applied to analysis of the Canadian chemicals industry and its adjustment to regionalization under the North American Free Trade Agreement (NAFTA): see D'Cruz, Gestrin, and Rugman (1995), and also Chapter 9 in this book. Two broad findings emerged from this case study. The first is the significance for competitiveness of key supplier relationships for subsidiaries of MNEs, in the face of the rapid regional integration of the Canadian industry. The second is the significance for competitiveness of key customer relationships of small and medium-sized enterprises (SMEs) with flagship suppliers.

Many of the larger MNEs in Canada are now doing very well as key suppliers. For example, in the paints industry key suppliers such as PPG and DuPont Canada have profitable businesses as key suppliers to the US and Japanese automakers (the original equipment manufacturers—OEMs) in Canada. The strategic direction for these businesses is partly determined in the United States but the production mandate to implement these contracts can result in a successful Canadian business, with many jobs, profits for the company, and a net positive contribution to Canada's social and economic well-being. Therefore, managers of MNEs need to continue to adopt a North American 'regional' strategic vision. Especially important within the context of MNEs will be the ability of Canadian managers to articulate in the appropriate strategic forums of the parent the Canadian subsidiary's potential contribution as a key supplier.

Within the institutional format of NAFTA the Canadian MNEs are adopting new and relevant regional strategies and any new Multilateral Agreement on Investment (MAI)-based rules for FDI should be NAFTA consistent to minimize further adjustment costs. An MAI will need not only to enshrine national treatment and right of establishment but to go well beyond these. To secure truly contestable conditions on a North American regional basis, or a global basis, additional domestic discriminatory practices must be ended and replaced by new trade, investment, and competition rules.

Somewhat in contrast to the dramatic retrenchment affecting the larger MNEs there is a more subtle change affecting SMEs. These are often 'niche' players driven by entrepreneurs who have a sense of the market. The SMEs are close to their customers; they can build and maintain long-term successful businesses through their marketing skills and flexibility. The SMEs act as intermediaries between the larger MNE suppliers and the wholesale or national distributors. Their flexibility and marketing know-how are vital firm-specific advantages. They can use their laboratories to customize products and/or respond very quickly to customer demands. They can manage these service functions better than larger MNE suppliers. As 'key customers' of the MNEs, they can actually expand the total market for the MNEs, while not acting as a threat to them. In this sense, the SMEs have to manage the key supplier role with skill and foresight. They can develop close working relationships with a variety of MNEs provided they preserve secrecy and develop a reputation for discretion and non-disclosure to rival MNEs.

SMEs therefore promise to be a source of considerable growth and dynamism in the Canadian chemicals industry as MNEs seek to rationalize the productive structure of their global (or regional) operations while at the same time accessing as many markets as they can. In effect, SMEs are the keys to new markets in so far as: (a) they are able to penetrate markets that are simply too small for MNEs to cater to, given the scale of operations to which most MNEs are committed; and (b) they allow for more rapid roll-out of technological advances by making smaller, more specialized product development economically viable. Once again, the lesson from the Canadian chemicals industry is that even SMEs can adjust to a new institutional framework, such as NAFTA.

Conclusions

The flagship model is characterized by the flagship firm's asymmetric strategic leadership over the network partners in common areas of interest. The MNE sets the priorities of the partners in regard to their participation in this flagship firm's business system. Only the flagship firm has the global perspective and resources to lead a business network and to establish the global benchmarks necessary to lead the development of the network. The network's 'key' (flagship) relationships are the organizational mechanisms for achieving the strategic purposes of the network.

Another distinguishing feature of the flagship model is the deintegration of business system activities from the flagship firm—a *de facto* re-engineering of the value chain. This feature is a reflection of the complexity of competition in the global markets of today. Rather than internalizing ownership of core competencies and FSAs (Rugman 1981), firms are deintegrating selectively those aspects of their value chains which they feel, for cost or strategic reasons, can better be performed elsewhere (Rugman, D'Cruz, and Verbeke 1995).

As a result of deintegration, key suppliers can expect to experience increased volumes through the flagship firm's outsourcing of activities. There is a reduction in the total number of suppliers serving the flagship, thereby creating value added to key suppliers outside the MNE; and a reduced business risk of more long-term contracts. The key supplier benefits through this partnership by having to benchmark its operations to the global standards of the flagship firm, for example, in adopting quality standards. The technologies, processes, and systems of the supplier will reflect global standards of competitiveness.

Key customers in the five partners business network, by virtue of ceding strategic control to the flagship, fulfil a valuable role beyond being a market for the flagship. These customers are the testing grounds for product and service development. Specifically, by having thick and tight relationships with network members, the customer provides market feedback and, in return, receives products which respond to its needs. Often the key customers will be intermediaries between the flagship firm and the end consumer, as is the case with car dealers.

For the NBI, the flagship firm provides leadership and vision in terms of resource allocation, competency exploration, and mobilizing financial resources (as they apply to the NBI organization's participation in the flagship's business system). Such organizations contribute human resources, facilities, equipment, and institutional arrangements as their role in business network activities.

Relationships with key competitors include joint ventures in new markets, market-sharing arrangements, technology transfers, supplier development, etc. Unlike static contractual arrangements of the past, flagship model relations depend more on joint working teams and managerial interaction to elaborate and operationalize strategic purpose. This more fluid approach recognizes the adaptability required to change with the market but does not hinder the accrual of benefits through interaction. As with the other 'flagship' relationships, key competitors share in a mutually beneficial co-operative relationship, thereby increasing the amount of trust present in the flagship model.

PART III

Case Studies of Flagship Business Networks

7

The Canadian Telecommunications
Network

Introduction

In this chapter, we introduce and develop a framework, the five partners model of a 'business network' for an alternative governance structure to hierarchies and markets. We argue that the business network has mechanisms to reduce the costs inherent in hierarchies and markets; and in particular, asset specificity and opportunism, respectively. Moreover, we propose that the asymmetric strategic control of the business network by a flagship firm increases the efficiency of the governance structure. Specifically, we argue that this asymmetry increases interorganizational trust, network stability, and interorganizational learning.

In the latter half of the chapter, we examine the Canadian telecommunications industry as a case study of this theory. We chose the telecommunications industry because, globally, it is undergoing significant and rapid environmental change. Therefore, we expected that the demands placed on the efficiency of current governance structures of industry firms would be high. The Canadian industry also represents one which faces pressures from firms in the large US market. We conclude by distinguishing between relationships which are truly of a business network variety and those which only appear to be so.

The theory of business networks

A business network is a governance structure for organizing exchange through co-operative, non-equity relationships among firms and non-business institutions. The business network's five partners include: the flagship firm which is a multinational enterprise; key suppliers; key customers; selected competitors; and the non-business infrastructure (NBI). The latter partner includes the service-related sectors, educational and training institutions, the various levels of government, and other organizations such as trade associations, non-governmental organizations, and unions. The business network is shown in Figure 7.1. This framework has been developed in D'Cruz and Rugman (1992a, 1992b).

The business network is characterized also by the flagship firm's asymmetric strategic control of the business network (Rugman and D'Cruz 1994a). This asymmetry entails leadership and direction setting, a 'strategic hand' effectively, in setting the priorities of the partners in regard to their participation in the network's business system. Those aspects of the partners' businesses which are not

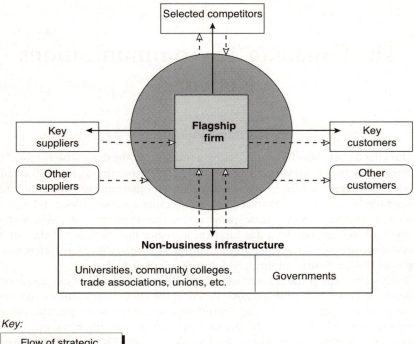

Figure 7.1 The five partners business network model

pertinent to the business system of the network will be operated autonomously by the partners. The flagship firm's influence extends only to those partner activities which are germane to the business network's strategic intent (Hamel and Prahalad 1989). Asymmetric strategic control by the flagship firm is consistent with the idea that international competitiveness demands global strategies from firms. It is the flagship firm, a multinational enterprise (MNE), which has the global perspective and resources to forge a business network and to establish the global benchmarks necessary to lead the development of the network. The business network's relationships are the facilitating mechanism for achieving the strategic purpose of the network.

In addition to asymmetric strategic leadership by the flagship firm, the business network is characterized by the deintegration of value-added activities from the flagship firm to the network partners—a *de facto* re-engineering of the value chain. Traditionally, the hierarchical MNE has been organized to capture and retain proprietary control over intangible firm-specific assets (FSAs) which are difficult to protect in market transactions. Through internalization in which internal governance mechanisms are embedded in organizational structures, systems, and processes, the MNE has replaced market mechanisms to ensure these FSAs are not dissipated.

Increasingly, however, rapid changes in markets are testing the effectiveness of the hierarchy as a governance structure. The internal mechanisms of the hierarchy, its rules, procedures, and systems, were designed originally to organize economic activity in more 'stable' competitive environments. Ironically, it is those very governance processes and structures which limit the hierarchical firm's ability to innovate and adapt. In his discussion of industrial districts, Harrison (1992) raises a similar point about 'institutional inertia' and the difficulties that large firms have in adjusting to changes in competition. Consequently, rather than internalizing ownership of core competencies (Prahalad and Hamel 1990) and FSAs (Rugman 1981), firms are deintegrating selectively those aspects of their micro business systems (value chains) which they feel, for cost or strategic reasons, can better be performed elsewhere.

In a business network, *key suppliers* can expect to experience increased volumes through the flagship firm's deintegration of value-added activities and through a rationalization of the number of suppliers serving the flagship.

Key suppliers should benefit from the reduced business risk of more long-term, open-ended contracts (Fama 1980) and from the flagship firm's assumption of some risks associated with technology and capital expenditure. The key supplier also benefits through this partnership by having to benchmark its operations to the global standards of the flagship firm. The technologies, processes, and systems of the supplier, therefore, will reflect global standards of competitiveness.

In regard to its relationship with the NBI, the flagship firm provides leadership and vision in terms of resource allocation, exploitation of competency, and the mobilization of financial resources (as they apply to the NBI organization's participation in the network's business system). The NBI contributes human resources, facilities, equipment, and institutional arrangements. The NBI, particularly government and educational institutions, provides a valuable forum for the business network's partners to foster co-operative relationships. Moreover, the bureaucracies of government, educational institutions, trade associations, etc. can serve as 'the loci of social memory' (Ouchi 1984, 29). Participation by network partners in such bodies, therefore, contributes to a pool of knowledge and understanding which facilitates interorganizational partnering. The traditional North American perspective of 'government as interference' has ignored the benefits of institutionalized memory and non-market forums for co-operative exchange.

Relationships with *selected competitors* include joint ventures in new or common markets, market-sharing arrangements, technology transfers, supplier development, etc. Unlike static contractual arrangements of the past, business network relations depend more on joint working teams and managerial interaction to elaborate and operationalize strategic purpose. As with viewing the NBI with a new perspective, relationships with competitors need not default to wary competitiveness protectionism. Commercial success in the future is likely to be predicted on a firm's ability to learn and adapt. In fact, Kogut and Zander (1992, 1993) suggest that the boundaries of the firm depend upon the generation of knowledge from current capabilities or from a recombination of them. The question that must be asked is: Can firms learn and stay competitive solely through the internalization of activities? We propose that the answer is negative and that firms must share knowledge with competitors and, thereby, contribute to a redefinition of their own boundaries.

Key customers in a business network, by virtue of yielding strategic control to the flagship firm, fulfil a valuable role beyond just being a market for the flagship. Specifically, by having close relationships with network partners, the key customer acts as a valuable market feedback mechanism for the network. Often, the key customers will be intermediaries between the flagship firm and the end consumer, as is the case with car dealers. Presumably these key customers, like the other network partners, believe that it is in their best interests to follow the flagship firm's strategic leadership. For example, if telecommunications services are an integral aspect of a customer's operations, then the key customer may be more willing to have its telecommunications strategy set by the telecommunications network's flagship firm. The key customer follows the strategic hand of the flagship firm in terms of its (the customer's) participation in the network's business system.

The distinction between strategic cluster and business network

In this section, we differentiate between our concept of a business network and the strategic clusters of Porter (1990). Through a brief discussion of economic geography and the localization of industry, we distinguish the business network by emphasizing its international, interindustry relationships as opposed to nation-bound, intraindustry clusters.

It is important to understand the distinction between our business network and the strategic clusters of Porter (1990). The latter represent a descriptive and statistical characterization of historical economic activity and organization. The development of clustered industry owes as much to social, cultural, and political forces as to economic factors. Krugman (1991) also supports this idea in his treatment of economic geography, arguing that the location of economic activity owes a great deal to 'historical contingency'. Porter's clusters, in analytic retrospect, are illustrative of the benefits of geographically bound economic activity. Moreover, they provide examples which strongly support Porter's (1990) diamond framework for understanding the success of industries and national competitive advantage.

Porter's strategic clusters are statistical aggregations which measure international competitiveness by export trade. Unlike these industry clusters, business networks are designed explicitly to address the issue of achieving international competitiveness (D'Cruz and Rugman, 1993, 1994*b*). These business networks reflect the trade and investment patterns which affect the Canadian economy. Specifically, the economic features of the Canadian economy are dominated by approximately 50 MNEs which account for 70 per cent of the country's trade (Rugman 1991). These MNEs typically generate 70–90 per cent of their revenues outside Canada, with the USA accounting for 70 per cent of their trade. Given this evident dependence of the Canadian economy on a relatively small number of MNEs, it is apparent that economic growth and international competitiveness issues cannot be separated from the role of the MNE. This argues, therefore, for a business network structure which includes the MNE as a key player (flagship firm) and which recognizes the salient feature of the MNE—its organization, investment, and trade across national borders (Rugman 1981).

The business network, with an MNE as its flagship firm, is not geographically bound. More specifically, the business network does not view Canada (or even worse, a province or region of Canada) as the 'home base' for competitive advantage as Porter (1990) does, especially in his Canadian study (Porter and the Monitor Company 1991). The flagship firm operates and develops linkages across borders and benchmarks its activities globally. Because the business network is conceived as a re-engineering of the business system (accessing the resources of others, deintegration, etc.) through linkages with partners, the benefits to those partners reflect the global benchmarking of the flagship firm. The network partners of the flagship, in turn, will demand similar levels of service and quality from their suppliers and alliance partners.

One of the primary advantages of the business network is that deintegration to core competencies (Prahalad and Hamel 1990) and linkages to partners foster responsiveness and adaptability. In contrast, Porter's strategic cluster concept cannot be readily operationalized. While in strategic clusters there are benefits to having firms close to each other (for example the spawning of related firms, the pooling of knowledge, etc.), Porter does not explain how these new firms, or the original ones for that matter, will be organized to compete through a salient structure in the global economy of the twenty-first century. It should be noted that attempts have been made to implement Porter's cluster theories. In The Netherlands, the government, the chambers of commerce, and the SMO Foundation have collaborated to build an infrastructure which facilitates cluster development. The success or failure of this project is not yet evident. Regardless of the outcome, the governance structure of firms in these intraindustry clusters are likely to be hierarchical. Therefore, the issue of outdated governance mechanisms and structures still has not been addressed. A business network approach does address these organizational issues since an interindustry, internationally oriented governance structure is developed to replace large vertically integrated MNEs.

Enright (1993*a*, 1993*b*) examines the relationship between localization (geographic concentration) and the co-ordination of economic activity within industries. He supports Krugman's (1991) view that there is no one progression or path along which geographically clustered industries evolve. By improving co-ordination and communication across firms in an industry, localization may influence, but not solely determine, the boundaries of these firms. Enright's case studies of localized industries indicate that surviving industries change organization and co-ordination mechanisms to reflect changes in the competitive environment, be they in markets, technology, government involvement, etc. Hence, Enright implicitly suggests that Porter's advantages of local rivalry, demanding customers, etc., are dynamic and are more dependent on the information flow among individuals and organizations than on geographic space. We argue that the business network, through its cross-border relationships, expands the geographic scope of competitive advantage beyond tightly constrained regional clusters.

The business network's asymmetric strategic leadership

In this section, we develop the arguments for asymmetric strategic control of the business network by the flagship firm. The management of a business network requires a commitment from all the partners to the strategic direction of the network. In effect, the network partners must accept the asymmetry of strategic control because the resultant strategic interdependence among the five partners is paramount to the efficacy of the governance structure. We argue that the business network's asymmetry increases the credible commitments (Williamson 1985) of the five partners and, in so doing, lessens certain governance costs such as those associated with opportunism.

Avoiding the transaction costs, such as opportunism, in short-term, transaction-oriented relationships is a key benefit of the network mode of organizing economic activity. There may be increases in governance costs related to managing the network and co-ordinating production; however, these governance costs are bearable for they are matched by concomitant gains in the success of the network, rather than being 'lost' as the transaction costs of opportunism are.

We argue that asymmetry serves to increase: (a) interorganizational trust; (b) network stability; and (c) interorganizational learning. The literature on interorganizational relations, and particularly that relating to network theory, has stressed the important role of trust in relationships. Specifically, the contribution of high levels of trust often is tied to a decrease in transaction costs associated with opportunism. We propose that due to the asymmetric business network's high degree of transaction exclusivity, the accumulation of transactional experience is enhanced. In turn, this experience creates opportunity for the development of trust. Ring and Van de Ven (1992) theorize a similar dynamic—that lasting and high-trust relationships result from cumulative transactional experience.

In terms of network stability, we argue that agreement on a narrowed strategic agenda reduces conflict associated with competing strategic objectives. In effect, asymmetry reduces the inclination of network partners to protect their own sovereignty through non-cooperation. This helps to ameliorate the risk that the sovereignty of hybrid organization partners will detrimentally influence the stability and continuity of the hybrid (Borys and Jemison 1989).

We argue that asymmetry enhances the quality and content of the flow of information among network partners; and, thereby, facilitates interorganizational learning. Moreover, we propose that communication in the business network need not be less 'efficient' than within a firm. The reasonableness of this assertion is grounded in work on: (a) the embeddedness of economic action in social relations, and (b) the codification of knowledge and its transmission (Kogut and Zander 1992, 1993). The literature contends that the effective organization and transmission of knowledge is more dependent on the development of a 'common language' than on organization structure *per se*. Moreover, this knowledge is embedded in the social relations of the organization because it is these very relations which help to create the shared code or language.

We challenge the outdated idea that intraorganizational communication (in a hierarchy) is necessarily more efficient than interorganizational communication (in a network). The homogeneity of a monolithic MNE often is not based in fact when the culture, norms, and social relations of subsidiaries are examined. Therefore, the transmission of knowledge between culturally diverse units of an MNE cannot readily be assumed to be more efficient than that among separate organizations (Bower 1993). We believe that business networks will develop their own language for sharing of knowledge and for learning. As the strategic focal point, the flagship firm's asymmetric leadership facilitates the development of such a language. Powell (1990) agrees that the relational, open-ended features of networks enhance the process of acquisition of knowledge and learning of skills.

The most important management issues for the flagship firm in a business network are: (1) to deintegrate, organize, and co-ordinate economic activity to the most core competent partner; (2) to manage relationships so as to promote trust and co-operation; and (3) to encourage interorganizational learning (a key component of which is the global benchmarking of activities).

In the final two sections we apply our theory of business networks to the Canadian telecommunications industry. We pay particular attention to how the structure of relationships affects the process of governance.

Competitive forces in the Canadian telecommunications industry

Recent changes in the regulatory framework for telecommunications in Canada have created new strategic management challenges for existing telephone companies (telcos) and new entrants. The Canadian telecommunications industry has long been heavily regulated and protected. Beginning in 1990, telecommunications resellers began to enter the market and the regulated telephone companies, especially Bell Canada, started to experience slight erosion of market share. In June 1992, the Canadian Radio and Telecommunications Commission (CRTC), the regulating and licensing body for the industry, ruled that the Canadian long-distance telecommunications market was open to competition. Moreover, the CRTC decided that new competitors such as Unitel Communications Inc. were to be given access to the local switching networks of the telcos. These telcos, led by Bell Canada, had long maintained that their profits from long-distance (toll) service enabled them to offer low-price local service to customers. They argued that the effective cost of this local service per household far exceeded the charged rate. (Note that the CRTC had long held that the level of service for all citizens should be uniform. Therefore, given Canada's vast geography and relatively small population, the telcos maintained that the cost of providing local service for many of their subscribers was very high.) Nevertheless, the CRTC ruling indicated that it was desirable for long-distance rates to decrease and that competition in the marketplace would be the most effective mechanism. Also, while local rates could possibly rise, the CRTC believed that competition would raise productivity levels and offset the need to raise local rates.

The formerly regulated Canadian industry leaders such as Bell Canada face increased competition not just from within Canada's borders but also from outside. The threat of competition from the USA is significant if the industry is viewed from a global perspective. In January 1993, AT&T purchased a 20 per cent equity interest in Unitel by agreeing to a technology investment worth $Cdn150 million. This agreement will allow Unitel, with AT&T, to offer their business customers a seamless cross-border service. It should be noted that after its equity purchase, AT&T installed one of its American executives as President of Unitel. Before this agreement, Stentor concluded a deal with MCI for technology purchases and development flowing both ways. In August 1993, Sprint and CallNet Enterprises signed a technology and services sharing agreement worth $Cdn60 million, giving Sprint 25 per cent ownership of CallNet.

Telecommunications firms have formed partnerships of various sorts quite rapidly in the three years to 1993 (for example: Bell and Mercury (Britain), AT&T and Unitel, Stentor and MCI, and British Telecom and MCI). Moreover, US telecommunications firms are linking themselves to other media providers. For example, AT&T, in its desire to dominate the 'communications network' business, acquired NCR in 1992; created a joint venture with cable operator Tele-Communications and with General Instruments to decompress cable channels; purchased McCaw Cellular Communications in 1993 and became a major force in the cellular phone business; made a deal in 1993 with Novell (network software leader) to connect AT&T switchboards to LANs (local area networks); and entered into a joint venture with 3D, Time Warner, and Matsushita to develop interactive media. In February 1993, Southwestern Bell purchased cable operator, Hauser

Communications, for $US650 million. US West invested $US2.5 billion in Time Warner in May. In October, Bell Atlantic and the largest cable company in the USA, Tele-Communications, announced a merger valued at $25–30 billion. Pacific Telesis, the parent of Pacific Bell, confirmed that it intends to spend $US16 billion to build an information superhighway in California. In December 1993, Southwestern Bell Corp. and Cox Cable Communications announced a cable television partnership valued at $US4.9 billion to own and operate 21 of Cox's cable TV systems.

In Canada, the pace of industry restructuring has been limited by the telcos' scope of activity as defined by the CRTC. Nevertheless, the Canadian industry's boundaries of economic activity also are broadening. In December 1993, Bell Canada Enterprises Inc. (BCE Inc.), the parent of Bell Canada, agreed to acquire 30 per cent of Jones Intercable Inc., one of the ten largest US cable TV companies. At the same time, BCE announced its intention to divest its real estate and financial services businesses in order to focus on telecommunications. In December 1993, Stentor and Kodak Canada Inc. announced they would form an alliance to transmit images via the public switched telephone network, private data networks, and LANs.

Deregulation also will affect the relationship between telcos and their equipment suppliers. Through cross-ownership and tight product-development relationships, Northern Telecom dominates the Canadian telecommunications equipment market. This will change as global suppliers enter the market, just as the market changed in the USA. The competitive role of the equipment providers may also be altered, because of the increasingly commodity-like nature of basic telecommunications services. Extra services and options and the needs of customers operating in competitive, global markets may place the equipment suppliers in a more strategic position as they provide the solutions to help telcos serve customers better.

Deregulation is forcing telcos to manage for the market, not for a stable return-on-equity environment characterized by artificial revenue allocation systems between telcos. One benefit of the piecemeal development and the fragmented Canadian market is the experience of managing relationships among the Telecom Canada (now Stentor) members. In setting technical and technology standards for connecting their systems and allocating revenues from shared traffic, the Canadian telcos have valuable experience in intercompany co-operation.

Stentor: Nascent business network?

In this section, we describe the structure of the Stentor alliance (Figure 7.2). In light of the discussion above of the competitive dynamics in the industry, we then analyse the Stentor structure in relation to our own theory of business networks.

The Stentor alliance is a clear example of organizing economic activity to deliver to customers that which they could not otherwise receive and/or to

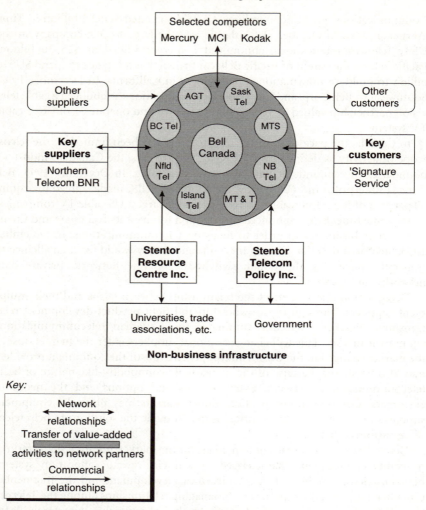

Figure 7.2 The emerging business network of the Canadian telecommunications system

deliver it at a lower cost (D'Cruz, 1993). The macro business system (value chain) of the Canadian telecommunications industry is unique in comparison to most other industries. The connectivity of the telephone system and co-ordination of service among the telephone companies and other telecommunication firms is essential to provide the ultimate consumer with adequate levels of service. This is primarily the case with long-distance (toll) service, including overseas transmission. Seamless service means that the industry structure forces the telcos to be interdependent. Any one telco cannot provide adequate levels of service without the participation of the other network partners. (For a thorough examination of business network theory in the telecommunications industry, see D'Cruz and Rugman's (1994*b*) treatment of France's industry.)

As the customers of the telcos increase their commitments to competing globally, so must the telcos themselves in order to be able to serve these customers. The boundaries of service and product delivery are becoming broader and in fact, arguably, nationless. This global orientation is also made more dramatic by the fundamental redefinition of what it means to communicate. As the lines between computer telecommunications and entertainment become increasingly blurred, a process called convergence in the communications industry, it is evident that industries and companies will be redefined. This does not mean that individual firms will choose the industry in which they will compete. It means that complete business systems in an industry will be fundamentally altered and that different industries will have overlapping and interlocking business systems. Where value is found and perceived to reside is likely to change. Is it hardware or software; the transmission of images, data, and voice or the images themselves?

The Stentor alliance consists of eight provincial telephone companies and one company, Bell Canada, which serves Ontario and Quebec. The relationships among network partners is also more formalized through ownership positions. Bell's parent, BCE Inc., owns 53 per cent of Northern Telecom; 34.3 per cent of Maritime Tel&Tel; 37 per cent of NB Tel; 55.3 per cent of Newfoundland Tel; 100 per cent of Northwest Tel; and indirectly through MT&T's 52 per cent ownership of Island Tel, 17.8 per cent of the same. Before the establishment of Stentor in January 1992, a loose alliance of the same companies existed as Telecom Canada. Originally, Telecom Canada evolved through a series of *ad hoc* agreements among the telcos. These agreements dealt with technical standards for interconnection and with a revenue-allocation system for toll traffic between their systems. The conversion to Stentor Canadian Network Management was driven by the need to create an alliance that was more strategic in nature than was Telecom Canada. Specifically, it was meant to provide a seamless national service and to support each company's commitment to its customers.

Through its 'Signature Service' programme, Stentor meets customer requirements by offering solutions from the network as a whole. For example, the 300 Signature customers can order service and equipment needs centrally and the appropriate Stentor telco partner will implement the order. The telco that provides the service is essentially a national account manager (NAM) to the customer. It is the management of the linkages among the Stentor members, however, that distinguishes this Signature Service offering from merely being considered good marketing practice. While it is true that Stentor's Signature Service is about getting close to its customers, this is being done in quite a different manner than previously. Stentor determines the overriding priorities of the national service offering and the local telco operationalizes the offering.

Linkages with the NBI for marketing and development and government relations are explicitly addressed through two new network companies—

Stentor Resource Centre Inc. and Stentor Telecom Policy Inc., respectively. The Stentor network's management process, in addition to being operationalized through the two newly formed companies, is embodied in two other structures—the Council of CEOs and the Strategy Committee (Stratcomm). The Council of CEOs has representation from all the telcos in the country and operates on a one telco, one vote approach. The Strategy Committee has different representatives from the telcos but also is organized with equal status among members.

The organization of the Stentor alliance, as we have detailed it in Figure 7.2, appears to be structured in the manner of a business network. However, there are fundamental flaws in its conception and execution which minimize the benefits of the alliance. First, the core relationships among the Stentor alliance members (the nine telcos) are driven more by the need for technical interdependence than by strategic purpose. In effect, the old Telecom Canada relationships still dominate but under a different name. Informal discussion with Stentor managers indicates that the smaller telcos (that is, all except Bell Canada) are wary of Bell Canada's power. Their wariness can be attributed partially to their relatively small size, which decreases any significant leverage in terms of influence on the whole of the system. Moreover, they are uncertain how they will fit in a system that may extend beyond Canada's borders. Bell Canada's unilateral negotiations with Mercury and other companies have extended the boundaries of the industry without their direct influence. In fact, the international alliances with Mercury and MCI were negotiated by BCE Inc., not by Stentor.

Communication among Stentor members is hampered also by the role of Stentor Resource Centre Inc. (SRC) and Stentor Telecom Policy Inc. (STP). These companies have been established as separate entities with their own hierarchical management structures. While the companies do communicate with their respective constituencies, that is educational institutions and government, they do not effectively represent a coherent communications strategy from all the Stentor members. Instead, they place another layer of management between each telco and the Stentor alliance itself.

In terms of the relationship between Stentor and government, it still is driven by regulatory compliance, not long-term infrastructure and competitiveness needs. The telcos view government, especially as embodied in the CRTC, as a source of great marketplace friction which hinders the ability of the Canadian industry to participate in opportunities outside the telecommunications field (such as cable) and to restructure for a more rapidly changing competitive environment. In no way can the relationship between Stentor and government be viewed as an effective arrangement to ensure the competitive response capability of the Canadian industry.

Despite Stentor's Signature Service programme, customers are still not viewed as partners. While the new orientation is a better marketing focus, it still does not represent an attempt to lead customers' telecommunications strategies.

Conclusions

One of the most important aspects of economic competitiveness is the conception and execution of global strategies. Given the foregoing and the dependence of the Canadian economy on a small number of multinationals, it is logical to conclude that MNEs should play a leading role in fostering international competitiveness. The business network, with the MNE as flagship, is an organizational structure which capitalizes on the MNE's organization, trade, and investment across national borders and its ability to create the strategic direction and purpose of the network.

The business network is a form of organization which addresses the realities of trade and investment patterns that dominate small, open economies such as that of Canada. Business networks, with MNEs as flagship firms, can conceive and execute global strategies. The success of a business network depends upon asymmetric strategic control by the flagship firm; the deintegration of value-added activities from the flagship firm to the network partners; and the development of high-trust, long-term relationships to facilitate interorganizational learning.

The Canadian telecommunications industry represents an industry with compelling reasons for movement towards a business network structure. Rapid technology change, convergence, increased exposure to global competitors, and the reality of technical interdependence would suggest that the hierarchical structures and competitive isolation of the past are not sufficiently adaptive to respond effectively to change. This is especially the case for the small, provincial telcos. In the not too distant future, the shape of the Canadian telecommunications industry is likely to have changed to reflect the influence of convergent technologies. Development of co-operative relationships predicated upon a common strategic purpose, as opposed to technical need, is one way for the Canadian telephone companies to survive the onslaught of global competitors.

Update to Chapter 7

To update the preceding analysis of the flagship relationship in the Canadian telecommunications industry in the period 1991–3, two more recent major developments must be considered: the new regulatory environment and Northern Telecom's network relationships.

The new regulatory environment

There has been further change in Canada's regulatory framework. In 1997 the CRTC allowed limited competition in the local-phone market, a decision which was similar to its 1992 decision to open up the market to long-distance competition. The 1997 decision on deregulation will eliminate the regional monopolies of Canada's telephone companies. This will lead to the entry of new competitors into the local market, driving down prices and eventually leading to consolidation into two or three main service providers. By 1999 Bell Canada (and its parent, BCE

Inc.) bought 20 per cent of the Manitoba telephone company. In April 1999 BCE Inc. offered to sell part of Bell Canada to the Chicago-based Ameritech Corporation, the largest US local-telephone company. Both Bell and AT&T Canada now compete with BCT Telus Communications Inc. (which was formed by a merger of the British Columbia and Alberta telephone companies in early 1999). Twenty-seven per cent of this is owned by the Bell Atlantic telephone company, based in Philadelphia. This merger was the last event in the dismantling of the Stentor alliance. In retrospect, true flagship relationships did not develop in the Stentor alliance. As a result of fierce price competition, in May 1999 AT&T Canada announced the sale of the consumer segment of its long-distance business to Primus, leaving AT&T Canada with its business customers.

The emerging picture is that Canada's regional telephone companies (most of which were originally in the Stentor alliance) failed to form a true flagship network, despite the pressures of deregulation, globalization, and the entry to Canada of US firms. Four major players have emerged, all affiliated with large US companies. These are:

- Bell Canada, owned by BCE Inc., with revenue of $Cdn13 billion and 43,000 employees, affiliated with Ameritech.
- BCT Telus Corporation, with revenue of $Cdn6 billion and 25,000 employees, affiliated with Bell Atlantic.
- AT&T Canada, 31 per cent owned by the US AT&T Corporation, with revenue of $Cdn1.4 billion and 4,000 employees.
- Sprint Canada, a Canadian-owned company, which has licensed the Sprint name and has elements of a flagship relationship with US Sprint.

The company to benefit most from these changes is AT&T Canada. It is the first company in Canada to be positioned to offer a full range of telecom services (local, long-distance, data, wireless, internet) to businesses across Canada. Both Bell Canada and BCT Telus lack local networks in some regions of Canada. The domestic increase in the competitive strength of AT&T Canada is an amazing achievement in four years. From an initial focus on the cellular and mobile phone market, AT&T Canada has broadened its product scope to take away large segments of the Bell Canada/Stentor business. The leading position of Bell/Stentor has been eroded by AT&T Canada as Bell Canada has been slow to respond to its loss of a dominant monopoly in long-distance and local calls. In 1999 AT&T Canada bought Metro Net Communications of Calgary for $Cdn5 billion and is still hoping to buy part of Rogers Cantel Mobile Communications. It is constrained by the foreign ownership rule which restricts US ownership to 20 per cent of a Canadian telecommunications company.

Northern Telecom's network relationships

Developments at Northern Telecom (Nortel) itself have moved it along as a major 'transnational' corporation, operating as a network rather than with a North

American home base. A major move was its acquisition, in 1998, of the Silicon Valley internet provider, Bay Networks, for $Cdn11.2 billion. This has resulted in a change of Nortel's name to Nortel Networks, with a focus on being one of the world's largest suppliers of digital networking solutions. Nortel Networks in 1998 had sales of $US18 billion, 80,000 employees, and 42 R&D facilities in 17 countries, along with numerous joint ventures and alliances.

Northern Telecom, or Nortel Networks, has transformed itself from a Canadian-based MNE in 1977 to a North American-based MNE by 1987 to a transnational corporation by 1997. The early strategy and structure of Northern Telecom has been analysed by Rugman and McIlveen (1985) and by others. Between 1985 and 1995, revenue increased from $US4.2 billion to $US10.7 billion and total employees from 46,500 to 63,000.

In 1985, over 90 per cent of its sales were within North America. Today Nortel has 92 per cent of its sales outside Canada, and 40 per cent of all its sales outside North America. It has a very large ratio of R&D to sales of over 20 per cent (R&D spending in 1995 was $US1.6 billion on revenues of $US10.7 billion). Today one in four of Nortel's employees focuses on R&D. Overall, the number of knowledge workers has increased from 42 per cent in 1985 to 66 per cent in 1995, rising to an expected 75 per cent by 1998.

While Nortel competes globally in the telecommunications sector, it is not operating as if borders do not exist. Despite the globalization in the telecommunications sector, there remains a very high degree of government regulation and a set of regionally separated national markets. Even with the World Trade Organization's International Technology Agreement of 1995, there is no single world market for telecommunications. Nortel must be flexible enough to respond to differences in national regulations and consumer tastes, so it has adopted a policy of national responsiveness postulated by Bartlett and Ghoshal (1989). Other companies which are nationally responsive include Unilever and Asea-Brown Boveri (ABB). With a national responsiveness strategy, a firm like Nortel can be 'close to the customer' and responsive to the local regulator. Such decentralized firms are called 'transnational corporations' (TNCs).

Nortel qualifies as a TNC on three grounds. First, Nortel has decentralized decision making, to reflect the regional nature of the telecommunications market for products and services. A large degree of autonomy is given to product-sector managers and country managers.

Second, Nortel has an internal managerial resource strategy which decentralizes key decision making to some 200 top executives in more than a dozen markets around the world. As recently as ten years ago, Northern Telecom was run by five to ten people from its head office in Mississauga, Ontario. The 200 top managers making key decisions today operate with the large degree of autonomy typical of a TNC.

Third, Nortel's decentralized top management structure is held together by heavy use of the internet for interoffice communication. Nortel has its own internal electronic voicemail and data network, which is heavily used by senior managers, as well as all other employees. The senior managers are members of the President's Council, which conducts its business through the corporate internet.

The key managerial challenge for Nortel today is how to organize effective 'networks' with allies and strategic partners across the segmented regional markets that characterize the telecommunications sector. Nortel's vision is to be the global resource for digital network solutions and services. It is building and integrating both wireline and wireless digital networks on a global basis. Nortel has three types of network: wireless networks; enterprise networks; and broadband networks. Nortel attempts to deliver a 'total network solution' (of technical assistance, training, customer service, and documentation) in partnership with its customers.

Mature flagship relationships

The flagship linkage of national telecommunications operators to domestic key suppliers is a general feature of the telecommunications industry. These linkages are show in Table 7.1.

Nortel

Some of these key suppliers are now flagships, due to their new digital technology capabilities. The telecommunications operators were flagships in the days of the old analogue networks. Northern Telecom is now developing flagship-type relationships by reducing its own manufacturing and developing its own key suppliers.

For example, in software, Nortel has developed key suppliers in India. Nortel has started to develop elements of a mature, 'tiered', flagship network, as shown in Figure 7.3.

Nortel's key supplier of software in India has now started to develop a 'tiered' set of flagship relationships with independent software subcontractors in the Bangalore area. These tiered, key supplier–flagship relationships are also beginning to be developed by Lucent, the US-based supplier of AT&T, and to a lesser extent by the suppliers of Alcatel, Siemens, and Ericsson.

Nortel has also developed flagship relationships with the NBI. For example, in

Table 7.1 Flagship linkages in the telecommunications sector

Country	Key supplier	Telecommunications company
Canada	Northern Telecom	Bell Canada/Stentor
France	Alcatel	France Telecom
Germany	Siemens	Deutsche Telekom
Japan	NEC and Fujitsu	NTT

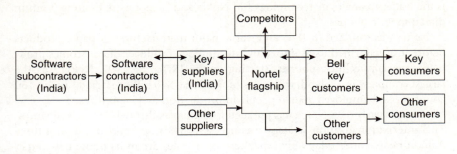

Figure 7.3 A tiered network at Nortel

China, it has a number of laboratories and teaching and research programmes in universities. It also has a set of joint ventures with Chinese competitors (state-owned enterprises in the telecommunications equipment industry).

In Canada, Nortel has developed a flagship relationship with the Engineering Faculty of the University of Toronto. This includes:

- endowed chairs in telecommunications;
- a specialized masters programme in network engineering and the hiring of graduates;
- advanced engineering and management development—non-design, post-university education;
- the sale of communications technology developed at the university;
- buying technology (patents, know-how).

Telecom Italia

Telecom Italia was privatized in 1997. It was more difficult for this company than it was for other national telecommunications operators to modernize its old regulated monopoly culture. In 1999 it was acquired by Olivetti in the largest hostile takeover bid in post-war Europe. The successful mobile phone subsidiary, Telecom Italia Mobile (TIM), was also acquired by Olivetti, whose own mobile phone company, Omnitel, has now come under the control of Germany's Mannesmann. An unsuccessful defence against Olivetti would have linked Telecom Italia with Deutsche Telekom.

Nokia and Ericsson: Building flagship relationships

The largest producer of mobile phones is Nokia, based in one of the world's smallest countries, Finland. Its major rival is the Swedish-owned firm, Ericsson. Nokia is the leader in Europe and is second to Motorola in the United States. Motorola is the leader in analogue technology but Nokia and Ericsson are fighting it out in digital mobile phones.

Nokia was founded in 1865 and was a major manufacturer of paper products before it transformed itself into a high-technology producer of electronics products, especially cellular phones, starting in the 1970s. By 1997, Nokia was the largest company in Finland, with sales of nearly $US10 billion. It had sales in 130 countries and employed 36,000 people in production in 45 countries.

From its early days Nokia has pursued foreign sales through network alliances. This internationalization strategy was necessary because Finland only has three million people and today only 5 per cent of its sales are in its home base. First, Nokia became the mobile phone leader in Scandinavia, despite competition from Ericsson of Sweden. Next it became the leader in Britain and then the rest of Europe and formed strategic alliances with US distributors such as Radio Shack and also with US telecommunications companies like AT&T. Nokia has also developed special phones for Chinese and Japanese companies. Some of these strategic alliances have budding flagship linkages.

Nokia spends a large amount on R&D and it is attempting to provide mobile phones which can use 'global roaming', that is, they would be usable across different telecommunications systems around the world. This requires that Nokia also works closely with different political regimes in order to try to develop an industry standard. In this interaction with the NBI, Nokia needs to work with its great rival, Ericsson. They are now attempting to establish Groupe Spécial Mobile (GSM) as the standard for mobile phones across Europe, and as one of the global standards. The next generation of mobile phones will build on a system like GSM, so a flagship-type linkage between rivals is necessary to change public policy.

L. M. Ericsson has over 100,000 employees and sales of $US20 billion in the 130 countries in which it operates. In 1997, Ericsson was the world's largest producer of digital mobile phones. Only 6 per cent of its sales occur in Sweden: nearly 40 per cent of its sales are in Europe, 27 per cent to Asia, and 16 per cent to North America. Unlike Nokia (which started as a paper and rubber producer) Ericsson has always been in telecommunications, starting in 1876 as a telephone manufacturer. It has always been innovative and, today, one-fifth of all employees work in R&D, a similar proportion as in its other rivals such as Northern Telecom. In other areas of business Ericsson developed telephone switches, in which it competes with firms such as Canada's Nortel and France's Alcatel. Ericsson was well positioned to benefit from the telecommunications deregulation of the 1980s and 1990s. This has created new demand, especially for new equipment like mobile phones, an area where there were few local monopoly producers.

Ericsson has formed strategic alliances with Compaq, Intel, Hewlett Packard, and Texas Instruments. Again, these are budding 'tiered' flagship linkages. These firms act as key suppliers of components and products that Ericsson uses for voice and data transmission. The relative weakness that Ericsson has is a weak brand name, compared to Nokia and Motorola. It has the production technology but needs to improve on its marketing side.

The link between Ericsson and Nokia will benefit from the alliance between AT&T and British Telecom, and that between Sprint, France Telecom, and Deutsch Telekom. These big alliances help set standardized services with which mobile phone producers can then be involved as key suppliers, even tiered key suppliers. In the future mobile phones will become even smaller, but the two producers from small countries, Nokia of Finland and Ericsson of Sweden, will become even bigger.

8

The French Telecommunications Network

Introduction

This chapter uses the D'Cruz and Rugman five partners model (D'Cruz 1993, D'Cruz and Rugman 1993) to show how France Telecom has effectively partnered with suppliers, customers, competitors, and the non-business infrastructure (NBI) to develop France's telecommunications cluster. The five partners model is a framework based on co-operation, for organizing economic activity to create international competitiveness for globally-oriented firms. It is compared with the more traditional framework based on competition, used by multinational corporations. A contrast is drawn between Alcatel and France Telecom in their attempts to craft national, regional, and, eventually, global strategies for competitiveness in telecommunications. The comparison is useful and timely, because of the increasing convergence of the technologies of communications, the impact this will have on the strategies of other firms, and the implications for the strategic management of large firms competing in global markets.

A comparison of the competitive strategies of France Telecom and Alcatel illustrates two very different means of positioning for competitiveness in the global telecommunications industry. Moreover, the organizational structures of these companies embody fundamentally different approaches to achieving international competitiveness. France Telecom embraces a more co-operative strategy which depends upon sharing and accessing resources with partner organizations. Alcatel adheres to the more traditional structure of a multi-divisional, multi-national corporation.

The five partners model

The five partners model is a means of organizing economic activity among partner organizations through co-operative relationships in a business network. The five partners include the flagship firm, which as the leading partner is usually a multinational firm, key suppliers, key customers, competitors, and the NBI: see D'Cruz and Rugman 1992a; Rugman and D'Cruz 1994b. The NBI refers to the non-traded service sectors, government, education, healthcare, social services, and not-for-profit cultural industries. (See Figure 8.1.)

The flagship firm has the resources and perspective to develop global strategies for the network. Moreover, the flagship firm's global scope and experience enables it to provide the strategic direction for the network. This strategic direction is a

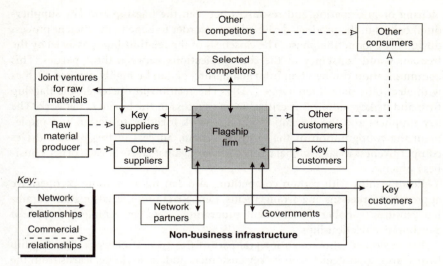

Figure 8.1 The flagship firm provides strategic leadership for its partners in the business system

vision of competitiveness for the network as a whole. The flagship firm plays a large role in determining the markets to be served and the products/services to be produced by the network. This strategic hand, so to speak, orchestrates the relationships among the network partners to achieve the strategic purpose envisioned by the flagship firm. The leadership of the flagship firm, in this network model of competitiveness, is manifested in several key activities, including:

- adopting a relationship-based, co-operation paradigm for network activities;
- restructuring and relocating the loci of production and service provision for numerous activities;
- benchmarking network activities and processes to global standards.

The partner organizations yield the strategic leadership role to the flagship firm because it is the global strategic purpose of the network as a whole that prompted the partners to join the network initially. Therefore, presumably, it is in the best interests of the partners and the network as a whole to operate under this umbrella of strategic intent. These partners undertake much of the responsibility for executing and operationalizing the network's strategy.

Typically, network relationships entail close co-operation and the sharing of resources and information. In the case of key suppliers, this tight relationship with the flagship firm often is manifested in near or total exclusivity of supply to the flagship. In return for this dedication of resources, the key supplier is rewarded with production responsibility for a greater share of the value added in the product/service and with more business in total from the flagship.

Sharing of information and resources between the flagship and key suppliers often occurs in the product-design phase, in order to benefit an efficient process during the production phase. The closeness of the relationship is assisted by the frequency and constancy of the communications between these parties. This communication can be of an informal nature, or can be highly ordered such as with electronic data interchange (EDI). The relationship between the flagship firm and its key suppliers is critical to the success of the business network. The key suppliers and the flagship essentially work together to design and implement the configuration of the business system. Success in this process drives competitiveness as large global firms compete against facets of each other's business systems.

Relationships with certain competitors also can follow a more co-operative approach. Market-sharing arrangements, joint R&D projects, co-operative training ventures, supplier development programmes, etc. are simple examples of collaborative relationships.

Key customers also are an integral part of this type of network. The flagship firm shares its strategies with its key customers and, in so doing, learns from the customers' input and achieves buy-in on the network strategy. The key customer accepts the flagship firm's leadership in regard to that area of the customer's business that is supplied by the flagship. For example, the telecommunications strategy of a large firm will be shaped by the recommendations of the flagship.

The NBI contributes to the network by providing human and technological capital. Institutions such as universities and government laboratories can provide equipment, facilities, and other arrangements in return for capital funding from the flagship firm. Members of the NBI also may receive assistance in obtaining other resources such as physical space and human resources.

Rationale for the five partners model

The highly integrated and interdependent global economic system of today has meaningful consequences for the organization of economic activity. The role of the nation state and the treatment of national borders are changing in order to accommodate the global flows of international trade and investment. The role of the multinational enterprise (MNE) is changing in a concomitant manner. Because the MNE plays the primary role as a co-ordinator of international production and investment, it is reasonable to expect that it must somehow evolve to reflect this borderless world. Specifically, one would expect that the structure and systems of the MNE would change in order to allow the enterprise to be more responsive and adaptive to its external environment.

The concept of isolated and completely independent firms competing against each other in the bid to optimize individual economic gain may be outdated. It must be questioned whether individual firms have the resources and capabilities to compete effectively against global competitors which are already benefiting from the co-ordination of strategies, resources, and competencies in network-like structures. Obviously, the Japanese *keiretsu* and Korean *chaebol* are examples of this latter approach to competition.

Another important aspect of international competition is the manner in which firms define their business. The above challenges in the marketplace have prompted many firms to focus on their core competencies (Prahalad and Hamel 1990; Hamel 1991) and capabilities (Stalk, Evans, and Shulman 1992) in order to develop a competitive advantage. Consequently, businesses often are defined by aspects of the value chain (Porter 1985) rather than by the industry in which they operate. When companies determine that they are competing in value chains (or business systems), not in industries, then it opens the way for them to forge linkages with other organizations which have advantages in other parts of the value chain. In this manner, the service produced is delivered to the customer through a business network, not through a single, integrated firm.

The five partners model is responsive to this way of understanding competition and competitive advantage. It explicitly fosters co-operative relationships among numerous partners as a means of exploiting each partner's competence in a business system. Long-run competitiveness, therefore, depends upon achieving mutually beneficial relationships which attempt to assist each partner in becoming competitive in its chosen business system activity (or activities).

The five partners model, as a co-operative model of behaviour, necessarily embraces dimensions of interorganizational behaviour which usually are not considered important, namely, aspects of competitiveness formulae. Specifically, these dimensions include trust, relationship stability, relationship longevity, and shared interorganizational purpose.

France Telecom and Alcatel are an example of competitiveness based on a network characterized by co-operation, as opposed to competitiveness based on rivalry among single firms which depend upon the internalization of economic activity (Buckley and Casson 1976).

Profile of France Telecom

France Telecom became a state-owned company on 1 January 1991. It evolved from its predecessor, the DGT (Direction Générale des Télécommunications), a publicly administered apparatus of the national government. DGT's role in the 1970s and 1980s was to develop France's telecommunications infrastructure and, essentially, to build an internationally competitive industry. The catalyst for this centrally directed industrial policy was the poor state of France's telecommunications infrastructure in the 1960s. During the period of 'the reconstruction' after the Second World War, France concentrated on rebuilding roads, railways, water, and electricity infrastructure, as well as primary industries. Telecommunications, as a state monopoly, suffered as a result of the short-sighted and negative view of it held by the De Gaulle government (Duch 1991). Consequently, France's telephone system was one of the least advanced among OECD nations at the end of the 1960s.

Despite the weak infrastructure, France had one of the world's leading telecommunications research institutes in the Centre National d'Etudes de Télécommunication (CNET). The CNET was founded in 1944 to co-ordinate civilian and military R&D in telecommunications. Since that time, it has played a leading role in researching transistors, micro-processors, integrated circuits, digital switches, optical fibres, satellite technology, and video communication. A second specialized institution, the Ecole Nationale des Télécommunications (ENST), is an élite engineering school which trains telecommunications engineers and managers for the industry (comprising private firms, the DGT, and the CNET).

Pressure from DGT managers and the CNET in the late 1960s forced the government to address the poor condition of France's telecommunications industry (Palmer and Tunstall 1990; Barreau and Abdelaziz 1987). In the early 1970s, the French government decided to invest heavily in order to develop a national telecommunications industry (Barreau and Abdelaziz 1987; Duch 1991). Its commitment to this programme was evident in the restructuring of DGT into a separate division of the Ministère des Postes, Télécommunications et Télédiffusion (PTT). The DGT received autonomy from the Ministry of Finance for budgets and employee compensation, thereby depoliticizing DGT and protecting it from changing political priorities.

The strategy adopted by the DGT to develop France's telecommunications infrastructure consisted of the following elements:

(1) *Design of long-term infrastructure programmes.* These programmes would be based on French technology and would allow French companies to enjoy the growth in a large domestic market. Examples of long-term programmes included digital switching, videotext (Minitel), ISDN, and fibre optics.

(2) *Protection of the domestic market.*

(3) *Involvement in R&D.* This included the DGT's relationship with CNET, and also the funding of telecommunications projects for other organizations.

(4) *Development of competition among equipment suppliers.* In the 1960s, equipment contracts were dispensed in accordance with quotas for a small group of suppliers established by DGT telecommunications engineers. The DGT unbundled its R&D and production contracts in order to promote more open competition (Palmer and Tunstall 1900). Using CNET's Central Service of Price Control, the DGT was able to apply pressure on suppliers to reduce prices. Third, the DGT pressed for the purchase of Ericsson France and LMT by the French company Thomson in 1976. This purchase placed Thomson ahead of Compagnie Générale d'Eléctricité (CGE), ITT (International Telephone and Telegraph Corporation), and AOIP in terms of market share (Barreau and Abdelaziz 1987). In the late 1970s, the DGT favoured the development and strengthening of the telecommunications sectors of two French firms, Matra and Sagem.

(5) *Assistance to export through political and financial support.*

The DGT business network in the 1970s and 1980s

Figure 8.2 indicates that the DGT had developed close relationships with suppliers and the NBI in the 1970s and 1980s. In particular, the DGT's relationships with the research community and educational institutions were well developed. In addition to CNET and ENST, the DGT created another engineering school, the Institut National des Télécommunications, in 1979. Two management schools specific to telecommunications also were administered under the DGT—the Ecole Nationale Supérieure des Postes et Télécommunications (ENSPT) and the Cadre Supérieur de Gestion de l'Institut National des Télécommunications. Industrial policy co-ordination with government ministries was highly developed. The DGT's relationships with key suppliers, primarily Thomson and CGE, consisted of technology transfers, assistance to export, and cost control.

The DGT's relationships with its customers or competitors were not close (unlike those that it had with the NBI). With regard to its competitors, the DGT depended on international standards organizations (such as the Comité consultatif international télégraphique et téléphonique (CCITT)) to co-ordinate relations with other PTOs (public telecommunications operators). Customers were viewed as users and their input was not actively solicited. The DGT was a technology-driven enterprise, organized on a geographic basis to match its operational organization. Moreover, its monopoly position left it free from external market constraints and demands.

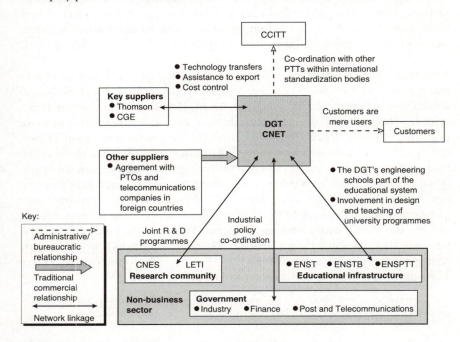

Figure 8.2 The DGT's business network during the 1970s

The DGT becomes France Telecom

While the DGT was considered a technological success in the 1970s, it became apparent in the mid-1980s that its administrative structure was a hindrance to continued success in the next decade. Changes in regulation, technologies, and economics had increased international competition, created more demanding customers who could 'shop around', and increased the need for network management.

Regulation   The liberalization of telecommunications regulations in the USA, the UK, and Japan opened up the competitive field to new players. Movement towards European integration and harmonization of regulatory infrastructures had shifted the power of telecommunications policy making from national bodies to the European Commission: see Carpentier, Farnoux-Toporkoff, and Garric 1991. The liberalization of telecommunications services in other countries prompted foreign carriers to adopt aggressive pricing strategies and new services. The DGT's administrative status prevented it from responding to the competition, leading the government to conclude that 'state-guided' liberalization was required (Duch 1991).

Technology   Advances in technology spawned the development of numerous new services. As network-penetration rates and first-line installations reached high levels, growth in traffic depended on increasing usage by customers. Customers were becoming sophisticated users and demanded useful and accessible services.

Economics   The slowdown in network growth rates[1] required better network management to increase productivity; and capacity growth could no longer correct forecast errors (Cayla-Boucharel, Ciceri, Heitzmann, and Pautrat 1990). With new technological developments, distance became less important as a cost driver for toll calls (Duch 1991). Consequently, the cross-subsidization of local calling costs with toll revenues needed to be rebalanced. It became obvious that the international competition and rapid technological changes demanded operational flexibility, financial freedom, a marketing focus, and international expansion by the DGT. In 1992, only 3.3 per cent of France Telecom's revenues were generated abroad (Bessières 1993). France Telecom was created at the beginning of 1991 as a state-owned company. This autonomy from the public administration infrastructure gave France Telecom the flexibility to develop a corporate strategy independent of the Ministry of Finance. The objectives of France Telecom, as stated during the 'corporatization' process, were:

(1) to reduce indebtedness (the highest among the Western PTOs in 1990);
(2) to restructure telecommunications rates;

---

[1]   The compound annual growth rate was 3.9 per cent between 1986 and 1991: France Telecom 1992.

(3) to modernize the network;

(4) to internationalize (France Telecom 1992).

The independence would allow for professional marketing and product/service development and investment, divestiture, and joint ventures internationally.

Figure 8.3 shows the business network of France Telecom. It indicates that France Telecom has established joint ventures with international competitors such as Deutsche Telekom, Southwestern Bell, and US West. Stronger links with key customers have been established through the newly developed marketing and sales programmes. France Telecom, Alcatel, and Matra have jointly developed and launched a mobile phone system. France Telecom's close relationship with its key suppliers can be seen in the division of France Telecom's purchasing profile—Alcatel 56.1 per cent, Matra 16.1 per cent, Sagem 9.7 per cent, and Philips 7.9 per cent (Bessières 1991). In terms of the links to educational institutions, France Telecom still retains control over the administration and teaching at the specialized schools.

Alcatel: The multinational equipment supplier

Alcatel is the largest telecommunications manufacturer/supplier in France and in the world. It was formed in 1983 when CGE and Thomson merged their telecommunications businesses under CGE's control and the new name of Alcatel. While France is its home base, 75 per cent of its revenues come from foreign sales. Alcatel

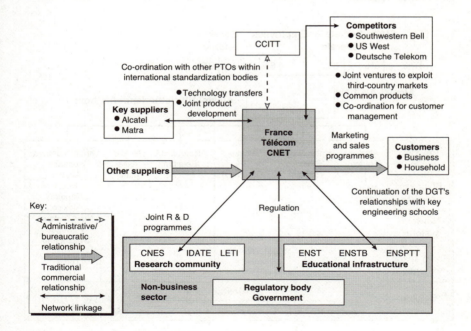

Figure 8.3 The business network of France Telecom

has benefited from the vast investments made in France's telecommunications infrastructure since 1960. The French telecommunications infrastructure is almost 70 per cent digitalized and its productivity rates and levels of service quality are among the highest in the OECD. There are more than 300 firms, employing 48,000 people, in the telecommunications equipment industry (Syndicat des industries de télécommunications 1993; Ministère de l'industrie et du commerce extérieur 1992). Matra, the second-largest producer, manufactures primarily in Europe for European sales. The third-largest producer, Sagem, manufactures in France and sells in Europe. Other competitors include Philips, Siemens, Bosch, and IBM.

Unlike the public telecommunications operator, France Telecom, Alcatel has a vision that is not a nationalistic vision for France. While France Telecom wishes to push the development of the French telecommunications industry in much the same way as did its predecessor, the DGT, Alcatel's vision is decidedly global. Alcatel wants to use France and later, the European Community (EC), as a base for global telecommunications manufacturing. It is important, therefore, for Alcatel to be able to have access, as required, to the French telecommunications infrastructure, such as the engineering schools, in order to fulfil its vision.

Through an export-driven strategy, Alcatel wants to be a dominant player in the global telecommunications equipment industry. Figure 8.4 shows that Alcatel is structured as a typical multinational, as opposed to the network that characterizes France Telecom.

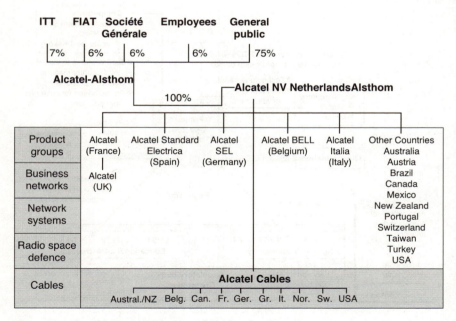

Figure 8.4 Alcatel is structured as a multinational corporation

Alcatel's business strategy is:

(1) To be active in every product segment, using focused divisions:
   - PBXs, public switching, microwave, mobile, space, fibre, etc.
(2) To pursue a global scope for each business:
   - presence in all major markets except Japan;
   - increased North American presence via purchase of Rockwell's Network Transmission Systems Division, 15 per cent of Loral;
   - first position in world equipment markets in switching, cable, microwave, cables. Major seller in space and mobile equipment.
(3) To use the EC as a home base:
   - 85 per cent of its employees and 75 per cent of its revenues are in Europe;
   - 30 per cent market share in Europe, 6 per cent of US market, 7 per cent of world market.
(4) To grow by acquisition:
   - 1986 merger with ITT European subsidiaries;
   - 1990 joint ventures with Aerospatiale and Alenia Spazio;
   - 1990 purchase of FIAT's Telettra;
   - 1993 joint venture with US Sprint.

France Telecom and Alcatel: Different visions

At the time of writing, Alcatel and France Telecom are not direct competitors. France Telecom is a service provider and Alcatel is an equipment manufacturer. However, as the line between hardware and software (manufacturing and service) blurs, it is a very real possibility that they will become direct competitors. The likelihood of this scenario happening is high when it is considered that Alcatel's R&D budget increasingly is focused on software. In 1992, 80 per cent of its R&D dollars were spent on software development, as compared to 50 per cent in 1987 (OECD 1993). To date, Alcatel has undoubtedly benefited from the DGT's network strategy and the development of the French telecommunications infrastructure. In terms of that strategy, the DGT was unquestionably successful in:

(1) developing a large and technologically competitive industry in France;
(2) creating a significant knowledge base in telecommunications engineering and management;
(3) building a dominant company in the domestic market.

Arguably, the DGT's strategy had several significant weaknesses:

(1) The DGT was technology, not market, driven and it missed some key areas, including mobile communications.
(2) The DGT dominated the industry and few other large competitors emerged. The industry is comprised of numerous small firms which are not internationally competitive on their own and which are dependent on the DGT. (Ninety per cent of firms account for only 5 per cent of exports

and 20 per cent of employment: see Barreau, Le Nay, and Abdelaziz Mouline 1986.) The ten leading companies, all of which are part of an industrial group (Alcatel, Matra, Sagem, Philips, and Bosch), account for 90 per cent of exports and 60 per cent of employment: see Ministère de l'industrie et du commerce extérieur 1992.

(3) The development of the French telecommunications industry does not seem to have acted as a catalyst, either as an example or as a facilitator, in developing the international competitiveness of other French industrial sectors.

The question remains, however, whether France Telecom's business network structure or Alcatel's multidivisional MNE structure places either firm at an advantage in the global trade of telecommunications products and services.

Summary and conclusions

This chapter presents a clear example of two quite different strategies for global competitiveness—the DGT/France Telecom co-operation-based strategy and Alcatel's competition-based strategy. Each firm is attempting to position itself to be competitive by becoming a dominant player in the global telecommunications industry. Whether France Telecom's network structure or Alcatel's multidivisional MNE structure proves to be superior has yet to be seen. It is apparent, however, that the forces of globalization are pushing each corporation to look well beyond France's borders. France Telecom still obtains only a small portion of its revenues (less than 5 per cent) from outside France; and, therefore, it faces the challenge of competing with firms which already are more globally oriented. Alcatel is still an EC-dependent company (75 per cent of its revenues are in Europe) that has yet to develop a truly global strategy that includes a significant presence in all the Triad markets.

The five partners model presents a different way of thinking about both strategy and structure. It says that a co-operation-based strategy in a business network structure is a viable approach to follow in order to achieve international competitiveness. The model challenges the effectiveness and appropriateness of the traditional multinational structure in today's rapidly changing global economy.

Update to Chapter 8

Siemens and Deutsche Telekom

Another set of flagship relationships links Siemens to Deutsche Telekom. For example, the 'component' division of Siemens, one of its eight strategic business units in 1997, has worked with Deutsche Telekom AG to supply semiconductors and it is jointly developing future telecommunication solutions. Siemens is, in fact, the only major semiconductor manufacturer in Germany and its level of production is well under half that of any one of the world's largest producers such as NEC, Motorola, TI, and Toshiba and only one-sixth of that of the industry leader, Intel. In terms of the Porter (1990) home country 'diamond', there are few related and supporting industries in semiconductors for Siemens, in contrast to the US and Japanese home bases of rivals like Intel, IT, NEC, Motorola, Toshiba, Lucky Goldstar, and Fijutsu. Siemens is even smaller than the South Korean semi-conductor producers, Hitachi and Samsung.

The Siemens components division maintains flagship relationships with some 50 key suppliers. These are small and medium sized firms (part of Germany's 'Mittelstand') which work exclusively for Siemens in its Dresden home-base area. Siemens also has a flagship-type joint venture for the development of new semi-conductor substrates and processes with ATMI/Symetrix. Besides its long-established linkages with Deutsche Telekom, Siemens is also a key supplier to German automobile makers such as Robert Bosch GmbH and Mannesmann.

Siemens has some developmental joint ventures with Triad rivals such as IBM, Toshiba, and Motorola, the last for wafer manufacturing technology. It is not clear if these are long-term flagship relationships, or a means for Siemens to access the know-how of the US and Japanese markets. Siemens also has a manufacturing joint venture with Motorola in the United States, which allows it to split risks and obtain access to the US market.

Finally, Siemens has strong flagship relationships with parts of the NBI of its home base of Dresden. It has educational linkages with the Technical University of Dresden, which specializes in electronics, and a strong network link in intellectual property. Siemens has a business alliance with the Federal State of Saxony, which is helping to develop the Dresden region as a high-tech cluster. There are also links with BMBF (the German federal ministry of education, science, research, and technology). The BMBF helps to fund basic research projects at Siemens.

Siemens has tried to develop flagship relationships across too many areas, indeed across all electrical sectors. As a result it has too many, poor, flagship relationships in:

- electrical power;
- automobiles;
- telecommunications;
- computers;
- semiconductors.

This lack of focus means that Siemens is weaker than Northern Telecom. To improve its competitive position, Siemens would need to reposition itself on a narrow, more specialized basis, and attempt to develop deeper flagship relationships.

9

The Canadian Speciality Chemicals Network

Introduction

The Canadian chemicals industry is composed of two types of firm: multinational enterprises (MNEs) and small and medium-sized firms (SMEs). Both types are faced with the same challenge and overarching strategic objective: how to become useful participants in the increasingly internationalized structure of the global chemicals industry. However, for each type of firm, either MNE or SME, the appropriate strategy to adopt in order successfully to attain this objective is heavily influenced by the structure of the network relationships that characterize each form.

Our analysis reveals that Canadian managers of MNEs are confronted with a dual challenge. During the current phase of global restructuring by these firms, Canadian managers must find ways to sell the benefits and capabilities of the Canadian operation effectively, on the basis of the needs of the parent's plans for a rationalized global network. Unless they succeed in this objective, they will not have sufficient resources at their disposal to fulfil the second objective, which is to refocus and concentrate the contribution of the Canadian operation to the MNE's global network. In other words, Canadian managers of MNE subsidiaries need to find a niche within the global operations of the company. This niche will usually consist of establishing key supplier relationships, either directly with the parent (an intrafirm key supplier relationship) or with independent MNE flagships in the form of regional or global supplier arrangements (an interfirm key supplier relationship).

For SMEs, healthy key customer relations with relevant MNE flagships are critical for survival in an economy increasingly driven by global benchmarks of competitiveness. We have found that SMEs are, in several key respects, better placed to benefit from globalization than some subsidiary operations of MNEs. For example, SMEs can help MNEs to gain access to small markets that require flexibility and quick response. This natural correspondence of interests means that SMEs have been and can continue to be a source of dynamism and growth in the Canadian chemicals industry.

In the next section, we summarize the five partners model as it is relevant for chemicals. We then apply the model to the five key chemical sectors in Canada. We conclude with a series of recommendations aimed at policy makers in government and managers in the industry.

Speciality chemicals and the flagship/five partners model

The flagship-five partners model of business systems is becoming increasingly common in industries where internationalization and globalization are advanced. By 'business systems' we mean the chain of companies that interact with each other from the manufacture of basic raw materials to final consumption. Conventional relationships in such systems are characterized by arm's-length competition between firms as they buy and sell. Such relationships, which are well explained in the 'five forces' model of competitive advantage (see Porter 1980) are based, to a large extent, on the development and exercise of market power. They tend to foster a short-term orientation among participants, with each participant being concerned primarily with its own profitability.

The flagship model, in contrast, is based on the development of collaborative relationships among major players in a business system. Its focus is on strategies that are mutually reinforcing. By their very nature, such relationships tend to foster and depend upon a collective long-term orientation among the parties concerned. Hence, they form an important facilitating mechanism for the development of long-term competitiveness (D'Cruz and Rugman 1992*b*, 1993).

There are two key features of the five forces business network: (a) the presence of a flagship firm that pulls the network together and provides leadership for the strategic management of the network as a whole; and (b) the existence of firms that have established key relationships with that flagship. These relationships are illustrated in Figure 9.1 by black arrows that cross organizational boundaries, symbolizing the nature of interfirm collaboration that characterizes them. Conventional arm's-length relationships stop at organizational boundaries. We will now apply this framework to the chemicals sector.

Flagship firms in chemicals

The flagship firm is the heart of the five partners business network. The flagship is usually an MNE that provides the network with strategic and organizational leadership. Flagship firms are critical to competitiveness in so far as they provide direction and leadership beyond the resources that, from an accounting perspective, lie directly under the flagship's management control. In other words, flagship firms extend their influence throughout the network in such a way that the quality of business leadership provided by the flagship will directly affect the competitive position of the other key players in the network, namely the flagship's key suppliers, key customers, and selected competitors. The relationship between the flagship and the non-business infrastructure (NBI) can also affect the competitiveness of the overall network. Each of these relationships within the network is described later in this chapter.

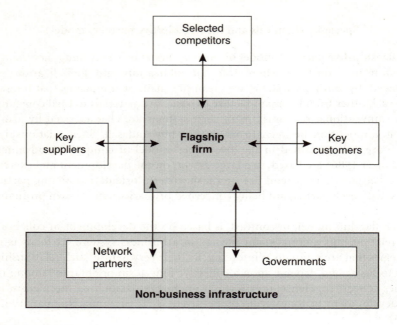

Figure 9.1 The five partners network model

In our investigation of sectors of the Canadian chemicals industry in Ontario, the strongest instance of a flagship firm operating from a home base in the province was a subsidiary of Sterling Chemicals, Inc. known as Sterling Pulp Chemicals, Ltd. This company has its Canadian head office in Toronto and operates a chlorine dioxide-based business in two sectors—bleaching systems for the pulp industry and disinfection systems for water treatment. The technology and commercial vision for this business have been developed in Canada by Sterling Pulp and its predecessor companies. In operationalizing this vision, it has made extensive use of network relationships with its partners in the business system, as we show below.

Key suppliers in chemicals

Key suppliers have established long-term relationships with the flagship of the network. In other words, although these firms may be completely independent of the flagship from an ownership perspective, a close convergence of the strategic interests of the two gives rise to a business relationship that is more stable and involved than one based purely upon arm's-length transactions. This type of relationship has become increasingly common in the global economy since the mid-1980s.

The role of the flagship in the key supplier-flagship relationship is to direct key suppliers with respect to:

(a) the supplier's role and mandate in the value chain;
(b) the quality standards and product specifications to which the key supplier must adhere; and
(c) the organizational parameters of the key supplier-flagship relationship.

The flagship will direct the key supplier in these three areas in accordance with the strategic objectives of the network as a whole. For example, with respect to the organizational parameters of the key supplier-flagship relationship, flagships that have recently been concerned with reducing inventory costs have started to require their suppliers to adopt electronic data interchange (EDI) systems to streamline the supply network.

Sterling's relationships with its key suppliers are instructive. Sterling has designed the technology for production of chlorine dioxide by its customers using generators which have also been designed by Sterling. However, the generators are produced by suppliers that have long-term relationships with Sterling. Similarly, Sterling works with a network of general contractors that have the expertise to install the generators at the customer's site.

In contrast, Sterling's relationship with Ontario Hydro has become a major strategic issue that threatens its future competitiveness. Electric power is a major input for Sterling's plants which produce sodium chlorate, the raw material from which its customers produce chlorine dioxide. Ontario Hydro's rates for Sterling's Thunder Bay plant have risen to the level where they make production in Ontario uneconomic. Unless it can obtain power at competitive prices, Sterling may have to consider locating expansion capacity in the United States where power rates are substantially lower.

With respect to the role of the flagship in establishing the key supplier's mandate in the value chain, recent developments in the relationship between automotive original equipment manufacturers (OEMs) and their key suppliers are also instructive. In the late 1980s, the automotive OEMs, in their capacity as flagships, sought to shift greater responsibility for the quality of their output to selected parts producers by mandating that a few of these firms would be designated as 'tier one' parts manufacturers and would be responsible for complete subsystems rather than just individual components in the final product. In this case, the flagships in the network initiated a fundamental reorganization of responsibilities throughout this business system, highlighting the degree to which flagships can exert influence beyond their own corporate 'boundaries' and throughout the network.

Key customers in chemicals

The relationship of flagships with their key customers is based on the former developing strategies to support the prosperity and profitability of the latter. The flagship provides broad strategic guidance to the customer and essentially dictates what the customer should be buying and, by implication, producing. The flagship firm–key customer relationship with which the five partners model is most concerned is one in which the key customer is a producer that is using the output of the flagship firm as an intermediate input. Usually, the flagship–key customer relationship revolves around the flagship firm's production of a critical input for the key customer's own production. Key customers are often SMEs and their network relationships need to be carefully explored.

Sterling's relationships with its customers in the pulp industry offers a number of useful lessons. Sterling is working with one of its key customers to find ways to develop closed loop systems for using chlorine dioxide for bleaching pulp. These systems allow pulp mills to meet and exceed government emission regulations regarding free chlorine, a major environmental concern for the pulp industry. By addressing an important strategic issue facing its key customers, Sterling not only helps the Canadian pulp industry maintain its competitiveness but also consolidates it own position in the business system.

Key competitors in chemicals

The flagship firm in a network can interact in various ways with selected competitors, which in turn are often also flagship firms. While the inclusion of competitors is uncommon in traditional business models, they are included in more modern analyses such as the five partners framework to reflect the growing complexities of the international economy and the fact that MNEs (recall that most flagships are MNEs) are rarely singular in their strategic objectives. In reality, all MNEs pursue several strategic objectives at any given time and some of these are often best served by co-operating with firms that have complementary objectives—even though these same firms might be rivals with respect to other strategic objectives. Research at pre-competitive levels of product development is one area where co-operation between 'competitors' has become increasingly common.

Non-business infrastructure

The final relationship identified in the network in Figure 9.1 is that between the flagship and the non-business infrastructure (NBI). The NBI consists of both government and a group of institutions we have named 'Network Partners'. These include: independent research centres, universities, community colleges, and industry associations. The government NBI includes all government-based granting agencies, support services offered through various arms of the government infrastructure, as well as any *ad hoc* programmes and initiatives. The NBI-flagship firm relationship is critical to the competitiveness of the network and to the ability of the flagship to lead the network effectively. On the one hand, government has ultimate responsibility for shaping major elements of the economic environment within which the business network must operate (through its control over fiscal policy, monetary policy, and the legal environment in which business must be conducted). On the other hand, the other network partners can be conducive to (or discourage) collaborative research projects, can supply business with a pool of skilled labour (the education system), etc.

Again, an example from Sterling's experience is informative. Much of the fundamental technology for using chlorine dioxide in the pulp process was developed by collaboration between Sterling and the Pulp and Paper Centre of the University of Toronto. This collaboration has been in existence for many years and was inspired by the work of Dr Howard Rapson of the University of Toronto, an acknowledged intellectual giant in the field. Over the years, Sterling and the university team have developed improved processes to manufacture chlorine dioxide and are developing the technology for the closed loop system for use in pulp mills. Without the latter, it might not be possible to meet current and future environmental standards. Both Sterling and the university have had essential roles in this collaboration. Sterling provided the strategic leadership for the commercial aspects of the project and made important financial contributions to the research, while the university provided the research environment and talent for the projects.

The relevance of the five partners model to competitiveness lies in the contribution of network relationships and the roles of key suppliers, key customers, and flagships. An understanding of where a particular firm, or, in some instances, an entire industry, lies with respect to the particular network with which it is associated is critical for the formulation of a business strategy that makes sense. Strategies aimed at increasing competitiveness need to be based upon an understanding of the importance of establishing 'key' status with a flagship for firms that are not in a flagship position themselves.

The Canadian chemicals industry

In this study five segments of the Canadian chemicals industry (SIC 37)are considered; paints and varnish (SIC 3751), soaps and cleaning compounds (SIC 3761), adhesives (SIC 3792), agrochemicals (SIC 372), and the more general inorganic and organic chemical groups (SIC 371 and 3799). The first four segments accounted for approximately 21.7 per cent of the entire chemicals industry's shipments in 1992, which were valued at $Cdn21,489.4 million (preliminary data for 1993 value shipments at $Cdn22,515 million). Of this share, adhesives accounted for 1.3 per cent of the total ($Cdn276.9 million), soap and cleaning compounds 7.7 per cent ($Cdn1,651.3 million), paint and varnishes 6.7 per cent ($Cdn1,445.7 million), and agrochemicals 6.0 per cent ($Cdn1,282.4 million). In addition, the critical role played by producers of industrial inorganic and organic chemicals (SIC groups 371 and 3799) as suppliers to firms in these four groups are also considered in detail. However, due to the eclectic nature of the activities of firms in these two SIC groups, we have not treated them as a separate business system as we did for the other four groups. Organic and inorganic chemicals accounted for 43.9 per cent of shipments in 1992, or $Cdn9,437.1 million. The scope of this study therefore covers products which accounted for 65.6 per cent of the chemicals industry's shipments in 1992. The only major subgroups within SIC 37 excluded from the analysis are pharmaceuticals, plastic and synthetic resins, and toilet preparations. Relative to the other nine major SIC groups,[1] chemicals ranked third in terms of value of shipments in 1991, after transport and food.

The paint business system

The Canadian paint business system is comprised of two distinct segments: industrial and decorative. With respect to shipments, the segments are approximately equal in size. However, in terms of organizational and operational characteristics, they are quite different. The paint business system can be analysed using Figure 9.2. Key suppliers and key customers represent a source of value added in the industry, from the production of basic inputs to the retail or wholesale distribution of the final product, moving from left to right.

The paint industry made shipments worth $Cdn1,498.7 million in 1993, reflecting continued growth and recovery from the recession when industry shipments reached a low of $Cdn1,370.6 million in 1991. However, pre-1990 shipment levels ($Cdn1,659.6 million in 1989) have yet to be reattained. In 1992, there

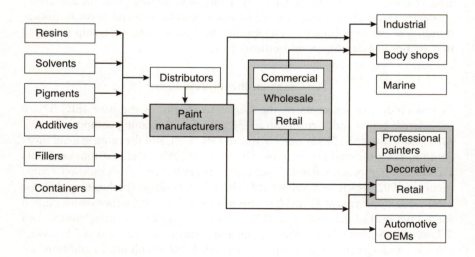

Figure 9.2 The business system of the Canadian paint industry

[1] Transport, food, paper, electrical, petroleum, primary metals, fabricated metals, wood, and printing.

were 131 establishments in this sector, wages and salaries accounted for 28 per cent of variable inputs costs, and value added for the industry as a whole equalled $Cdn829.6 million, or 57 per cent of the value of shipments.

The industrial segment serves primarily the automotive industry in both OEM assembly plants and the refinish aftermarket. The firms in this segment are essentially all large multinationals whose relationships with the automotive OEMs are organized to shadow the North American patterns of OEM operations. Output is concentrated in the hands of just a few large firms and a few smaller niche firms. The MNEs that account for most of this sector's output include BASF Coatings and Inks Canada Ltd., DuPont Canada Inc., PPG Canada Inc., and Akzo Coatings Ltd.

The key issues for paint manufacturers in the industrial segment revolve around the importance of the automobile OEMs as flagships. Indeed, in some instances, paint manufacturers have developed a strategy of serving only the automobile OEM market. For example, DuPont Canada Inc. produced paint for both the decorative and the broader industrial segments when it entered the business in 1956. However, its focus has progressively narrowed to the point where today it only produces for the automotive industry. PPG Canada Inc. is also highly focused in the area of automotive finishes, although the company does still manufacture some industrial coatings in Canada.

The suppliers to the automotive OEMs are responsible for researching colour trends, new product development, and technical support. Each of the major paint manufacturers serving the automotive OEMs is capable of covering all of the stages in the paint process. Yet, the automotive OEMs generally distribute different assembly lines among the different paint manufacturers and also distribute responsibility for the different layers in the automotive painting process (that is, E-coat, topcoats, clearcoats, primers, etc.) to different companies. Generally, each OEM facility has two suppliers. Only four Canadian automotive plants are sole sourced. One possible reason for multiple sourcing by the automotive OEMs is that the paint manufacturer may have led in the development of certain products. For example, PPG established an early market position in E-coat. Another likely reason relates to the efforts by the OEM flagships to keep their suppliers competitive and avoid becoming too dependent in any one area upon a given supplier.

In addition to dealing directly with the OEMs, paint manufacturers are also key suppliers to the automotive parts suppliers—which in turn supply painted parts to the OEM. In this instance, however, the paint manufacturer interacts with the parts manufacturer that has won a contract with an automotive OEM. In this case, the automotive OEM is still clearly acting as the flagship, even though the paint manufacturer is submitting its bid to the automotive parts manufacturer. One important technological development in the parts segment has been the increased use of flexible fascias. The widespread use of these products has required paint manufacturers to develop flexible finishes that have to match the colours of the rest of the body of the car.

Most of the paint manufacturers that have specialized in the automotive OEM segment have also developed relations with the Japanese transplants. In order to enhance their relationship with the Japanese automotive manufacturers, DuPont has established a joint venture with a major Japanese paint supplier—Kansai. In this case, the flagship status of the automative manufacturer and the key supplier role played by the paint manufacturer is again evident. To become a supplier to the Japanese OEMs, the joint venture was required to adopt a different technology—the technology with which the Japanese OEMs were familiar in their domestic operations in Japan. Furthermore, the joint venture was required to source its basic inputs from the traditional suppliers to Kansai Paint Co., Ltd. Even though DuPont would like to source more inputs from its own supplier network, the strategic force in this relationship has clearly been the Japanese OEMs.

The paint manufacturers that serve the automotive OEMs are organized to conform to the spatial organization of the OEMs themselves. In the case of DuPont, sales contracts with the automotive OEMs (both American and Japanese) are negotiated in Detroit (indeed, DuPont has a reputation in the industry for having regionalized the structure of its operations most rapidly). Likewise, all of PPG's contracts with the North American-based automotive OEMs are negotiated on a regional basis by the OEM office in Detroit. However, business with the transplants (mainly Japanese firms) is negotiated by the Canadian subsidiary. In the OEM paint segment we also find significant examples of horizontal integration. For example, in addition to being a major paint supplier to the automotive OEMs, PPG also supplies glass and DuPont supplies engineering plastics, fibres, and adhesive film for laminating windscreens.

In contrast to their role as key supplier to the automotive OEMs, the paint manufacturers act as flagships in the refinish business. The reason for this is that they control and support the technology used by the body shops to match paints in repair work. Body shops must usually enter into exclusive contracts with their paint suppliers.

The decorative segment is much less technically advanced than the industrial segment and is also dominated by MNEs. Producers in this segment can be distinguished according to the type of distribution channels they use: (a) those that distribute through their own retail outlets (for example Sherwin Williams); (b) those that produce private label products for, or distribute their own products through, mass retail outlets (for example Sico Inc.); and (c) those that distribute their products only through smaller independent retail outlets. With respect to the paint manufacturers that have positioned themselves in the upscale markets (such as Para Paints Canada Inc.), the critical business relationship is the key customer relationship they can develop with the large integrated chemicals manufacturers. Through these relationships, the paint manufacturers gain access to the output of research programmes that only the larger chemicals companies can support. The larger companies are willing to share this information with the smaller paint manufacturers because these do not represent a strategic threat to the flagship and because these SMEs are small enough to be able to access markets in which the MNE would otherwise not be able to sell its products (in the case of high-end decorative paint manufacturers, most could be classified as MEs, medium-sized enterprises).

One of the key issues in this segment concerns the strategic integrity of the distinction between low-cost/low-service producers and the high-quality/high-service producers. With respect to the former category, we find that these producers have established key supplier relationships with large retailers (for example Sico's relationship with Sears). As key suppliers, these paint manufacturers are mandated to supply the retail flagship with a reasonable product at very competitive prices. The product can be sold either under the original manufacturer's name (as with the Durral line sold through the Price Club/Costco chain) or as a private label brand (Canadian Tire's Mastercraft line of paints). The question that arises is whether the retail flagships will be content to continue to limit their activities to the high-volume/low-margin segment they have traditionally occupied, or whether they will attempt eventually to increase their share of the higher-quality segment of the decorative market. In several industries (including soaps and detergents), the large, aggressive mass merchandisers such as Wal-Mart are attempting to carve out a flagship role for themselves. It remains to be seen how the current shake-up in the retail sector and the flagship aspirations of several of the larger retailers will affect the decorative paint manufacturers.

In summary, Canadian paint manufacturers pursue their strategic interests by establishing key relationships with flagship firms. In this industrial segment, the predominant flagship relationship of the Canadian paint manufacturers is a key supplier relationship with the automotive OEMs. The strength and focus of this particular flagship relationship has led to considerable stability in this segment of the Canadian chemicals industry, a stability predicated upon the continued health of the Canadian automotive industry.

The decorative segment is more volatile. Depending upon which distribution network they are affiliated with, decorative paint producers have stronger key relationships either with the large integrated chemicals companies (mainly from SIC 371 and 3799) that produce the inputs for paint production or with the flagship mass merchandisers. The decorative paint manufacturers that have positioned themselves in the high end of the market must actively market their products— much of the distinctive value of the output from these paint manufacturers originates in the ability of their flagship chemicals suppliers to provide them with ingredients that impart to the final product its special qualities (such as zero volatile organic compounds, durability, washability, resistance to UV rays, etc.). The decorative paint manufacturers that have positioned themselves in the low-cost segment of the market are concerned with volume and have therefore benefited from their relationships as key suppliers to the flagship mass merchandisers.

The soap and detergent business system

The soap and detergent business system is comprised of two broad groups of manufacturers: name brand producers and private label producers. Name brand production accounts for approximately 80 per cent of industry shipments (with 60 per cent going to the consumer market and 20 per cent going to the commercial/institutional market); while private label production accounts for the remaining 20 per cent (most of which goes to the consumer market). Another way of describing the Canadian market, then, is that 80 per cent of it is consumer and 20 per cent of it is commercial/institutional. In 1991, raw materials accounted for 49 per cent of the cost of inputs, containers 19 per cent, wages 26 per cent, miscellaneous services and inputs 4 per cent, and fuel and electricity 2 per cent. Total shipments in 1991 were worth $Cdn1.7 billion. Value added equalled $Cdn887 million, or roughly 52 per cent of shipments. Figure 9.3 outlines the business system for soap and detergents.

The industry is dominated by MNEs. Procter & Gamble Inc. and Lever Brothers Ltd. are the predominant name brand producers for the consumer market, with approximately 75 per cent market share. The rest of the consumer market is divided between: (a) smaller, specialized producers (often regionally based) such as Lavo Ltée (Montreal); (b) MNEs that service a smaller share of the market through a distribution presence only (or minimal manufacturing) such as Colgate-Palmolive Canada Inc.; and (c) private label manufacturers such as Witco Canada Inc. and CCL Industries Inc. The industrial segment is also dominated by MNEs, such as Diversey and Ecolab Ltd., that specialize in producing cleaning and sanitizing products for the hospitality, institutional, and industrial markets.

Two MNEs have acted as flagships in the soap and detergent industry: Lever Brothers Ltd. and Procter & Gamble Inc. These companies are characterized by

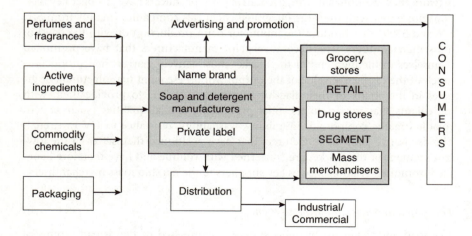

Figure 9.3 The Canadian soap and detergent business system

significant levels of both vertical and horizontal integration. Lever Brothers Ltd., for example, has integrated backwards into higher-value-added inputs such as isethion-ate and fatty acids and has sourced other critical inputs from third-party suppliers.

Key suppliers to these flagship firms are the large integrated chemicals com-panies. For example, Rhône-Poulenc has been a key supplier of surfactants to many of the major soap and detergent manufacturers in Canada (Procter & Gamble Inc., Colgate-Palmolive Canada Inc., Lever Brothers Ltd., Diversey Corporation, and CCL Industries Inc.). As a key supplier, Rhône-Poulenc interacts with its flag-ship customers on a North American basis reflecting the nature of flagship strat-egy in this industry.

In some cases, the soap and detergent flagships will closely co-ordinate the activities of several of their key suppliers. For example, the production of ethoxy-late for a major soap and detergent manufacturer involved the co-ordination of three key suppliers: one supplied the ethylene oxide; another supplied alcohol; and the third supplier provided the reactors on a service fee basis. Therefore, in addition to negotiating all of the contracts for the inputs with its key suppliers, the soap and detergent manufacturer also directed its key suppliers to do the blend-ing of a critical input for them.

Although Procter & Gamble and Lever continue to act as flagships, their long-standing flagship positions have come under attack recently and the networks for which they have served as a hub for so long are on the verge of radical transform-ation. Competition for flagship status in this industry has emerged in the retail sector, both from traditional retailers, such as Loblaws, and from the new entrants in the Canadian retailing scene, mass merchandisers such as Price Club and Wal-Mart.

The new entrants in the Canadian retail sector have set new standards for effi-cient distribution networks and heightened price competition. While the soap and detergent industry has always been subject to price pressure from retailers (since soaps and detergents are among the 'basic products' that retailers frequently feature as specials), the traditional soap and detergent flagships are likely to see their leverage with respect to retailers substantially eroded due both to the increased market power of the new retailers that have entered the market recently and to the rise of the private label segment. Furthermore, with advertising costs already accounting for approximately 25 per cent of the selling price, it is unlikely that the soap and detergent manufacturers will be able to improve their leverage with respect to the retailers by means of increased promotion at the consumer level.

The soap and detergent business in Canada continues to be viable. However, the traditional flagship status of the MNEs operating in this sector is under attack from the retail sector. The strategic question faced by managers in the soap and detergent industry then is whether to engage the retailers head-on in a battle to maintain flagship status or whether to adapt to fundamental changes in the network by developing key supplier relationships with retailers. In most cases, the confrontational approach will not be successful. We recommend that firms in the soap and detergent sector attempt to increase their leverage with respect to retailers through development of stronger name brand recognition while simultaneously seeking common ground with them.

The adhesives business system

The adhesives business system in Canada is dominated by MNEs. The industry can be roughly divided according to the quality of output; between low- and medium-performance products that are produced for local industrial and consumer markets and high-performance products that are produced for new industrial applications such as in the automotive and aerospace industries. The Canadian market is relatively small and therefore production in Canada is limited to the low- and medium-performance products. High-performance needs are served through imports. These products account for approximately 35 per cent of the Canadian market, and are associated predominantly with the automotive OEM sector. The industry does not export to any significant degree. Figure 9.4 illustrates the business system of the adhesives sector.

Shipments in 1993 were valued at $Cdn300.3 million. The total cost of inputs into the manufacture of these shipments was $Cdn200.1 million. Raw materials

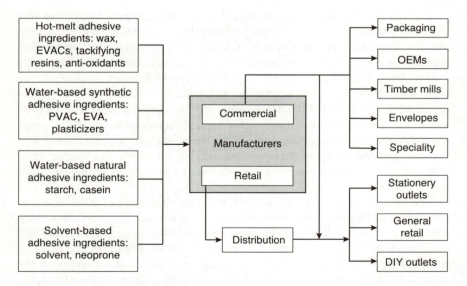

Figure 9.4 The Canadian adhesives business system

accounted for $Cdn124.8 million (62 per cent of total cost), wages $Cdn71.7 million (36 per cent), and fuel and electricity $Cdn3.7 million (2 per cent). The cost structure of the industry was affected considerably by the ratification of the Canada-USA Free Trade Agreement (FTA) in 1989 and by the continued liberalization of trade in the North American Free Trade Agreement (NAFTA). Before these agreements, basic inputs accounted for upwards of 76 per cent of manufacturing costs, while wages accounted for only 22 per cent of total cost. Trade liberalization has therefore contributed to a lowering of overall production costs and led to a significant increase in the relative share of wages in the sector's cost structure.

Canadian adhesives manufacturers usually specialize in producing either for the consumer market or for the commercial/industrial market. The principal producers for the industrial market include Nacan Products Ltd., Swift Adhesives Inc., H. B. Fuller Canada Inc., Helmitin Canada Inc., and Halltech Inc. The producers that dominate the retail/consumer market include Roberts Company Canada Ltd., Lepages Ltd., and Canadian Adhesives Ltd. A few firms produce for both segments; these include 3M and Dural. In value terms, the industrial segment accounts for approximately 80 per cent of the total adhesives market.

Adhesives manufacturers in Canada act as key customers to the large integrated chemical producers and as key suppliers to large manufacturers such as the automotive OEMs. In effect, the adhesives and sealants manufacturers play an intermediary role in the value chain that links the flagship producers of the basic inputs into the manufacture of adhesives and sealants and the flagship commercial end-users of these products. A stylized characterization of the new-product development processes in this relationship is as follows: (1) the end-user (for example automotive OEM, packaging facility, etc.) communicates a new need to the adhesives producer (such as a reduced volatile organic compound product); (2) the adhesives manufacturer tries to supply this product if the new specifications are not too technically demanding; (3) if the technical implications of the end-user's needs are more complex, then the adhesives producer will be dependent upon its suppliers of basic inputs to provide the required innovation (for example in the form of a new polymer system) to create a product with the qualities demanded by the end-user.

The Canadian adhesives manufacturers have established key customer relationships with the large integrated North American chemicals producers. In the four main product categories (hot melts, water-based synthetic adhesives, water-based natural adhesives, and solvent-based adhesives) the Canadian manufacturers have heavily integrated backwards for some products and not others. Further, where they have not integrated, there has been a strong trend towards a greater concentration of suppliers and the development of closer, more long-term relationships with those that remain.

With respect to the production of hot melts (which have been one of the fastest-growing segments), the main inputs are often sourced from independent suppliers. The three main inputs are wax, EVACs, and tackifying resins. A fourth input, that is more important from a quality perspective than a cost perspective, is anti-oxidants. The main producer of wax is International Waxes Inc. EVACs are produced by AT Plastics (the only major Canadian-based producer), DuPont, Exxon, and Atochem. Tackifying resins are all imported from the United States. The principal manufacturers of this input are Arizona, Eastman, Exxon, and Hercules. Finally, anti-oxidants are produced by, and mainly sourced from, Ciba-Geigy Canada Ltd. The significance of large integrated chemical MNEs as suppliers is clear. North American producers of hot melts, such as Nacan Products Limited, have not vertically integrated any of these basic inputs.

With respect to water-based synthetic resins, Polyethylene vinyl acetate chloride (PVAC) and Ethylene vinyl acetate (EVA) account for approximately 90 per cent of basic inputs by value. PVAC production has been integrated into the value chain of the large adhesives producers such as Dural, Nacan, and Reichold, which together account for more than 80 per cent of PVAC output in Canada. The principal producers of EVA are Nacan (National Starch), Reichold, and Air Products. An input into the production of water-based synthetic resins that has not been internalized by the adhesives producers is plasticizers. These are produced mainly by large chemical MNEs such as Monsanto and Velsicol.

With respect to production of water-based natural adhesives, the two most important inputs are starch (dextrins) and casein. Starch production for adhesives production is almost completely internalized, with only a few firms, including National Starch, accounting for the bulk of production in Canada. Casein, on the other hand, is imported. It is a traded commodity for which key supplier relationships have not been found necessary.

Production of solvent-based adhesives, which have been on the decline for environmental reasons, is characterized by linkages with large MNE chemical producers for all significant inputs: solvents and neoprene. Solvents account for approximately 80 per cent of the input for this product. The most commonly used solvents include xylene, toluene, MEK, and hexane. Imperial Oil and Shell are the main suppliers of these inputs. (It should be noted that a very small fraction of the output of these products by Imperial Oil and Shell is destined for the adhesives industry.) In the case of neoprene, which accounts for the other 20 per cent of the input into solvent-based adhesive production, DuPont is the only supplier of this input in Canada.

With respect to their role as key suppliers, the principal customers of the adhesive producers have been packagers (40 per cent of the industrial market) and the automotive OEMs (35 per cent of the industrial market). As is the case in the industrial paint segment, the adhesives producers have established key supplier relationships that reflect the growing need for product customization and high-quality service to accompany the product. In some instances, adhesives manufacturers develop such close relationships with customers that the adhesives manufacturer will assume responsibility for managing supply to the customer. For example, as a key supplier to some customers, Nacan will determine the adhesives needs of its customer on site and will initiate a shipment—the customer is not involved in the order process until the invoice stage.

A key issue facing Canadian adhesives manufacturers is the erosion of their Canadian customer base. For example, whereas furniture manufacturers used to be a significant market segment, this industry has been largely rationalized on a North American basis with very little manufacturing remaining in Ontario. A related problem concerns the Canadian industry's traditional emphasis on production of lower- to medium-performance products and the lack of technical capability, as a growing share of the adhesives market moves towards higher-performance products.

Therefore, in their role as key customers of the flagship integrated chemicals producers, the adhesives producers should continue to develop these relationships by finding niches where they may be able to market new products based upon new formulations developed by the flagships. With respect to their role as key suppliers to flagship customers, the adhesives producers need to focus upon the needs of their customers both in terms of technical requirements as well as with respect to organizational issues where their customers are in the process of integrating their operations on a North American basis.

The agrochemicals business system

The agrochemicals industry can be divided between fertilizer production and pesticide production. The two sectors are radically different from each other in terms of the structure of shipments. The fertilizer industry is characterized by low levels of imports (approximately one-fifth of the domestic market) and high export volumes (approximately two-thirds the value of total shipments). In contrast, roughly half of the domestic market for pesticides is served by imports, and exports account for only one-tenth of the value of total shipments. With respect to the industry's cost structure, in 1991 63.5 per cent of input costs were accounted for by raw inputs, 15.8 per cent by wages, 9.0 per cent by fuel, 1.6 per cent by containers, and the remaining 10.1 per cent by various other costs. Shipments were valued at $Cdn1,282.4 million in 1992 (preliminary data suggest that shipments for 1993 will be valued at $Cdn1,452.8 million). We will focus our analysis here upon the flagship relationships and the competitiveness of the pesticides industry, as indicated in Figure 9.5.

As with all of the other sectors examined in this chapter, the agricultural chemicals sector is dominated by MNEs. For the most part, the main function of the Canadian subsidiaries of these firms has been distribution and the mixing of active ingredients to create the final product. The principal firms that operate in this market are Ciba Geigy, Zeneca, Hoechst, Monsanto, Rhône-Poulenc Canada, Rohm and Haas Canada, Sandoz, and Uniroyal Chemical Ltd. Some firms in this market, such as BASF, DuPont, and ICI, do not manufacture pesticides in Canada but do act as distributors. Almost 90 per cent of the industry's output is for the

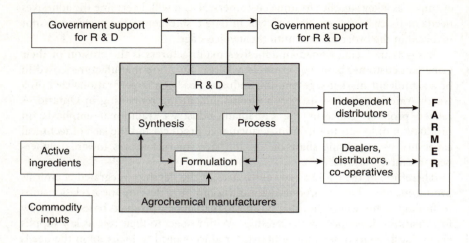

Figure 9.5 The Canadian agrochemicals business system

agricultural market and, of this, approximately 77 per cent is herbicides. Most firms do not conduct R&D in Canada or maintain only small research laboratories (a few significant exceptions will be discussed below).

This sector is characterized by some clear examples of flagship activity. In the 'greenhouse' segment, Plant Products Company Ltd. stands out as having several strong flagship qualities. With respect to suppliers, strong, co-operative, long-term relationships have been fostered with an emphasis on quality and trust. In terms of the direction of product development, the company has sought to develop relationships both with key competitors as well as with the NBI (namely a research relationship with Laval University) towards maintaining the ability to develop cutting-edge technologies in house (especially in the area of biological controls). As a result, Plant Products Company Ltd. is responsible for the first biological fungicide registration in Canada. In its relationship with Laval, the university laboratory does the basic research while Plant Products Company Ltd. takes care of patents, registrations, and market research.

Another example of flagship activity in the agricultural chemicals industry is Uniroyal Chemical Ltd. Uniroyal maintains a sophisticated R&D facility in Guelph which is integrated into Uniroyal's global R&D programme. The high level of technical ability at the Canadian operation has translated into two forms of flagship role. First, with respect to the parent R&D facility in Connecticut, the Canadian R&D facility plays a key leadership role (while at the same time also fitting into Uniroyal Chemical's international organizational structure). For example, the Guelph facility supplies all of the in-house compounds for biological screening in Connecticut, where environmental chemistry is conducted. In effect, the high technical capacity of the Canadian operation has made it an important part of Uniroyal Chemical's global R&D organization.

Another area in which Uniroyal Chemical's technical capacity has given it a flagship role is with respect to field testing and its relationship with customers. Its field testing programme is among the most sophisticated in Canada and the company works closely with customers to determine and then provide for their needs. In addition, Uniroyal will attempt to develop differentiated products for its customers.

Finally, Uniroyal Chemical's relationship with the NBI has been critical to the company's success, with respect both to competitors and to its internal relationship with the rest of the company's global operations. Whereas numerous examples can be found in the Canadian chemicals industry of MNEs reducing or completely eliminating the R&D capacity of their Canadian operations (for example the closing of Shell's R&D facility in Oakville and the moving of Diversey's R&D facility to Chicago), Uniroyal Chemical Ltd. is an example of a viable R&D operation in Canada and of the benefits of having good R&D conducted in Canada. Part of Uniroyal's success in this regard should be associated with government support of research programmes. For example, from 1962 to 1983, a National Research Council programme which supported R&D at the Uniroyal research laboratory was critical to the laboratory's success.

The Canadian agrochemicals industry is among the most competitive subsectors of the Canadian chemicals industry. This competitiveness derives from a combination of 'natural' factors (such as proximity to a large market, the availability of basic inputs at world-competitive prices, etc.) and less 'natural' factors (such as the positive contribution of government programmes to R&D efforts, favourable precedents for joint business-university research efforts, the good international reputation developed by the Canadian scientific community, etc.). This sector therefore provides other subsectors of the chemicals industry with examples of viable Canadian operations that are integrated into the global operations of their parents. However, to remain viable the agrochemicals producers must continue to nurture their network relationships.

Conclusions

Three broad conclusions have emerged from the previous analysis:

(a) the significance for competitiveness of key supplier relationships for subsidiaries of MNEs in the face of the rapid internationalization of the Canadian industry;

(b) the significance for competitiveness of key customer relationships of SMEs with flagship suppliers; and

(c) the importance of the non-business infrastructure to the continued dynamism and entrepreneurial contribution of SMEs.

These three conclusions persuade us of the analytical strength and predictive ability of the five partners business network model.

The key supplier relationships of MNEs

The chemicals industry has not adapted quickly enough to a rapidly changing international economic environment that has increased Canada's levels of international economic integration. More specifically, many Canadian chemicals companies have not understood clearly enough the need for a transition from their earlier stand-alone organizational structures (that had been fostered by means of high tariff barriers) to key supplier and key customer roles implied by internationalization in an industry dominated by MNEs. Even when managers did recognize this (for example in firms such as DuPont, Alkaril, Hart) they could not resolve the problem. Whether a firm is a subsidiary of an MNE or an independent and much smaller niche player, establishing strong relationships with flagships is the key to the future survival of Canadian chemicals companies.

Many of the larger MNEs in Canada are now doing very well as key suppliers. For example, in the paints industry key suppliers such as PPG and DuPont Canada have profitable businesses as key suppliers to the US and Japanese automobile manufacturers (OEMs) in Canada. The strategic directions for these businesses are partly determined in the United States but the production mandate to implement these contracts can result in a successful Canadian business, with many jobs, profits for the company, and a net positive contribution to Canada's social and economic well-being.

Therefore, managers of MNEs need to continue to adopt a North American strategic vision. Especially important within the context of MNEs will be the ability of Canadian managers to articulate in the appropriate strategic forums the Canadian subsidiary's potential contribution as a key supplier.

The key customer relationships of SMEs

Somewhat in contrast to the dramatic retrenchment affecting the larger MNEs there is a more subtle change affecting SMEs. These are often 'niche' players driven by entrepreneurs who have a sense of the market. The SMEs are close to their customers; they can build and maintain long-term successful businesses through their marketing skills and flexibility.

The SMEs act as intermediaries between the larger MNE suppliers and the wholesale or national distributors. Their flexibility and marketing know-how are vital firm-specific advantages (FSAs). They can use their laboratories to customize products and/or respond very quickly to customer demands. They can manage these service functions better than larger MNE suppliers. As 'key customers' of the MNEs, they can expand the total market for the MNEs, while not acting as a threat to them. In this sense, the SMEs have to manage the key supplier role with skill and foresight. They can develop close working relationships with a variety of MNEs provided they preserve secrecy and develop a reputation for discretion and non-disclosure to rival MNEs.

The SMEs therefore promise to be a source of considerable growth and dynamism in the Canadian chemicals industry as the MNEs seek to rationalize the productive structure of their global (or regional) operations while at the same time accessing as many markets as they can. The SMEs are, in effect, the keys to new markets in so far as (a) they are able to penetrate markets that are simply too small for MNEs to cater to given the scale of operations to which most MNEs are committed; and (b) they allow for more rapid roll-out of technological advances by making smaller, more specialized product development economically viable.

Support from the non-business infrastructure

While we have encountered exceptions, especially in the agrochemicals sector, generally MNEs have been consolidating their R&D functions outside Canada. This in turn has meant that there has been less opportunity for technical training 'on the job' in the Canadian chemicals industry. Therefore, more of the burden for technical training will shift to the Canadian educational system. However, the skills to be a successful MNE network manager are often missing in today's Canadian chemicals industry.

Managers who started their careers running branch plants, for which Canada was the market, now often find themselves in a radically different organizational and strategic environment. While Canada was a protected market, the reason for the existence of the Canadian operation was obvious and needed no explaining. Now, with much freer trade, the contribution of the Canadian operation to the company's global strategy is no longer so obvious (at least not to head office) and Canadian managers are finding that they need to justify their role. Canadian managers therefore need to develop the managerial skills relevant to international network forms of corporate organization.

Therefore, although Canadian universities provide the industry with an ample supply of graduates in engineering and chemistry, the radical change which the industry has experienced and the continued exposure of the industry to the forces of globalization and international benchmarking has given rise to the need for skill sets which the industry is not used to needing and which the NBI is not yet equipped to produce.

10

The Scottish Electronics Cluster

Introduction: Scotland's electronics cluster

In this chapter, the Scottish electronics cluster is analysed using the 'five partners' framework of international competitiveness developed by D'Cruz and Rugman (1992b, 1993). In this, a 'flagship' firm, usually a multinational enterprise (MNE) develops network relationships with four other partners: key suppliers, key customers, selected competitors, and the non-business infrastructure (NBI). The five partners/flagship framework has been applied to the telecommunications sectors in Europe and Canada (D'Cruz and Rugman 1994a, 1994b), and to the Canadian chemicals sectors (D'Cruz, Gestrin, and Rugman 1995). The relationship of the five partners/flagship framework to the theory of the MNE has also been explored recently (Rugman, D'Cruz, and Verbeke 1995), while Rugman and D'Cruz (1996) relate the model to the literature on business networks.

The Scottish electronics sector was built by foreign direct investment (FDI) by US MNEs such as IBM, NCR, Burroughs, and Honeywell. In 1990, the foreign-owned firms in the electronics industry accounted for 30 per cent of all jobs in foreign-owned companies in Scotland (Young, Peters, and Hood 1993). These firms were attracted partly by relatively low-cost skilled labour, but also to a large degree by government incentives justified for reasons of regional development (Hood, Young, and Truijens 1993; Hood and Young 1997). The electronics cluster failed to develop the higher-value-added end of the industry and it now faces a serious competitive threat from lower-cost producers in South-East Asia, such as Taiwan and Singapore (Peters 1995). The electronics industry in Scotland is focused on the hardware side, manufacturing computers and components, especially integrated circuits, and is weak in software. The cluster also failed to develop key supplier linkages or university research infrastructure (Hood and Young 1997). The creation of the Scottish Electronics Forum may help to foster better linkages with the NBI.

Applying the five partners model by sector

The Scottish electronics cluster can be analysed across its five sectors (or lines of business), which are:

(1) information systems;
(2) semiconductors;
(3) telecommunications;
(4) consumer electronics;
(5) software and other, including medical and military.

We shall now review the major firms active in these five sectors or lines of business and see how the five partners/flagship framework applies to each of the sectors. After this review, we provide a generalized analysis of the flagship framework across all the sectors.

Information systems

American computer MNEs, such as IBM, Honeywell, and NCR, have been active in Scotland since the 1950s. By the 1990s, Scotland produced one-third of all branded personal computers (PCs) sold in Europe, which represented about 7 per cent of world output. The MNEs operating in Scotland in 1997 vary in their degree of value-added activity in Scotland.

IBM at Greenock has the world's largest PC production facility, employing 2,300 people, with IBM portable and desktop PCs being distributed world-wide. There is, however, relatively little R&D or marketing autonomy at the Greenock plant.

While Honeywell and NCR are no longer active in Scotland, there are ten other manufacturing companies, in areas such as: processing systems (electronic fund transfers (EFTs) and automatic teller machines (ATMs)); peripherals (display monitors, keyboards, printers, data communications products); support products (disk drives, cable harnesses, switched-mode power supplies); software (computer to office applications).

The ten active companies in 1997 include:

- Compaq. Scotland is its first and largest foreign location and houses the international service and regional centre, employing 1,100 people;
- Digital. It employs 2,000 people at two plants; the one at Ayr designed the Alpha AXP PC 150;
- Sun Microsystems. Scotland is its largest manufacturing facility, employing 400 people making workstations;
- OKI Electric (a Japanese producer of dot matrix printers which came to Scotland in 1987 as an entry point for the European Union (EU) and to avoid a potential anti-dumping action by the EU. It employs 500 people);
- AT&T. Its Scottish subsidiary produces 38 per cent of the world's supply of automated banking machines, and has a world-product mandate involving design, manufacture, and marketing;
- Apricot (a PC manufacturer owned by the Japanese firm, Mitsubishi Electric).

Other firms involved in computer manufacturing include:

- Elonex (175 employees);
- Tandem (US-owned, 100 employees);
- Exabyte (US-owned, 150 employees; tape drives);
- Escom (German-owned; retailer).

Of these ten computer/information processing firms only two have 'flagship' relationships. The first is AT&T, which has a world product mandate and thus an independent value-added line of business in automated banking machines. The second is IBM, which is a large enough computer manufacturer to operate on a flagship basis within the 'internal network' of IBM. However, a relative lack of marketing skills may hinder IBM's ability to retain flagship skills. One way to develop IBM Scotland's flagship status would be to have its managers develop a regional/EU focus for R&D, production, and marketing.

Semiconductors

The Scottish electronics cluster has seven MNEs engaged in the production of semiconductors—from wafer fabrication to the manufacture of components used in microprocessors, memory devices, logic systems, linear devices, and power semiconductors. Scotland has 12 per cent of European production of semiconductors, in the highest concentration of semiconductor companies in Europe. Over 5,000 people are directly employed in the fabrication of semiconductors and they are supported by companies in related fields such as chemicals and gases, and by suppliers of substrate materials.

American MNEs such as Motorola and National Semiconductor established silicon production in Scotland in the 1960s and were followed by Digital and Hughes. Subsequently, Japanese MNEs such as NEC and Fuji Electric chose Scotland as their first European manufacturing location. The initial NEC Scottish facility for the assembly and testing of semiconductor components was upgraded to house the first Japanese wafer fabrication plant in Europe. There has been a programme of continuous investment by NEC to remain competitive in semiconductor manufacturing technology. Fuji Electric started the production of power transistor modules for use in control systems in 1991, Scotland being the company's first European location. For both NEC and Fuji Electric, it is clear that Scotland provides a low-cost production and assembly platform for entry into the EU market.

Motorola employs 2,500 people in manufacturing microprocessor and memory semiconductor products for UK and European markets. It has a sub-micron wafer processing capability for integrated circuits and·also produces digital signal processing chips. Digital has a semiconductor fabrication facility in Scotland in addition to its computer manufacturing plant; the latter uses much of the proprietary output of the semiconductor plant.

Other semiconductor firms in the Scottish electronics cluster are:

- National Semiconductor. It has been in Scotland since the 1960s, and its plant has a wide product range and has full design and development authority for its analogue products (logic and linear integrated circuits);
- Hughes Microelectronics. This makes custom integrated circuits, hybrids, subsystem assemblies, and interconnect products;
- Seagate Microelectronics. This designs and manufactures integrated circuits for disk drives.

There is a lack of flagship relationships in the semiconductor sector of the Scottish electronics cluster. The two Japanese MNEs appear to have located in Scotland to achieve more secure access to the EU market after their exports were threatened by anti-dumping measures. The Japanese firms see the UK government as a champion for their sales to Europe. This may represent a weak flagship relationship, in that the UK government also benefits in its regional policy by the jobs created in Scotland. The American MNEs in Scotland appear to lack managerial autonomy in developing flagship relationships. Indeed, they appear to be assembly platforms for Europe or to be in more mature product lines which are governed by low-cost manufacturing criteria, rather than by any marketing autonomy.

Telecommunications

Two American MNEs, Motorola and Hewlett-Packard, have major facilities in Scotland, with a wide degree of world-product mandating. In addition, there are two much smaller companies with little autonomy. These are:

- Cubix, which has a new plant in Livingston to make networked computer systems for remote access to local area networks;
- Phillips BSC Small Switching, which makes telephone equipment for private brand exchange systems.

Of the large MNEs, Hewlett-Packard was first involved in Scotland in 1967, and now employs 1,100 people in its plant near Edinburgh. It has gone through several stages of development and now has achieved a large degree of independence in the production of telecommunications equipment. It has total responsibility for the design, manufacturing, and world-wide marketing of products for testing telecommunications systems, measurement equipment, and microwave equipment. However, it has weak flagship relationships since it failed to find suitable independent local suppliers. There are only weak links in research for equipment development with Heriot-Watt University in Edinburgh, and these educational linkages do not yet involve any customized programmes. The R&D activity is limited to improvements of existing product lines and is much less than in comparable plants elsewhere, such as in Australia.

Motorola employs 2,000 people near Edinburgh, making cellular portable communications systems but nearly all of this product is sold in Europe, leaving little scope for flagship relationships in Scotland.

Consumer electronics

Japanese MNEs such as Mitsubishi Electric and Matsushita Panasonic produce colour television sets in central Scotland, attracted by the relatively low labour costs, government assistance, and access to the European market.

Mitsubishi first located in Scotland in 1979 and now has two plants employing

1,200 people in manufacturing colour television sets and video cassette recorders. Production of television sets includes 37-inch sets, the largest models in the world. The video cassette recorder plant is Mitsubishi's principal manufacturing facility for sales to world-wide markets outside Japan. Matsushita Panasonic opened in 1993 and manufactures flyback transformers for use in televisions and computer monitors.

Neither of these two Japanese firms appears to have developed any flagship relationships with key suppliers, key customers, or educational institutions in the Scottish electronics cluster. It is possible that Mitsubishi has sufficient managerial autonomy and/or influence to warrant a world-product mandate of the design, production, and marketing of large colour television sets; thereby having an internal-market flagship relationship with other parts of Mitsubishi.

There are four other smaller firms active in consumer electronics in Scotland. These have no flagship relationship. They are:

- Tannoy, which makes its entire output of loudspeakers in Scotland, as well as speakers for car radios;
- JVC, which manufactures standard television products and video drums;
- Linn Products, which makes high-quality audio equipment, such as record turntables, amplifiers, and loudspeakers;
- Alps, which produces tuners for televisions and video cassette recorders.

Software and other (including medical and military)

There are over 250 independent software-producing companies in the Scottish electronics cluster, with a wide product base across a variety of market sectors. Large firms active in Scotland include the French MNE, Groupe Bull, with a large systems integration service and custom software for UK and European customers.

There are some potential key customer linkages to be considered in these software producers. One example is Aldus, a US firm with its European headquarters in Edinburgh. Aldus has contracts for the development and marketing of desktop publishing software for both Apple Macintosh and IBM-compatible personal computers. Schindler, an elevator manufacturer, has its software research and development facility in Scotland. Other companies include: 3L, Office Workstations Ltd., and Ferranti Infographics.

In the areas of industrial and medical electronics there are many companies competing in international markets but few with flagship relationships. For example, Mitsubishi Electric produces air conditioning equipment for Europe from its Scottish base, but it has no key supplier linkages. One exception is OKI Electric. This Japanese company is a key supplier to the Honda plant in Swindon, England, making electronic controls for Honda car engines. There are also companies in niche markets, such as Osprey Electronics which has 70 per cent of the world market for underwater vision systems. Pilkington Optronics produces periscopes for submarines, as well as laser and thermal imaging systems. Marconi (now part of GEC) specializes in providing secret voice and data communications systems to armed forces, as well as its traditional radar and military products. These specialized, niche markets do not generate the potential for ongoing flagship relationships, although they are good examples of successful companies.

The flagship relationships in the electronics cluster

In this section we analyse the Scottish electronics cluster using the five partners/flagship framework across all its five sectors. We are looking for flagship relationships. These are long-term managerial-type linkages between private sector firms (such as key suppliers–MNE) or between a private sector firm and an education institution or government agency.

Flagship firms

Large foreign-owned firms, mainly US MNEs, are the dominant actors in the Scottish electronics cluster. These MNEs include:

- Hewlett-Packard;
- IBM;
- NCR (now acquired by AT&T);
- Motorola; and
- Honeywell.

Most of these US MNEs were attracted to Scotland in the 1960s and 1970s for two reasons. First, it was seen as a convenient location for entry to the EU and, second, it had relatively inexpensive skilled labour. These location decisions were also affected by generous regional development grants provided throughout this period by the British government.

More recently, several Japanese electronics companies have located in Scotland, again seeing it as a good assembly point for entry to the large EU market. These firms include:

- NEC;
- Mitsubishi; and
- OKI.

Within the European region, the Scottish electronics cluster has competitive advantages as a relatively low-wage, hardware-production assembly location, but it lacks value-added-software and marketing capabilities. Indeed, most of the MNEs producing in Scotland have their marketing divisions on the continent of Europe. Production in Scotland is of hardware such as personal computers, laptop computers, workstations, and components such as semiconductors and integrated circuits. In computers, Scotland accounts for 35 per cent of all European production and in components such as integrated circuits, it accounts for 20 per cent (Peters, 1995).

The major rival locations to Scotland for these products include other 'peripheral' areas with low labour costs and government assistance such as Ireland, Wales, Portugal, Spain, and North-East England (all within the EU) and newly industrialized central European countries (outside the EU) such as the Czech Republic. Outside Europe, rival electronics clusters exist in Singapore and Taiwan, while there are more fully developed electronics clusters in North America in Silicon Valley (California), Massachusetts, and Austin (Texas).

Large European MNEs, such as Philips, have not invested in Scotland, because they already have access to the EU market. The US and Japanese MNEs in Scotland have large exports from the UK to the EU (in the range of 80 per cent).

Both US and Japanese MNEs have located in the Scottish electronics cluster as a gateway to the EU market. The single market measures of 1992 made it even more important to have a secure, cheap labour, assembly platform within 'Fortress Europe'. The MNEs in Scotland source well under 20 per cent from local suppliers. Indeed, it could be as low as 12 per cent according to Monitor (as reported in Peters 1995). Less than 2 per cent of their output is used locally. In contrast, over 60 per cent of the output of the electronics MNEs in Scotland is sold in the rest of Europe and 18 per cent to the rest of the UK. Despite this, the Scottish electronics cluster can be said to have some value added since the raw materials and parts shipped to Scotland are transformed into finished, manufactured products for Europe.

Key suppliers

Despite very active government programmes to promote indigenous suppliers, the large MNEs operating in Scotland source over 85 per cent of the their procurement from abroad. The average local share of MNE procurement has varied between 10 and 15 per cent of total procurement over the 30-year history of the electronics cluster in Scotland (Peters 1995). One-third of all EU semiconductors are produced in Scotland, by Motorola, NEC, and National Semiconductor.

Through the efforts of the government regional development agency, Scottish Enterprise, local suppliers have been encouraged to upgrade quality standards and co-operate with MNE production process demands. Indigenous suppliers have been successful in plastic injection mouldings and in printed circuits for semiconductors. An example of a key supplier is Peter Tilling. This company makes plastic mouldings—a key component in the assembly of personal computers for MNEs such as IBM, Compac, Sun (and formerly Apollo). Another successful supplier in the assembly of personal computers is Mimtec (which is a key supplier to IBM).

Recently, Japanese MNEs such as OKI and JVC have used local suppliers. In addition, some of the recent Japanese MNEs have been able to develop key supplier relationships, an example being OKI Electric, which is producing exclusively for the Honda car plant in Swindon, England.

The small percentage of indigenous suppliers is perhaps not surprising given the internationalization of the electronics industry. The producers and assemblers in Scotland would be expected to source components and suppliers internationally, and also to sell (export) internationally. Critical components can be brought in quickly by overnight freight services. Otherwise, Scotland's location has been enhanced by recent improvements in logistics, such as the Channel Tunnel and better freight handling and co-ordination services. Some of these logistics problems have been overcome in partnership with the NBI, in particular due to government initiatives. Recently, in train and truck assembly, freight logistics have been improved by infrastructure improvements.

Key customers

There are very few relationships with independent key customers. The reason is that the MNEs in the Scottish electronics cluster are mainly in production and assembly; they are units of integrated MNEs whose 'customers' are the marketing divisions of the MNEs on the continent of Europe. The marketing and distribution decisions are not made in Scotland but in other parts of the EU. Both the US and Japanese MNEs produce in Scotland for sales in the rest of the EU. The production 'mandates' of the Scottish MNEs are thereby severely limited by the marketing budgets and decisions made elsewhere in the MNE networks. This is a critical weakness for the Scottish electronics cluster. The lack of flagship relationships in this area can only be understood by an investigation of the strategy and structure of the large US and Japanese MNEs active in the electronics cluster in Scotland.

Key competitors

There are few examples in Scotland of collaborative ventures with competitors in the areas of R&D, or market sharing. The reason, again, is that the MNEs in Scotland are in a self-standing production and assembly routine, so there is no budget for major R&D initiatives and no independent strategic planning on the marketing dimension. The lack of autonomy in the management of the MNEs in the Scottish electronics cluster is reminiscent of the 'branch plant' MNEs in Canada (Rugman 1980*b*; Safarian 1993). Of course, the MNEs located in Scotland derive benefits from the collaborative ventures of their parent firms, such as the strategic alliance between Motorola and Toshiba in semiconductor chips, or that between NEC and Samsung in semiconductors. But there are no examples of major R&D initiatives in the Scottish MNEs. One area of co-operation, now fostered by the new Scottish Electronics Forum, is over training and education policy. This is discussed below.

The non-business infrastructure

The Scottish electronics cluster has a mixed history of business–government collaboration in training and education. In addition to the recruitment of substantial numbers of electrical engineers and computer analysts, the MNEs have been very active in the design and development of customized educational programmes, delivered by major Scottish universities. Examples include:

- Honeywell and the University of Strathclyde: a £1 million programme for the training of managers for the EU 1992 measure.
- IBM and the University of Strathclyde: on-going in-house management development programmes, including an IBM 'MBA' and an MSc in purchasing for IBM suppliers.

In addition, there have been 'centres of excellence' programmes, such as:

- an artificial intelligence programme at the University of Edinburgh, involving Motorola; and
- the University of Dundee has been involved in designing visual display units (for example for retail banking), involving NCR.

These programmes have been helped by government assistance and subsidies, largely through the regional development mandate of Scottish Enterprise.

Other successful initiatives include the improvement of logistics (discussed earlier) and a venture capital fund for small suppliers. The Scottish Enterprise venture capital fund has helped in the commercialization of segments of the indigenous electronics supplier sector, for example with new software companies.

Conclusions

This application of the five partners/flagship framework to the Scottish electronics cluster provides five conclusions.

First, most of the US and all of the Japanese MNEs operating in the Scottish electronics cluster see it as a low-cost manufacturing base for access to the larger European market; consequently few of these manufacturing subsidiaries have developed long-term flagship managerial relationships with key suppliers, with key customers, or with key competitors and the non-business infrastructure.

Second, there are a few individual exceptions to the lack of autonomy and the overall branch plant mentality that precludes flagship relationship. In these exceptional cases, there is more evidence of internal MNE autonomy than of external flagship relationships. For example, IBM in Scotland has more clients in its internal MNE network than does Compaq; Motorola has more autonomy and value added in Scotland than does National Semiconductor; OKI Electric is a key supplier to Honda whereas Mitsubishi Electric and Matsushita Panasonic have very limited potential for any flagship relationships. The flagship relationships at IBM, Motorola, and OKI are the exceptions, not the rule.

Third, there is evidence that some of the MNEs have developed world-product mandates, including marketing independence, which could yield flagship relationships. The MNEs with mandates include: NEC in semiconductors; IBM in personal computers; Digital in the Alpha AAP PC 150; AT&T for automated banking machines, Hewlett-Packard and Motorola in telecommunications equipment, etc. In addition, some firms have identified niches and are successful in sustaining new product development.

Fourth, what is somewhat surprising is the lack of genuine flagship relationships with educational institutions. There is only a handful of customized executive education and training programmes. Instead, most of the MNEs, including software companies, have recruited computer science and electrical engineering graduates and have engaged in relatively little in-house upgrading of skills. This lack of human resource development reinforces the key strategic advantage of Scotland as a relatively low-wage export assembly platform for access to the European market by US and Japanese MNEs.

Fifth, the Scottish electronics cluster is also under threat because it has not developed as good flagship relationships with the logistics infrastructure as have competitive clusters emerging in Europe. Given Scotland's peripheral location as a manufacturing site, there is a real problem of a lack of international competitiveness for the cluster. An example is Compaq's decision to relocate all of its distribution activities to Holland (with a centralized European logistics management group) despite all of its manufacturing for Europe being done in Scotland. In general, logistics and marketing distribution for most of the electronics MNEs in Scotland are based in Europe, with manufacturing separated from these high-end value-added activities. Furthermore, there are much better integrated electronics clusters in areas such as Silicon Valley, Massachusetts, Austin (Texas), South Germany, Singapore, and Taiwan.

The overall conclusion is that the Scottish electronics cluster could be in trouble in the near future as it lacks most of the flagship relationships necessary to keep it internationally competitive. Scotland may soon lose its viability as a low-cost assembly platform for US and Japanese companies seeking entry to the EU market, unless it develops more value-added activities and 'deepens' the electronics cluster, especially on the marketing and distribution side. Today only a few firms have key supplier or key customer stature; there are no examples of key competitor strategic alliances, and only a handful of flagship relationships exist with the NBI. While there are linkages to the UK government through the regional policy initiatives of Scottish Enterprise, and a useful new advisory council in the form of the Scottish Electronics Forum, there is little evidence that the culture of building flagship relationships is any more than skin deep. The future success of the Scottish electronics cluster will be at risk unless there is a dramatic change in attitude towards the need to create flagship relationships.

11

The North American Automotive Cluster

Introduction

The automotive industry is often viewed as an engine of economic growth. In Canada the industry employs almost half a million people, has shipments of $Cdn65 billion, and accounts for 10 per cent of manufacturing GDP and 24 per cent of exports. It is also a global industry that is at the centre of change in manufacturing operations. The structure, strategies, and relationships of the companies in such a key industry are therefore good indicators of the extent to which business networks along the lines of the flagship/five partners model have been incorporated into mainstream business policies.

In this chapter, the flagship/five partners model is used as a benchmark for analysis of the Canadian-based automotive sector. The Canadian automotive industry is entirely foreign owned so this analysis of managerial competencies inevitably raises issues of parent–subsidiary relationships and the changing role of the subsidy within the network of the multinational enterprise (MNE). The chapter is an extension of research using the flagship model (D'Cruz and Rugman 1992b, 1993, 1994a; Rugman and D'Cruz 1996; and Rugman, D'Cruz, and Verbeke 1995). In the next section we discuss the nature of the global automotive industry, and the positioning of the Canadian sector within it. Then we apply the flagship/five partners model to the Canadian automotive sector and move on to detailed analysis of the managerial relationships in this case study.

The Automotive Industry

The Global Automotive Industry

The North American automotive industry—Canada, the United States, and Mexico—is one of three distinct global markets, the others being Europe and Japan (Industry Canada 1995a). Together these three major regions account for 90 per cent of world-wide production and 72 per cent of consumption, though other markets and production bases have started to emerge in Eastern Europe, South America, and the rest of Asia. The industry is highly concentrated, with five companies accounting for about 30 per cent of world production. North America produces about 31 per cent of the world-wide supply of motor vehicles (*Ward's Automotive Yearbook* 1995).

In the past, interregional trade in both vehicles and parts has been relatively small, around 11 per cent and 6 per cent of production respectively, due in part to trade barriers established to maintain the domestic industry's role in local economic growth, as well as to high transportation costs. Instead, companies wishing to supply a foreign market established production capacity in that country through foreign direct investment (FDI), often importing parts from their home country. Some of the parts trade into North America, for instance, is to supply Asian manufacturers' assembly plants located in Canada and the United States. Consequently, 'globalization' of the automotive industry has tended to involve the 'regional' export of capital and technology rather than goods and services.

In the early 1970s, the 'Big Three'—General Motors, Ford, and Chrysler—dominated the North American market. During the late 1970s and 1980s, this dominance was challenged as Japanese automobiles gained market share at the expense of the domestic manufacturers. First, the oil shocks of the 1970s enabled the more fuel-efficient Japanese imports to gain a foothold in the North American market. Second, the lean production techniques of the Japanese manufacturers resulted in quality and productivity advantages that were favoured by consumers (Eden and Molot 1996). Demographics were also a factor since the large cohort of 'baby boomers' seeking cheap vehicles such as those offered by the Japanese entered the retail car market at this time (Foot with Stoffman 1996).

During this period, voluntary export restraints negotiated with the Japanese, combined with an appreciating yen, encouraged Asian automotive manufacturers to establish assembly plants (transplants) in Canada and the United States in order to serve the North American market. The first transplant was established in 1982 and the number of Asian manufacturers in Canada and the United States has since grown rapidly. Recently, the German manufacturers BMW and Mercedes-Benz have also invested in assembly plants in the United States. Transplant production has increased from 1,500 cars in 1982 to 2.7 million cars and light trucks in 1995 and capacity is forecast to be 3 million by 1998 (*Ward's Autoworld* December 1995). By comparison, 1995 North American production by the Big Three totalled 11.6 billion, 86 per cent of capacity (*The 100 Year Almanac and 1996 Market Data Handbook* 1996).

Consequently, competition for the North American manufacturers is on two fronts: (a) between the Big Three, and (b) the Big Three versus the transplants and imports. This latter competition has driven the Big Three to form alliances, not only with each other but also with the Asian manufacturers. Examples involving General Motors include CAMI Automotive Inc., a joint venture with Suzuki Motor Co. to produce vehicles in Canada; NUMMI (New Motor Manufacturers Inc.) in the United States with Toyota; and an import franchise, Passport International Automobiles, to serve customers preferring imported cars. The Big Three also responded to the Japanese challenge by altering production methods, increasing investment and selling more captive imports (Roy 1991; Adams 1993). As a result, by the early 1990s they had succeeded in regaining some market share.

However, the competition remains intense. Traditional markets are saturated; world-wide capacity exceeds demand. Cost-reduction strategies are imperative. In North America, where the assembly to sales ratio is less than one, several transplants have announced capacity-enhancement strategies and are shifting more in-house component manufacturing to the United States. Meanwhile, markets are opening in China, Russia, and other emerging economies, so automobile manufacturers are rushing to develop a presence in those countries.

The North American automotive industry

The domestic automotive industry within North America has been highly integrated, particularly between Canada and the United States. The Auto Pact of 1965 accorded duty-free entry between Canada and the United States to vehicles, parts, and accessories from qualified manufacturers, provided those manufacturers met certain production and sales targets in Canada. (General Motors, Ford, and Chrysler, as well as AMC before 1987, were joined in 1989 by CAMI as qualified vehicle manufacturers in Canada.) The main provisions of the Auto Pact continue today, having been incorporated in the Canada-USA Free Trade Agreement and the North American Free Trade Agreement (NAFTA), though the benefits are less since the external trade barriers to non-Auto Pact participants have been considerably reduced: Rugman (1994), Eden and Molot (1996). Enterprise zones in Mexico and NAFTA have also facilitated movement across the Mexico–United States border. These preferential conditions facilitated a high level of vertical integration within the Big Three manufacturers—each of them has assembly plants as well as in-house parts suppliers in both Canada and the United States, sources from both sides of the border, and allocates North American product mandates.

A few statistics illustrate the extent of integration (Industry Canada 1995*b*):

- In 1994, Canadian manufacturers purchased $Cdn19.5 billion worth of parts from US suppliers; US manufacturers purchased $Cdn7.6 billion worth of parts from Canadian suppliers.
- Canada exports around 80 per cent of its motor vehicle production to the United States.
- In 1995, Canada exported $Cdn58.6 billion of vehicles and parts to the United States, and imported $Cdn41.6 billion from the United States (see Figure 4.1).

It is not only the industry as a whole that has been integrated. Production too has been organized vertically. The 12,000 parts required to make a vehicle first come together as elements of a complete system such as steering or electronics. Groups of these systems are then combined by the vehicle assemblers to form a motor vehicle. The parts suppliers are organized in three tiers:

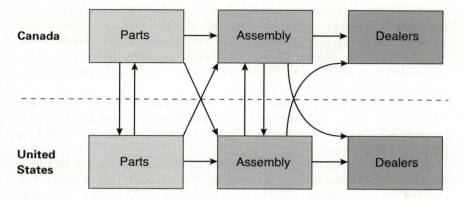

Figure 11.1 The Canadian-United States integrated automotive industry

- *Tier 1* producers are systems developers that deliver a finished product to the assemblers; they often own proprietary rights and are responsible for product design. Magna International Inc. is an example of the limited number of Tier 1 suppliers in Canada.
- *Tier 2* manufacturers build discrete parts or subsystems and supply these to Tier 1 producers. Most of Canada's parts suppliers fall into this category.
- *Tierr 3* suppliers provide raw materials and special services such as rolls of sheet steel or surface treatments.

The structure of the North American automotive industry has changed since the early 1980s. The rapid growth, first of imports and then of transplants has forced the Big Three to make significant structural changes. In their drive to reduce costs, the manufacturers are devolving more of the design and engineering work to Tier 1 suppliers and requiring them to become system integrators; they are also reducing the number of suppliers and making greater use of outsourcing. As it is in the United States, Canada's automotive industry is really two industries, vehicle assembly and parts production, and they are two of Canada's largest manufacturing industries.

In 1994, total Canadian light vehicle production was 2.3 million units, approximately 15 per cent of North American production. Sales amounted to around 1.3 million vehicles. Parts shipments were valued at $Cdn20 billion (Industry Canada 1995*b*).

There are seven car and light truck assembly plants in Canada, almost entirely foreign owned, while most of the 683 (in 1993) establishments in the motor vehicle parts and accessories manufacturing industry are small facilities. Each of the Big Three has some parts production located in Canada; other foreign-owned independent manufacturers include Budd Canada Inc., Hayes-Dana Inc., Goodyear Canada, Johnson Controls Ltd., Lear Seating Canada, PPG Canada Inc., and TRW Canada Limited. Amongst the major Canadian-owned companies are A. G. Simpson Ltd., Linamar Corporation, Magna International Inc., Stelco Inc., and Woodbridge Corporation. Financial data for a selection of Canadian automotive companies are shown in Table 11.1.

Amongst the vehicle assemblers located in Canada are three Asian transplants: CAMI (a joint venture between Suzuki and General Motors), Honda, and Toyota. Despite their presence, the Big Three still dominate the Canadian market, as Figure 11.2 illustrates.

As noted earlier, much (80 per cent) of the Canadian production of vehicles is destined for the United States, and essentially all of Canada's trade in motor vehicles and parts is with the United States. Canada has a large trade surplus in vehicles with the United States that is partly offset by a significant parts deficit, for a net automotive trade surplus of $Cdn17 billion.

The next section examines the business networks used by firms in the automotive sector to enhance their competitiveness and it applies the five partners model to selected examples. The analysis will focus as much as possible on Canadian companies but, due to the integrated nature of the North American industry, it will also include examples from the United States.

The flagship/five partners model and the Canadian automotive sector

The five partners flagship framework emphasizes two key features of a business network: the members that constitute the network and the nature of the relationship

Table 11.1 Light vehicle assemblers and selected automotive parts manufacturers in Canada, by total revenues and total assets, 1995 ($Cdn million)

	Motor Vehicle Assemblers			Automotive Parts Manufacturers	
	Revenues	Assets		Revenues	Assets
General Motors of Canada	30,775	10,994	Magna International	4,568	3,030
Ford Motor Co. of Canada Ltd.	21,255	6,001	Goodyear Canada (1993)	818	522
Chrysler Canada	13,619	4,875	Hayes-Dana Canada (1994)	655	254
Honda Canada	2,909	n.a.	ITT Canada (1994)	555	740
Toyota Canada	1,497	229	Linamar Corp.	547	330
Volvo Canada	459	128			

Source: Financial Post 500, 1996 (Toronto: Financial Post); 'Top 1000', *Report on Business Magazine* (Toronto: Globe and Mail, July 1995, 1996)

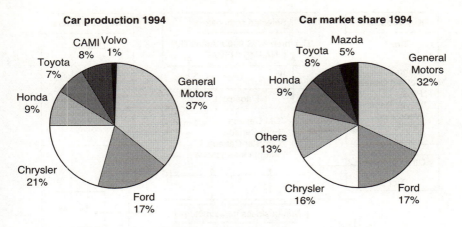

Figure 11.2 Canadian car production and market share by company, 1994
Source: Ward's Automotive Yearbook (1995).

between them. At the core of the network is the flagship firm which is usually an MNE, with key suppliers, key customers, selected competitors, and the NBI connecting to this central node. The strategic decisions and organizational considerations of the business network are led by the flagship firm. Figure 11.3 demonstrates these five partners in the flagship model, within the context of the Canadian automotive sector. These firms and organizations will be discussed in this section and their flagship relationship assessed.

The automotive sector exhibits many of the characteristics of the five partners business network. The flagship firms amongst the vehicle assemblers are establishing the parameters of the relationship with key suppliers by specifying quality standards, product specifications, and cost limitations to which those suppliers must adhere. They lead the relationship with their key customers, the franchised dealers. The Big Three competitors have also worked together in ways such as in developing common quality standards. Finally, the sector is widely represented on government advisory committees, well served with numerous industry associations, and developing relationships with education and research institutions. We shall now discuss each of the five partners in the flagship model in detail and relate these to the Canadian automotive sector.

Flagship firms

In the Canadian automotive sector, flagship firms are found primarily in the vehicle assembly industry. These consist of the wholly owned Canadian subsidiaries

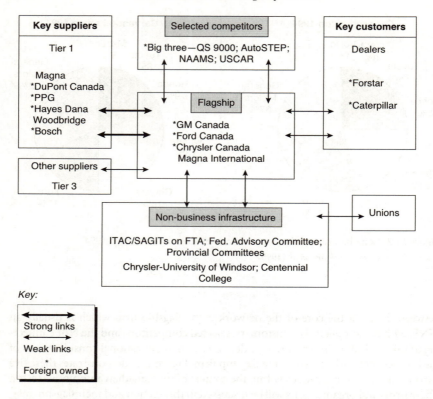

Key:

Figure 11.3 Flagship relationships in the Canadian-North American automotive cluster

of the Big Three—General Motors of Canada Ltd., Ford Motor Company of Canada Ltd., and Chrysler Canada Ltd.

Chrysler is a prime example among the vehicle assemblers of a flagship firm exerting leadership over the strategic interests of the broader business network. In 1994 Chrysler adopted the philosophy of 'extended enterprise' based on the Japanese concept of *keiretsu*. Under this approach, Chrysler views the roles, responsibilities, and relationships of suppliers and others along the value chain as an extension of the company. The system demands a high level of mutual trust and builds on the teamwork developed through Supplier Cost Reduction Effort (SCORE) which was initiated in 1989. Chrysler's 1994 annual report describes the new relationship as being one that 'provides closeness without control, unites and extends business relationships through supplier tiers'. It includes joint research projects, participation in process redesign studies together, and joint management of second- and third-tier suppliers. At the same time as changing supplier management, Chrysler has been trying to institute cultural change with its dealer network through the Customer One programme. Customer One is an intensive dealer training programme that covers not only product knowledge but also customer relations, and is aimed at improving customer (consumer) satisfaction. Overall, Chrysler's new culture aims to create methods to 'research, create, test and build world-class trucks, minivans and cars and improved ways to provide world-class treatment of the people who buy and own them' (Chrysler Comparation 1994, 1995).

Magna International Inc. is a Tier 1 supplier of automotive components and systems to the global automotive industry. It designs, develops, and manufactures automotive systems, assemblies, and components primarily for sale to OEMs of cars and light trucks in North America, Mexico, and Europe, and has 88 manufacturing facilities in ten countries. Magna conducts its operations through facilities which function as autonomous operating units. Facilities are grouped geographically and along product lines in order to align Magna on a product line basis with the purchasing groups of its OEM customers. Its North American operations have four automotive operating groups: Atoma International Inc. which focuses on interior systems; Cosma International Inc. which supplies body and chassis components; Decoma International Inc. which supplies exterior components and subsystems; and Tesma International Inc., a supplier of engine, powertrain (or driveshaft), fuelling, and cooling components (Magna International 1995). Although Magna is a multinational enterprise that dominates the Canadian parts industry, judging from public material, it does not appear to have strongly developed key relationships with the possible exception of its main customers, the Big Three. A part of the reason for this may be its strong entrepreneurial culture and decentralized operating structure. Many of its strategic alliances have taken the form of more traditional joint ventures or acquisitions. For example, its purchase of Britain's Marley PLC, an automotive component manufacturer that brings with it important new customers, is Magna's fourth European acquisition in three years (English 1996).

Key suppliers

The relationship between the three Canadian vehicle assembly flagship firms and their suppliers, like that of their American counterparts, has undergone a fundamental transformation since the late 1980s. The traditional, vertically integrated organizational structure that had been based on the Fordist approach to corporate organization, that is, the need for central control over all phases of production, has been replaced by a more deintegrated structure. As part of the shift to a lean production model, suppliers have been required to take on a larger role in designing, developing, and testing components, becoming responsible for aspects of the production process that the vehicle assemblers had traditionally reserved for themselves. Tier 1 suppliers are expected to be system integrators that supply modules or systems to the automobile manufacturers, and to manage the supply chain. In return they may receive longer-term supply agreements.

Suppliers are also increasingly being asked to service an automobile manufacturer world-wide. For example, Ford plans to source the majority of components for its common European/North American platform from multinational suppliers with production facilities in the United States and Europe (Industry Canada 1995*a*). As might be expected when flagship firms are developing key relationships, at the same time as they are shifting greater responsibility to suppliers, they are reducing the total number of suppliers. Chrysler plans to reduce its North American supplier base from 1,900 in 1992 to 750 in 1995, and eventually to reduce the number of Tier 1 suppliers from 1,250 to 150. Similarly, Ford plans to reduce the number of suppliers from 900 in 1992 to 750 in 1995; the majority of its components will be sourced from only 100 suppliers world-wide (Industry Canada 1995*a*).

In their drive to reduce costs, the flagship firms have opened the door to increased sourcing from independent producers, despite union protests. Consequently, the in-house producers' share of parts shipments in Canada has declined from 41 per cent in 1980 to 26 per cent in 1991. Of the Big Three, Chrysler outsources the most, purchasing 75 per cent of its components from independents; Ford outsources 50–55 per cent and GM 40 per cent (Industry Canada 1995*a*). Delphi Automotive Systems, a GM subsidiary, dominates the global parts suppliers with 1995 revenues of $US26.4 billion, almost twice as much as the next supplier, Robert Bosch GmbH (*Automotive News* 1996). Delphi's size is perhaps a reflection of GM's use of in-house suppliers.

The price of materials purchased from suppliers is the single largest cost component in the price of a car. Managing the cost of suppliers' materials is therefore an important strategy for the flagship firms, and each of the Big Three has set supplier cost-reduction targets/requirements and established a process to accomplish these targets. For example, teams under General Motors' Purchase Input Concept Optimization System (PICOS) visit supplier plants and suggest/require improvements. Similarly, Chrysler's SCORE mandates cost savings from suppliers through efficiency improvements. Chrysler launched SCORE in 1989 in an effort to reduce costs throughout the system. Under the programme, suppliers were encouraged to find ways to improve value for the customer without reducing supplier profit margins, by eliminating waste and inefficiencies. The programme was based on teamwork: Chrysler undertook to implement the ideas quickly or to refer the issue back to the supplier if the idea would not work; any cost reductions would be shared equally by Chrysler and its suppliers; and suppliers were promised long-term relationships (Kobe 1994). Chrysler mandates that a specific percentage, for example 5 per cent in 1995, of a supplier's business with the company come from suggestions on how they can do business more cost effectively. By July 1996, Chrysler had received more than 16,000 proposals from suppliers and achieved cumulative cost savings of $2.5 billion (Chrysler Corporation 1996*a*). The company has earned the reputation of being the lowest-cost producer amongst the Big Three.

Dyer (1996) describes Chrysler's new model of supplier management, the extended enterprise or American *keiretsu*. The model is based on an understanding by senior management that people at both Chrysler and its suppliers must have a common vision on how to collaborate to create value jointly, and that both must share in the rewards, not just the risks. He outlines the process changes Chrysler made to accomplish this: reorganizing the company into cross-functional, vehicle-development teams which include suppliers; presourcing suppliers early in the concept-development phase and giving them significant responsibility for design of the component; target costing; total value chain improvement through SCORE; long-term commitments; and enhanced communication and co-ordination through, for example, having suppliers' engineers work side by side with Chrysler's employees. There are approximately 300 suppliers' engineers resident at Chrysler facilities.

Chrysler pushes the collaborative relationship with its suppliers by using catalysts such as lean production workshops, classroom training, and sharing of lessons learned at other suppliers. In the first phase of its Chrysler Lean Operating Supplier Enterprise (CLOSE) programme, Chrysler ensures that its top 150 suppliers understand lean manufacturing and apply its principles in the same way that Chrysler does. In the second phase, Chrysler and its key suppliers co-host workshops for other suppliers, and finally the key suppliers introduce the workshops to their suppliers (Chrysler Corporation 1996*b*). As an example, Chrysler and Eaton Corporation, the valve train system integrator for its new truck family, hosted a workshop at Eaton's Saginaw facility in which several non-competing suppliers learned common lean production techniques.

A second example is Chrysler's relationship with Freudenberg-NOK in the United States. Freudenberg, a partnership between Freudenberg & Co. of Germany and NOK Corporation of Japan, supplies precision seals, vibration-control devices, and moulded rubber and plastic components to the automotive industry. It has the reputation of being a leader in lean production processes. Modelling its operations on theories and practices developed at Toyota, it adapts a manufacturing process to lean production by assigning small teams to analyse and improve the process during four-day workshops held throughout the year. These *kaizen* teams, which include front-line workers, are reported to have generated an average of $US40,000 savings per project. In 1994, Freudenberg offered to train Chrysler executives in these lean production processes, and by the end of the year had trained 200, including two vice presidents. These Chrysler employees will pass on the techniques to Chrysler operations and other key suppliers, who in turn will teach the concept to the smaller vendors as part of Chrysler's extended enterprise programme (Jackson 1994).

In other instances, automotive paint suppliers such as PPG and DuPont Canada are well integrated with their key customers, the vehicle assemblers. As discussed in Chapter 9 on chemicals, the paint manufacturers are responsible for researching colour trends, new product development, and technical support. They work closely with the vehicle assembler and may sit on OEM teams which create strategies for the global business. Hayes-Dana, the Canadian subsidiary of Dana Corporation which manufactures and distributes both original equipment and replacement parts for the automotive industry, asserts that close relationships with suppliers, customers, and its parent are the key to the future. For example, a group of Hayes-Dana, Dana, and General Motors personnel worked closely together to develop the equipment and tools necessary to build the frame subassembly for a new GM van (Hayes-Dana 1994). The Woodbridge Group, which manufactures automotive polyurethane foam products and considers itself a speciality rather than a Tier 2 company, believes that it must develop sophisticated, innovative working relationships with customers and suppliers which will lead to greater interdependence (*Ward's Autoworld* December 1995).

The development of long-term, collaborative relationships with their suppliers has been an important competitive strategy for the flagship firms. While aspects of the relationship between the Big Three and their suppliers are becoming more collaborative, at least from the flagship firm's perspective, there remain many elements of the power asymmetry typical of flagship firms with their partners. The vehicle assemblers establish the quality and design parameters. They require suppliers to invest in additional capital equipment and technology to meet the assemblers' deintegration policies at the same time as demanding cost reductions. The flagship firms bestow awards. They rate the suppliers according to their performance. Chrysler, for example, qualifies suppliers on past performance as well as operating a rating system that considers technology, delivery, price, and quality. Ford Tier 1 suppliers get individual report cards, including data on the supplier's role in recall campaigns, delivery performance, and defects; Ford then meets with each supplier and charts a plan to improve its rating. In all these ways, the assembly flagship firms are exercising their power over the supplier network.

Key customers

Close relationships with key customers play a vital role in the success of the network as a whole. According to Donald Fites (1996), Chairman and CEO of Caterpillar, the biggest reasons for Caterpillar's success in combating the cost advantage of Japanese manufacturers are its distribution network and close relations with its dealers. Local dealers can get closer to a customer than can a global company, but to benefit from their knowledge of the market, the dealers must be integrated into critical business systems. He writes: 'The quality of the relationship between a company and its dealers is much more important than the contractual agreements or the techniques and tactics that make the relationship work on the surface. What matters is mutual trust.' This view echoes the findings of Cross and Gordon (1995), that trust is the most important attribute in a long-term supply agreement between a supplier and a vehicle assembler. It is also an element that the five partners model requires for the network to be successful.

Each of the motor vehicle assemblers in North America has dealers which operate franchised retail outlets that carry the manufacturer's product lines. There are over 3,700 manufacturer's dealers in Canada, 55 per cent of which are associated with the Big Three (Canadian Automobile Dealers Association). In most, if not all, cases new vehicles are sold only through franchised dealers; these effectively are the key customers. While the characteristics of a franchise relationship and a single supplier necessarily align the strategic interests of the manufacturer and the dealer, some flagship firms are extending the relationship into a more collaborative one.

In Canada, Ford and its dealers are closely linked through an exclusive agreement which is based on mutual benefit, with Ford gaining access to the retail market and the dealers the opportunity for financial return. Each is dependent on the other—the dealers for quality products delivered in a timely fashion, and Ford for strong representation in the market-place. In the contractual agreement between the company and the dealers, there are specific performance criteria referenced on customer satisfaction, market share, and corporate image and reputation. To help dealers achieve these performance criteria, Ford makes available training, technology, and tools, the cost of which is often shared.

In the past, the relationship between Ford and its dealers has at times been contentious. However, in Ford's view, the culture has been gradually changing over the years so that the relationship is becoming more trusting and collaborative. A number of factors have influenced this change at Ford:

(1) In 1993 separate training programmes were blended into a single integrated system, the Professional Training System (PTS), which now covers product knowledge, customer standards, leasing, and technical training for technicians as well as sales and service personnel. The training curriculum is based on input from dealers on what they require, and Ford spends three months each year re-engineering the programme. Each dealer is free to select the type and level of training desired and for which employees, and pays a subsidized fee for it.

(2) Ford receives continuous feedback from the dealers through quarterly surveys, focus groups, and round table sessions.

(3) Technology has been an enabler of a more collaborative relationship at the operational level. Particularly innovative is the FORDSTAR dealer communications network, initiated in the United States and launched in Canada in January 1996. FORDSTAR is a private satellite network that not only has data communication capabilities which give immediate access to parts, service, and technical information, but also makes interactive training with one-way video, two-way audio broadcasts available to each dealership. For example, using the network, all dealers have immediate access to up-to-date technical and parts information; dealers' technicians and Ford's engineers can communicate quickly and effectively to solve problems.

(4) The national dealer council with regional councils, each comprised of dealer and company representatives, has been in place for 45 years; its purpose is to resolve issues and help with forward planning. The council has been viewed with mistrust by local dealers who felt that their issues

were not being addressed, there was a lack of frankness, and decision making was slow. Following the shared decision of a steering committee composed of eight senior dealers and company management, the process is, at the time of writing, being restructured into a more collaborative, round table approach that increases accountability, requires consensus decisions, and speeds resolution of issues.

In summary, Ford of Canada continues to influence its key customers, the dealers, though codification of the standards it requires in the sales and service agreement. However, the means by which those standards are met is changing, with more open, two-way communication and problem solving on an individual basis.

Chrysler Corporation has also intensified its efforts to incorporate the dealers into its competitive thinking. It has invested in the Customer One training programme, as described earlier, and established performance standards for its dealerships. Advanced-level training for service and general managers includes methods for achieving Chrysler's strategic initiatives. Like Ford, it has a satellite system which broadcasts to both dealers and employees but which appears to be more of a one-way communication device than an interactive tool. In the United States, Chrysler's 1992 'Adopt-A-Dealer' programme provided for each assembly plant manager to adopt a specific dealership (McElroy 1992). Small groups of assembly workers regularly met with the service manager, found out what problems had arisen, and solved those problems back at the plant. Typically, the group could solve the most difficult problem within two to three hours, compared to the two to three days it may take the dealer. At the plant, records are kept of the dealers visited and the types of problems encountered.

The dealers tend to think of themselves as entrepreneurs or independent businesses. However, the behaviours they can exhibit, the standards to which they must adhere, the performance-appraisal measures applied by the manufacturer, and the limitations on products they can sell, particularly in exclusive franchises, point to an organizational form that has limited autonomy and is closely tied to the manufacturer. In terms of the five partners model, the flagship firms exert considerable influence over the strategic interests of the dealers, their key customers. While there has been some movement towards seeking a more collaborative relationship on a day-to-day level, the drive, initiatives, and controls appear to remain with the vehicle assemblers.

Selected competitors

As noted in earlier chapters, flagship firms within one industry often have multiple strategic objectives, some of which may be pursued in conjunction with other flagship firms without loss of competition. In the North American automotive industry, the threat posed to the domestic vehicle assemblers by the Asian manufacturers has caused the Big Three to work together in a variety of ways that include common standards or pre-competitive research.

In 1994, General Motors, Ford, and Chrysler announced their long-awaited common quality system for their suppliers, QS 9000. The system is an adaptation of ISO 9000 standards and is specific to the automotive industry. It combines the ISO 9000 quality assurance with industry-specific guidelines drawn from former automotive industry programmes for quality—GM's North American Operations Targets for Excellence, Ford's Q101 Quality System Standard, and Chrysler's Supplier Quality Assurance Manual (Zuckerman 1994).

The Big Three are determining a strategic element of the network, quality, by requiring Tier 1 suppliers to become QS 9000 certified (though in practice, mandatory certification has been delayed while issues around the training of registrars are resolved). In turn Tier 1 suppliers are expected to ask their suppliers for QS 9000 certification. Only third-party registrars trained by the Big Three will be able to issue QS 9000 certificates. Since QS 9000 certification is more stringent that ISO 9000 certification, the latter is not acceptable to the Big Three. Consequently suppliers will have to incur substantial additional costs in order to be eligible as a supplier, illustrating once again the ability of the flagship firms to affect the internal operations of network partners and, indeed, the network itself.

Another area in which manufacturers and suppliers are becoming more integrated is in the electronic exchange of data. STEP (Standard for the Exchange of Product model data) is an international communications standard being developed to enable industrial engineers to exchange electronic data. Under an AutoSTEP pilot project initiated in 1995 by the Automotive Industry Action Group (which represents North American vehicle manufacturers and suppliers), the Big Three and six Tier 1 suppliers exchange product data and graphics using parts of the STEP programme. An additional nine suppliers have since joined the project. Cost is a driving force behind the project since separate CAD systems can cost up to $US100,000 each, not including training and maintenance.

Similarly, representatives from the Big Three joined with their suppliers and the Auto/Steel Partnership to standardize tooling within the automotive industry. After three years' work, the team created a manual, *North American Automotive Metric Standards (NAAMS): Forming and Stamping*; a similar team is addressing common assembly tooling standards. The manufacturers want the suppliers to follow the standards so that they can interchange the same component from multiple suppliers without retooling.

At the pre-competitive research level, Chrysler, Ford, and General Motors formed the United States Council for Automotive Research (USCAR) in 1992 to manage collaborative research. There are, at the time of writing, 13 consortia working on technological and environmental concerns. A year later the Big Three joined with the US government and defence laboratories in a Partnership for Next Generation Vehicle (PNGV). The PNGV has three goals: to significantly improve national (United States) competitiveness in automobile manufacturing; to apply innovations to commercial vehicles; and to develop a vehicle that travels up to 80 mpg. The Big Three in Canada have established CANCAR to co-ordinate

Canada's involvement in this Supercar, and work has begun on pre-competitive R&D projects (Industry Canada 1995*a*).

In the parts industry the changing nature of the business, in which a smaller number of Tier 1 suppliers are being asked to supply larger systems, means that a parts manufacturer may be the Tier 1 supplier for one contract but act as a Tier 2 supplier to a Tier 1 competitor for another. In one estimate, only 25 per cent of today's global Tier 1 suppliers will exist by the end of the 1990s; of the remainder, 25 per cent will be acquired or enter partnerships with each other, 30 per cent will go out of business, and 20 per cent will leave the automotive industry altogether (International Business Development Corporation, quoted in Chappell 1996). *Ward's Autoworld* reported nearly 100 globalization initiatives in 1995 among suppliers including acquisitions, joint ventures, and strategic partnerships. One recent example of a partnership among competitors is the ABS Education Alliance formed in 1996 by Robert Bosch Corporation, Delphi Chassis Sytems, ITT Automotive, and Kelsey Hayes to promote a joint nationwide campaign that will educate drivers on how to use the new braking technology (Kisiel 1996). Thus there appear to be shifting alliances amongst the suppliers during a shake-out of the industry and it is not clear at this point whether any of these alliances will develop the characteristics of a key customer–key supplier relationship.

Overall, while there are some elements of collaboration amongst selected competitors in both assembly and parts industries, these relationships are often tentative and not strongly developed.

The non-business infrastructure

Since the automotive sector is such a significant component of the economy, it has long attracted attention from governments seeking to enhance the economic health of their constituencies. Assistance has traditionally taken the form of investment incentives, loans, and subsidies, and the role between an organization and the government has primarily been of a lobbying rather than collaborative nature.

There have, however, been some opportunities for the industry to work with government on public policy issues. During the Free Trade Agreement (FTA) negotiations, the International Trade Advisory Committee (ITAC) and the Sectoral Advisory Group on International Trade (SAGIT) were influential in maintaining key elements of the Auto Pact. The automotive sector has also had the opportunity to work with the Canadian government through the Automotive Advisory Committee. This committee, formed in 1989, is composed of a broad representation of manufacturers, importers, dealers, and industry associations and gives sectoral policy advice to the Minister of Industry. Participation is at the CEO level. Industry Canada provides the organizational and co-ordinating services, and the Ontario and Quebec governments have observers on the committee. The executive co-chairs are from the automotive parts and assembly industries—currently the President and CEOs of Magna International and Chrysler Canada Ltd. Specific issues are dealt with at the subcommittee level. The committee provides a forum for government–industry communication as well as co-operation amongst competitors on issues of mutual concern. Ultimately, however, it is an advisory not a decision-making committee.

Provincially, efforts at co-operation have been less successful. The Canadian Independent Automotive Components Council, which grew out of the Components sub-committee of the Automotive Advisory Committee, began work on a strategic action plan for the automotive parts industry with the financial support of Ontario's Sector Partnership Fund, Industry Canada, and Quebec's Ministry of Commerce, Science and Technology. However, the council has not been able to complete its work, largely because it was unable to resolve strained relationships among its members. Hostility amongst the primarily non-unionized manufacturers to the inclusion of the Canadian Auto Workers (CAW) union as a partner, and competitive rivalries between the diverse parts manufacturers, hindered any collaborative efforts. With the change in Ontario's government in 1995, the Sector Partnership Fund was cancelled, and the Council no longer exists. Given the Ontario government's policies of reduced involvement in the economy, it appears unlikely that further sectoral initiatives will be forthcoming.

As one might expect, given its size and the interest of the government, the automotive sector is well served by industry associations whose primary role is to represent the interests of their members to government. Among the major associations in Canada are:

- Motor Vehicle Manufacturers' Association, whose members include nine major companies producing cars and trucks in Canada: General Motors of Canada, Ford Canada, Chrysler Canada, Freightliner of Canada Ltd., Mack Canada Ltd., Navistar International Corp., PACCAR Canada Ltd., Volvo Canada Ltd., and Western Star Trucks.
- Japan Automobile Manufacturers' Association of Canada, which was established in 1984 to promote greater understanding between Canada and Japan on economic and trade matters relating to the automotive industry. Its members include manufacturers, importers, and distributors in Canada of Toyota, Honda, Nissan, Mazda, Subaru, and Suzuki vehicles and Hino diesel trucks.
- Automotive Parts Manufacturers' Association, which represents OEM producers of parts, equipment, tools, supplies, and services. It has recently formed a Federation of Associations with its counterparts in the United States and Mexico, and established a liaison in Japan and an office in Europe.
- Canadian Automobile Dealers' Association, which represents franchised new automobile dealerships (domestic and import).
- Canadian Association of Japanese Automobile Dealers, which works on behalf of Canadian businesses that sell and service Japanese-designed vehicles.
- Automotive Industries Association of Canada, which represents suppliers, warehouse distributors, wholesalers, retailers, and exporters in the automotive aftermarket industry.

By co-ordinating and facilitating interaction among their members, these associations also enhance collaboration between competitors on issues of mutual interest. The previously described work on AutoSTEP and QS 9000 by the Automotive Industry Action Group is a good example of the role an industry association can play in developing relationships amongst competitors and others. The strength of that role, however, is dependent on the level of commitment and seniority brought to the table by the members. According to some in the industry, that level is not always high enough to be effective.

One of the areas in which flagship firms can influence the NBI is through collaborative ventures with universities and colleges in which the research and training is directed to the company's needs. Some of this occurs in the automotive sector though perhaps not as much as its importance dictates.

Chrysler Canada is showing leadership with respect to research partnerships, as demonstrated by its collaboration with the University of Windsor. In May 1996, Chrysler and the university opened the first jointly operated automotive research facility in Canada, the University of Windsor/Chrysler Canada Automotive Research and Development Centre. This facility will allow Chrysler to pursue niche research in new automotive product technology with university facilities and at the same time enable the university to offer hands-on experience for its students. As an example, the road test simulation laboratories will allow Chrysler engineers to develop and evaluate structural characteristics of automotive products under laboratory conditions. Chrysler has also sponsored two industrial chairs in the engineering department, in conjunction with the Natural Sciences and Engineering Research Council of Canada; one chair is in design and one in alternative fuels, with potentially a third chair in acoustic imaging. The incumbents will not only carry out R&D based on Chrysler's needs but also teach students, thus helping to produce graduates who have the skills sought by Chrysler. Chrysler is not the only flagship firm involved with academic institutions; Ford has also sponsored a chair in aluminium casting at the University of Windsor to promote R&D.

General Motors and Ford, as well as Honda, Toyota, and Canadian Tire, have taken a different approach in their interactions with the education sector. Each has formed a partnership with Centennial College, a community college in Toronto, by which the college delivers a company-specific, modified apprenticeship programme to employees of each company. Each programme has courses ranging in length from a few hours to four days, may be offered at the college, the company site, or through distance learning, and is intended to upgrade the mechanical skills of a company's employees.

At an industry rather than firm level, key players in the automotive industry are represented on the boards of industry-wide research and educational institutions. The Industrial Research and Development Institute is an industry-driven organization established to give advanced technical and research support to Canada's tool, die, and mould industry which is a significant supplier to the automotive sector. At the other end of the value chain, the Canadian Automotive

Institute offers an educational service to dealers and distributors in the automotive industry. The Institute is part of Georgian College of Applied Arts and Technology and operates with the advice of a National Advisory Board representing automotive industry associations, manufacturers, and dealer associations across Canada.

At the high school level, General Motors in the United States announced an initiative in 1996 to address its need for skilled graduates—GM Youth Educational Systems. This programme, which is intended to be the catalyst for nation-wide school-to-work automotive educational programmes, brings together GM, its dealers, and high school and vocational technical students. The rationale is that, with technology moving so fast, the skills needed at the dealerships are far advanced beyond those currently acquired by school graduates. For example, most repair jobs now require electronic engineering skills rather than the mechanical ability to use a wrench. General Motors provides expertise in curriculum development, donates vehicles, and brings in technical engineers to work with the instructors. The students do curriculum work in Grades 9 and 10, then an internship (apprenticeship) at a dealer in Grade 11. The programme is intended to provide qualified entry-level technicians and other service personnel for GM dealerships. General Motors hopes that the programme will extend across the United States and that ultimately Ford and Chrysler will join in an industry-wide programme.

In summary, the flagship firms are beginning to develop some long-term, company-specific relationships with the research and education sectors. While interaction with government in the past has been effective in trade policy, the current relationships often show more form than substance.

Conclusions

The technical and operational changes made by the vehicle manufacturers, coming as they did after a period of insulation and stability, have transformed the North American automotive industry. Productivity has increased and the quality gap has narrowed between Japanese and North American brands (Ballew, Schnorbus, and Hesse 1994). These structural changes have not only involved internal business processes and technological improvements, but also restructured the relationships in the business network. The Big Three, typically the flagships in the network, have each sought competitive advantage by incorporating key suppliers and customers (dealers) into their strategic thinking. Where a network previously existed primarily between the parent company and its Canadian subsidiary, with in-house parts manufacturers supplying assemblers on either side of the border, now the network has been simultaneously extended (more outsourcing) and constrained (long-term, global sourcing from fewer suppliers).

As mentioned earlier, Cross and Gordon (1995) surveyed manufacturers, parts companies, government, and industry associations on the importance of various attributes to the supplier-OEM partnership. Trust, a necessary ingredient in the five partners model, was ranked as the most important characteristic in a long-term supply agreement, indicating an understanding among the respondents of the interdependence between partners.

The changed supplier relationship stems in part from observing the effect of the relationship between Japanese suppliers and manufacturers. Helper has estimated that superior relations with suppliers gave the Japanese a cost advantage of $US300 to $US600 per car cost in the 1980s (Taylor 1994). Early involvement of suppliers in product design was the key to faster introduction of new models using fewer labour hours. In a more recent survey of 600 US and almost 500 Japanese automotive suppliers, Helper and Sako (1995) found that a voice-based relationship, one where problems are resolved jointly, produced significant cost reductions for suppliers. Better performance was found among suppliers that provided detailed process information to their customers, saw their customer commitment as long term, and expected to engage in joint problem solving with the customer. This voice-based relationship, however, applied to only 29 per cent of US and 32 per cent of Japanese suppliers. They concluded that the automotive industry in both countries reveals a tension between the automobile manufacturers' desire to select the best supplier at any particular time while creating good suppliers by working with them over a long period of time.

A review of the trade press echoes this view—the relationship is frequently uncomfortable as suppliers face simultaneous demands for higher quality and lower costs while assemblers fight for market share. Thus the form and shape of the supplier–customer relationship in the network is in a state of flux. While the principle espoused by the automobile manufacturers may be one of partnership and long-term collaboration, the practice encountered by some suppliers is more dictatorial.

The introduction of Japanese lean production management techniques has not been easy, and has required the flagship firms to hold fast to the strategic aims for the network. A flexible production system with integrated quality control, a leaner supply system, and labour–management relations based on work teams has forced the suppliers and unions to reconsider their role in the network. According to Yanarella and Green (1994), much of organized American labour has moved from the more adversarial model towards a more co-operative approach, in contrast to the Canadian unions. While this statement may be directionally true, the spring 1996 strike by workers protesting at General Motors' proposal to make greater use of outsourcing affected production levels throughout North America and temporarily threatened the overall network. Similarly, the CAW strike against GM in October 1996, and the issue of outsourcing, also affected production. A co-operative labour–management relationship in the Big Three is not strongly developed, if it exists at all, and this lack of collaboration represents a major weakness in accomplishing the long-term strategic objectives of the network. The unions' position is neither new nor surprising, since their key role is the protection and improvement of their current members' jobs, with less emphasis on future members' benefits. The challenge remains for the flagship firms that are unionized to manage that relationship in a way that recognizes the short- and long-term needs of both parties in order to provide some security to the network.

Since the automotive industry is often the major if not the sole customer for many of the suppliers, and the dealers are franchisees of the assemblers, the success of these network partners is dependent on the success of the flagship firms. Consequently, the relationship between them is asymmetrical, characteristic of the five partners model. Another key feature of the model, the development of long-term, collaborative relationships between and among the partners, is also evident, albeit in a transitional stage between suppliers and OEMs. The increasing role of the flagships in ensuring that their education, research, and development needs are met, and the initiatives of the numerous industry associations, both testify to the presence of an active network. Overall, the automotive industry is on the way to developing partnerships that align the strategic objectives of the partners, though some nodes are more advanced in this process than others.

On a final note, a recent study by the Office for the Study of Automotive Transportation at the University of Michigan and A. T. Kearney (1996) speculates that the structural changes in the automotive industry are only half complete. The first stage was the acceptance of higher levels of responsibility by suppliers with no change in responsibility at the vehicle assembly level. The second stage, which the authors estimate should be completed around 2000, will see a far greater change in supplier/OEM roles, with the assemblers shedding some of the responsibility and the power. At that point, the Tier 1 system integrators, as co-ordinators of the supply chain and with long-term agreements with the assemblers, will exert more influence. Thus, the central node in the five partners model could change from assemblers to system integrators.

Update to Chapter 11

Flagships are regional, not global

The material reported in this chapter was gathered by a process of field research involving a large number of interviews with senior executives in the flagship automobile sector 'Big Three', as well as new flagships like Magna. In addition, a series of interviews were held with key suppliers in the components and parts business, with key customers, and with government–business advisory groups in the non-business infrastructure. Interviews also involved other stakeholders, such as union leaders. In this process we were assisted by Anne Anderson and Michael Gestrin and summaries of interviews we have synthesized and incorporated into our original conceptual framework of the flagship model. How relevant is the Canadian experience for other regions? Can this North American case study be generalized for Europe and Asia? We believe that it can for the following three reasons.

First, as regards Asia, the flagship model is a North American version of the tacit *keiretsu* relationships behind the dominant Japanese-style production and distribution system in Asia. In the automotive sector, it was this Japanese ability to link partners that helped revolutionize the quality standards in the sector. To a large extent, North American firms have been playing catch-up to the Japanese system. We believe that the flagship model now fully captures the strategic perceptions and operational reality of the North American system, in which, of course, a large number of Japanese producers also participate through subsidiary operations. The flagship model is probably less applicable to Korean *chaebol* and Chinese family-clan systems, although further research is needed to assess this.

Second, as regards application to Europe, we believe that the flagship model, as developed in a North American context, is precisely the model now being followed in Europe. Later in this section we will explore several examples of this. The flagship constellation of North America is very much reflected in current European experience, in which both collaboration and power asymmetry exist.

Third, the evidence that we have gathered from corporate interviews, reinforced by publicly available information on company performance, indicates that the flagship model is a 'Triad' system. Rather than operating globally, in the automotive sector firms are organized 'regionally' in the relatively segmented Triad markets of North America (NAFTA based), Europe (the EU), and Japan. It is through foreign direct investment (FDI) and subsidiaries, coupled with new mergers and strategic alliances (such as Chrysler-Daimler Benz), that the automotive sector produces and sells to customers, not through international trade. Of all the cars sold in Europe, over 90 per cent are produced there, by foreign-owned as well as domestic producers. The same statistics hold for North America and Japan, revealing strong 'home-base', Triad markets. So, today, automobile production and sales are Triad regional, not global. The flagship network's internal relationships are regional, not global, as is the degree of government regulation. These data are explained in more detail in Rugman (2000).

European and North American automotive components suppliers

Federal-Mogul Powertrain Systems (FMPTS), an automotive components manufacturer, has built key supplier linkages with Ford and GM. FMPTS was formed in 1998 when North American based Federal-Mogul acquired T&N plc of Europe. Amongst its major product lines are pistons, rings, liners, and bearings. It designs, develops, manufactures, and delivers these components to major OEMs, either as individual units or as systems. It now has a large global network, operating across two parts of the Triad, with rival automotive components manufacturers being Dana in North America and Mahle or KS-Piersburg in Germany.

The key supplier relationships of FMPTS were initiated by Ford and GM. Both MNEs were attempting to replicate this North American network in Europe. Anticipating difficulties in finding European key suppliers who were willing to perform to their USA-based standards (and capable of doing so), they frequently took their US key suppliers to Europe. Both MNEs aimed to deintegrate their businesses and wanted a set of high-quality key suppliers, producing a more advanced product at greater efficiency. To maintain key supplier (Tier 1 status) FMPTS built a new plant in North America and dedicated it to business with Ford and GM. Because of the high quality and technology base of FMPTS the two OEMs did not insist on exclusivity and FMPTS was not limited in making sales into other markets or to competitors of the OEMs. Its other key customers include Mercedes, Nissan, and Cummins, while it is a non-flagship supplier to BMW, Toyota, and Caterpillar. The technology base of FMPTS allows it to respond quickly to new customer imperatives of Ford and GM and helps it maintain its key supplier status.

Bundy Corporation   The British-based engineering firm TI Group plc acquired the US-based Bundy Corporation in 1988. Bundy is a leading component maker for automobile, especially of double-wall brake tubing and of single-wall tubing for fuel lines and related low-pressure applications. Bundy is a key supplier to North American OEMs, especially Ford and GM. It has built a network of several dozen satellite assembly facilities adjacent to key customer plants, which supply just-in-time tubes. The acquisition of Bundy by TI led a move towards consolidation of suppliers, of which a more recent development was the merger of Lucas and Varity in 1996. A major competitor of TI is GKN, which is also looking for acquisitions of well-established suppliers in other parts of the Triad.

Bundy Corporation in 1970 anticipated the new US car emission laws and developed the world's first stainless steel tube for car exhaust gas recirculation (EGR) systems. By the early 1980s, Bundy was a key supplier to Ford and had virtually all of Ford's EGR business. About the same time Bundy developed new zinc 'Z coat' coating in response to tighter anti-corrosion demands by OEMs such as Ford and GM. It became a technical leader in anti-corrosion technology and developed a large range of new tube-coating technology. It was the first to develop brake and fuel 'handles' to supply to the OEMs. In order to maintain upstream co-operation with OEMs, Bundy formed a strategic alliance with the rival firm Freudenberg to develop and supply new brake systems to GM. Bundy has local relationships with raw materials suppliers for imports such as sheet steel. None of these appears to be a flagship relationship.

TRW and ZF   TRW of Cleveland, Ohio is a major supplier of steering systems to the automobile OEMs (as well as to the aerospace sector). The OEMs prefer to have their key suppliers of component/modular systems located close to their assembly plants in order to optimize just-in-time (JIT) delivery. The strategy of TRW is to be a key supplier. It is dedicated to being located close to its major customers and as a Tier 1 key supplier it will develop full modular (level 4 major module) assembly and take on design responsibility and selection of Tier 1 suppliers in co-operation with the OEM.

The major competitors for TRW in North America include Dana, Saginaw, and Visteon. In Europe, the major competitors are ZF in Germany, Lucas Varity in the

UK, and SMI in France. In Japan its competitors include Koyo, NSK, and Honda. In order to spread risk and develop complementary capabilities TRW has formed several strategic alliances with competitors, including Koyo in the United States and Lucas Varity in the UK (for electric power assisted steering). As a response to the latter, ZF has set up a joint venture with Bosch in Germany. In Europe, TRW is a Tier 2 supplier to the Rover Group and its local plants have not yet progressed to key supplier status.

The main global competitor of TRW is the German manufacturer, ZF. In complete steering assemblies, ZF has set up a plant in Tuscolusa to be a key supplier to Mercedes. In 1998, ZF formed a joint venture with Ford to supply continuously variable automatic transmissions (CVTs). Ford also buys CVTs from Visteon.

The European experience

As American OEMs like Ford and GM went to Europe and Asia they required their Tier 1 key suppliers to follow and build facilities in order to develop networks which replicated the American system, in areas such as:

- paints;
- seats;
- pistons and rings; and
- fabrics.

The Japanese did the same as they expanded into North America and South-East Asia: for example Nissan brought the wire business supplier, Yasaki, to North America.

Some Tier 1 and Tier 2 suppliers are now MNEs themselves, with networks in Triad regions. As such they mirror the OEMs. They are now 'mature' key suppliers. This has two effects:

(a) an increase in the strategic direction of the OEMs, which builds on their capabilities in their product and process technology;
(b) a decrease in the real production by Tier 1 producers, as well as OEMs, as Tier 2 suppliers are capturing a greater share of the value-added production from key suppliers in Tier 1.

The tyre companies are a good example of firms that have successfully resisted the efforts of the automotive OEMs to draw them into a flagship network. Two aspects of their businesses have been responsible for the ability of the leading tyre companies to stay away from becoming key suppliers to a flagship. First, there is a significant market segment—the aftermarket—that the tyre companies can access without involvement with automotive OEMs. Not only does this provide opportunities for implementing strategies that are not dependent on the automotive OEMs, but also the higher prices and margins available to the companies in the aftermarket account for a large portion of their profits. Second, the major tyre firms (with the exception of Coopers) have assiduously developed their own brand franchises, thus bypassing one of the most potent tools that the automotive OEMs use to maintain their flagship control over network partners. This brand franchise is a critical intangible asset of a flagship firm. The countervailing power of the tyre brands has played a critical role in their strategic independence.

PART IV
Conclusions

Managerial Implications of Flagship Relationships

The objective of this chapter is to extend the theory of Parts I and II, pull together the case studies of Part III on telecommunications, chemicals, automobiles, and electronics, and extend the flagship thinking to other sectors (especially in Europe). In particular, throughout this chapter, we shall draw out the strategic management implications for managers of the flagship model.

In the first section of this chapter we shall synthesis the case studies, which are principally North American. In the next we shall expand the flagship model to other sectors and countries, especially Europe. In the third we shall expand the flagship model to include 'tiered' flagship relationships. In the last we draw out implications for managers.

Building on the North American experience

What is the most important priority for the CEO of a large firm that faces intensified global competition? Today, for many CEOs, it is the question of how to convert a bloated, inefficient bureaucracy into a lean and effective operation. One of the most effective ways of doing this is to adopt the 'business network form' of organization. In a business network, a large firm forms a series of alliances with other firms; it transfers many operations to these network partners, but retains strategic leadership of the network. This form of organization is proving highly effective in developing global competitiveness in a variety of industries. Consider the following:

- Continental Bank of Chicago has decided to outsource the operation of its computer systems, using outside vendors to operate, maintain, and expand the hardware infrastructure of its information technology systems, and retaining only a small core of bank employees to manage the process. It has done this at a time when many other banks insist that they are in the 'information business'.
- A Dutch chemical company, DSM, has set up a subsidiary to provide the majority of the office services for its headquarters complex and its businesses located in the surrounding area. The subsidiary was given three years to become competitive, after which it was required to bid for the company's business against third parties.
- Jack Welch, the CEO of General Electric, has disbanded many of the large corporate service groups at headquarters. Strategic planning, for example,

once had over 600 employees, most of whom no longer have a job at GE. On the other hand, Welch decided to enlarge the budget of the corporate training facility at Crotonville, which is now teaching over 10,000 GE managers a year how to make their businesses globally competitive. Crotonville uses outside instructors to deliver most of its courses.

Key strategic decision making

Welch, and other leaders of large corporations, have recognized the strategic importance of decisions about what should be done inside the corporation and what is more effectively done through a network of alliance partners. As Ron Morrison, then President of Kodak Canada, put it:

When Kodak first came to Canada more than 60 years ago, we did everything ourselves. We had our own machine shop to manufacture parts to repair our equipment, we employed people to plough the snow and we printed our own stationery. We had to do these things because there were no suppliers we could rely on to do them. Today, we rely heavily on outside suppliers for many of these goods and services we need to run our business.

In their drive to enhance their global competitiveness, large corporations are discovering that it pays to find ways to get others to do what was once considered a necessary part of the business. Business leaders are finding that assumptions they made in the past about these functions no longer apply.

The first assumption they question is that the firm can produce these services more cheaply internally than it can purchase them from outside suppliers. This argument was often used to justify the establishment of mainframe computer centres by large companies. Citing the economies of scale that each new generation of mainframe promised, corporate computer centre managers claimed that their unit costs of computing would decrease each time they purchased bigger, faster mainframes. While this may be true of the direct costs of operating a mainframe, the argument falls apart when total costs are evaluated. As the overheads of managing a computer centre within a large company are substantial, the total costs of computing are usually higher when done inside a large corporation. Even IBM has discovered that it can purchase standard or commodity computing services more cheaply than the total costs of providing those services internally.

Second, most large firms have adopted some form of a Total Quality Management (TQM) system and pride themselves on the quality of the products and services they provide to their customers. These firms often make the mistake of assuming that the same should apply to the services they produce for internal consumption. As the Dutch chemical firm, DSM, has discovered, this assumption often does not hold true. For many services, the reverse applies. Corporate service units often take on a life of their own. They become rule bound and bureaucratic and lose sight of the need to treat those who use their services as customers. Service quality is poor when measured by speed of response, flexibility to meet evolving user specifications, or the ability to deliver on time for a reasonable price.

In particular, the quality of customer service usually suffers badly when a large firm attempts to reduce the costs of operating the service. The temptation to effect economies by reducing responsiveness is hard to overcome. Alternatively, if an internal transfer pricing system is used, service units often charge exorbitant premiums for anything beyond the standard level of service they are designed to provide.

Finally, the assumption that internal suppliers of products and services will be more flexible than outside suppliers has to be questioned. Close examination frequently reveals that the opposite is true. Once the internal unit has made substantial capital investment, it becomes inflexible. Change is seen as costly and difficult and, in any case, unnecessary. Outside vendors are more likely to be willing to consider changing the way they produce and deliver their output.

Flexibility and lower costs can sometimes be achieved by shifting from using an internal system with full-time employees to an external system with part-timers on contract. In the UK, for example, a packaged food company has begun using part-time contract sales persons. They work from their homes, use the family car for transport, and usually put in from 15 to 24 hours a week. During peak periods of sales activity, however, they are willing to work longer hours; compensation is strictly on a commission basis. Not only does the firm gain greater flexibility in the deployment of sales effort, but its retail customers report that service quality has improved.

Forging a business network

A business network can be an effective way of bringing together a group of firms for the purpose of creating a system for outpacing competition in a global industry. At the centre of such a network will be a flagship firm that has some unique contribution to make to the working of the network. Usually, this contribution includes:

- *Managing the network as a whole.* The flagship is responsible for deciding the mission and product/market focus of the network, the location of various production activities, and the strategic moves that the network will undertake to improve its international competitiveness.
- *Fostering and developing core technologies.* This role includes deciding on technology priorities and the allocation of resources for technology development. It does not necessarily require that the R&D function reside within the flagship. Instead, many flagships are assigning the conduct of research to network partners, including participants from the non-business infrastructure (NBI). University research laboratories, for example, are becoming partners in business networks.
- *Managing government relations.* Members of business networks often conclude that they need to co-ordinate the relations between the network and various government bodies. Regulation, trade policy, and competition

policy have become more complex as industries globalize. Business networks, therefore, must ensure that policy makers understand where national interests lie and act accordingly. The CEO of the flagship firm is naturally seen as the spokesperson for the network as a whole, and has special responsibilities to ensure that communications with government are effective.

Business networks are built through alliances between the flagship firm and its network partners. Often called strategic alliances, the partnerships involve the creation of long-term, mutually beneficial relations. But these alliances are not partnerships of equals; in fact, these relations are asymmetric. Strategy formulation for the network is a highly centralized process that is mainly the prerogative of the flagship. Strategic direction flows from the flagship to the network partners in a top-down manner. The role of the network partners is the efficient implementation of strategy. Unless the network partner is willing to accept this fundamental asymmetry, its membership in the network is unstable.

Under this arrangement, it is natural for technology development priorities and strategies to flow from the flagship to its network partners. The smaller firm can expect a better pay-off from collaborating with the flagship than from confrontation. For example, accessibility to technology by all partners is a valuable benefit of collaboration. This arrangement is well understood, for example, by suppliers to the automotive industry. They take direction from the automotive flagships—firms with global perspectives and strategies.

Helping the daughter grow up

A new type of network partner is the 'daughter' that has been spun off from the parent. When a firm creates a subsidiary from existing operations, the processes of establishing proper working relationships are difficult. Initially, many of those whose jobs are transferred to the daughter experience a sense of resentment at being separated from the parent. Having grown used to the support systems that are typical in large firms, they find it difficult to operate in the leaner environment of the subsidiary. If the daughter has been told that it will have to compete with other firms for the parent's business after a fixed period of time, there are also fears about job security. This is a new experience for many who had assumed that they had an implicit lifetime employment arrangement with the parent. Finally, having to sell their services on the open market is itself a new and disturbing experience for employees who had previously operated as monopoly internal suppliers.

How do these corporate daughters grow up? Figure 12.1, entitled 'Paths to competitiveness' illustrates two possible paths from adolescence to maturity. Before being spun off, internal service units such as computer centres usually

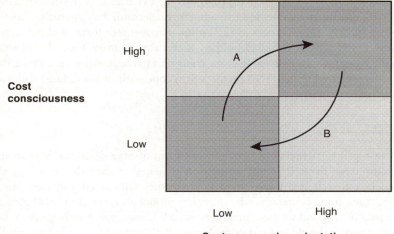

Figure 12.1 Paths to competitiveness

do not place priority on being cost competitive. Managers focus on technical excellence, and pay more attention to the integrity of their operations than the needs of their internal customers. Thus, high costs and low service levels are typical.

After the spin-off, these managers are likely to continue to operate within their comfort zones for a while, concentrating on the technical aspects of the functions they performed when their unit was part of the parent. Next comes the realization that spun-off units have to improve cost competitiveness. These daughters follow Path A. Managers eliminate expenses that are not core to the service, cut overheads and seek ways of producing more with less. Later, they realize that merely being cost competitive will not ensure their firm's survival. This is the point where they start to improve the customer service orientation of their operation. In effect, the daughter moves to the top right quadrant, as it learns to provide high-quality service at a low price.

Path B illustrates the second way of making the daughter competitive. This way involves concentrating on improving service to users before attempting to improve cost competitiveness. Path B is more likely to be followed when the parent itself is not under cost pressures. Given the recent recession and the aggressive pricing strategies of Asian competitors in global markets, we are likely to find more Path A daughters than Path B ones.

Only those daughters that end up in the top right quadrant will survive. Parents of daughters who fail to arrive at this quadrant quickly enough will turn elsewhere. There are several things that parents can do to help their daughters mature. First, they can set clear expectations for price and service performance, along with specific timetables for achieving them. Second, they can make sure that there are sufficient newcomers in the senior management team of the daughter before it is spun off. It is highly unlikely that a management team drawn solely from the parent will be able to effect the transition to competitiveness. Third, they should be prepared to help the daughter firm cope with initial failures and learn from them.

Need to get the balance right

The flagship/five partners business network form of organization is here to stay. For many large firms it is not a question of whether they should adopt this approach; rather it is a question of how far they should go and how fast to proceed. One thing is certain—the pressures of global competition will increase over time. To respond to these pressures, senior management in large firms will have to abandon the old ways of doing business. They must question assumptions about what should be done by the firm itself and what is better assigned to a network partner. Some will get the balance right and move quickly to the new form. They will prosper. Those that do not may not even survive.

Building on the European experience

A steel firm's flagship relationships: ASAB and BOC

There are strong flagship relationships in the steel business. For example, the European MNE, Avesta Sheffield AB (ASAB), which is the third-largest producer of bulk stainless steel in the world, has close key supplier linkages in its Sheffield home base with the British gas supplier, BOC. The BOC group itself is a global supplier of industrial gases and is a supplier to the chemicals, glass, and electronics sectors, as well as steel. BOC is the key supplier of hydrogen, a highly explosive gas which therefore requires the development of a long-term close relationship to focus on safety problems.

ASAB also has several key customer linkages. One is with Slag Reduction Ltd. This is a British company which removes the slag by-product produced by ASAB's steel-making process. They are completely dependent on ASAB for their business. Slag Reduction operates on the ASAB plant site and then uses the material for road building. ASAB has also undertaken joint research with other key customers, for example in the development of the stainless steel beer barrel, which is being developed to replace the aluminium barrel.

Another, so far underdeveloped, area for ASAB to build flagship relationships is with parts of the non-business environment dealing with environmental pollution issues. Disposal of by-products from the steel-making process presents major problems. In addition to the key customer-type relationship with firms like Slag Reduction, it is vital to develop shared long-term relationships with policy makers and environmentalists. If ASAB can help develop regulatory policies for the disposal of carcinogenic by-products, like nickel, then it could develop a 'first mover' green capability, as discussed by Rugman and Verbeke (1998).

BOC has difficulty in developing many key supplier relationships because most of its gas production is of 'commodity' gases. To put value for the customer into its product it needs to add specialized services, such as the development of firm-specific safety features, as it has done with ASAB. However, a strategy of being the low-cost supplier, or even of being the 'world class' supplier, is not enough to qualify as a true flagship relationship. BOC's goal is to be a key supplier, not a flagship.

Oil firms

In the oil sector there are many flagship relationships, because most of these MNEs have reduced their vertical integration. The oil sector has a history of strong vertical integration; indeed these MNEs were classic cases of internalization, in order to generate proprietary firm-specific advantages (Rugman 1981). More recently oil MNEs have moved from their hierarchical relationships towards flagship network ones.

In the exploration and production sectors (the 'upstream' part of the industry) a host of highly specialized key suppliers have emerged, often as part of the de-integration strategies of the majors. Firms such as Oil Tools International have emerged as mature multinational key suppliers, with capabilities for providing high-quality services wherever their major customers require them. There are several thousand small suppliers in the upstream part of the industry. These have not been organized into a multi-tiered network such as the one in automobiles.

One example of a quasi-flagship relationship occurred in a strategic alliance organized by the British Petroleum Company plc (BP). Starting in 1993 BP organized an alliance with Brown & Root to develop an oil and natural gas reservoir north of Aberdeen, Scotland. An integrated team of seven contracting companies was formed, as shown in Table 12.1.

To design, build, and install the platform facilities, plus subsea hardware and

Table 12.1 Partners in the Aberdeen alliance

BP Exploration	*Aberdeen field operator*
Brown & Root	Design procurement and management support
Trafalgar John Brown Oil and Gas	Integrated deck fabrication
BARMAC	Jacket, template, and pipes fabrication
Saipem	Platform transportation and installation
Allseas	Oil and gas export pipelines procurement and installation
Santa Fé	Drilling facilities design, procurement, and fabrication
Emtunga	Accommodation module design, procurement, and fabrication

pipelines, BP along with Brown & Root identified that the specialist skills of seven contracting companies would be required. BP moved away from the traditional tendering process and selected companies not only on their technical and commercial competences but also on less tangible qualities such as participants as members of a team. By September 1993 the team members were on board.

The cost of developing the conceptual platform design in 1991 was estimated at £450 million, but at the end of 1992 BP set an extreme target of £270 million to gauge the commitment of key suppliers to cost reduction. Finally in November 1993 a realistic target cost of £373 million was set for delivering the platform and pipeline facilities, with the first oil to be produced January 1997. Through close collaboration by BP with key suppliers the project came on-line six months early, the first oil being produced in June 1996 and £80 million below budget, at £290 million.

Tiered networks

In a mature key supplier relationship a key supplier can regain influence on the strategic direction of the business network. We have observed several examples of new 'tiered networks', especially in our research on the automobile sector: we shall report on Woodbridge Foam and Magna in this sector and also consider other sectors, such as pharmaceuticals, where tiered networks are also developing.

Tiered networks in the automobile industry

Woodbridge Foam is a Tier 2 supplier to two Tier 1 suppliers, Lear Seating and Johnson Controls. Initially, as a Tier 2 supplier, Woodbridge followed product design instructions from its Tier 1 customers and focused all its efforts on cost curtailment to respond to the aggressive cost-reduction targets which came down from the OEM and the Tier 1 suppliers. Once the cost-reduction possibilities of existing product designs were exploited, it became apparent that further improvements could only be achieved through close co-ordination of product and process technologies. However, the Tier 1 supplier had eliminated much of its product-development capabilities in its efforts to reduce its own cost base. Further, lacking production capacity in foam manufacture, the Tier 1 supplier had virtually no capability in process technology. Woodbridge saw an opportunity to add some product-development capability to its manufacturing capacity-based process technology skills. By combining product and process-development capabilities, Woodbridge came up with new innovative solutions which the Tier 1 supplier took to the OEM, thus expanding the scope of its supply capabilities. A diagrammatic representation of a tiered network with these mature flagship relationships appears in Figure 12.2.

Woodbridge and its Tier 1 customers are representative of the new form of mature supply network which is developing in the automotive industry. The flagship firm's monopoly on technological leadership functions is being replaced by a

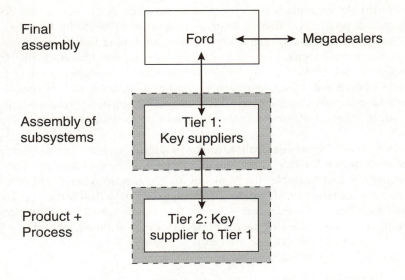

Figure 12.2 A tiered flagship model for automobiles

system that assigns the leadership role to that part of the network where it can be most effectively exercised. As the Japanese networks discovered many years ago, product and process developments have to be closely linked. As the automotive flagships and their Tier 1 suppliers ceased manufacturing components, their development capabilities atrophied because of a lack of linkages with process development, which can only take place in close proximity to operations. As the operations activities in automotive components supply migrate more and more to Tier 2 suppliers, it is conceivable that development activity should follow. In such mature networks, we are likely to find the following:

- Flagship firms will relinquish much or all of the technological leadership role they formerly performed.
- Tier 1 suppliers will become systems integrators and assemblers, and they will focus their resources on understanding and anticipating the systems requirements of the OEMs and managing a network of relationships with Tier 2 suppliers.
- Tier 2 suppliers will learn to play a leadership role in those areas of technology development that require a combination of product- and process-development capability.

Another example of a tiered network is Magna, the Canadian-based automotive parts producer. Magna is bringing to Europe the system it developed in North America. It organizes a total programme as a systems supplier (for an OEM's basic platform). An example is a seating programme such as car frames and doors. Magna will produce car frames, doors, and engine components for Chrysler.

Another example of a Tier 1 key supplier developing flagship relationships occurred when Magna developed hydro forming (a new manufacturing technology) in the 1990s for door frames. Magna has an exclusive contract for a Chrysler platform. Magna is now organized as a confederation of semi-independent companies, at plant level (each with only one flagship relationship). An example arises in Magna's foreign operations in Austria, as shown in Figure 12.3.

In Austria, Magna has a small network of suppliers, such as a key supplier linkage with the steel maker, Voest Alpine. Magna is a key supplier (to OEMs) in Germany. It also assembles the Mini van for Chrysler, in Austria, and sells this across the EU. However, Magna does not wish to become a rival to the large OEMs like Ford, GM, and Daimler Benz-Chrysler, so it has kept itself in a small niche. It can therefore survive against bigger competitors such as Bosch, which has a flagship linkage to BMW, VW, and Mercedes.

Tiered networks in the pharmaceutical industry

The pharmaceutical industry is currently in the process of radical restructuring as a consequence of the series of mergers which have led to the creation of a new type of pharmaceutical giant. Traditionally, the large, research-based pharmaceutical companies were highly vertically integrated, internalizing everything from new drug discovery to drug registration and, finally, production and marketing (Rugman 1981). These firms derived their competitive advantage from the ownership of patents and drug registrations, areas where the legal protection of property rights is particularly strong in countries which constitute their major markets.

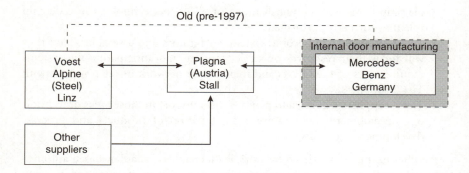

Figure 12.3 Magna's tiered networks in automotive parts

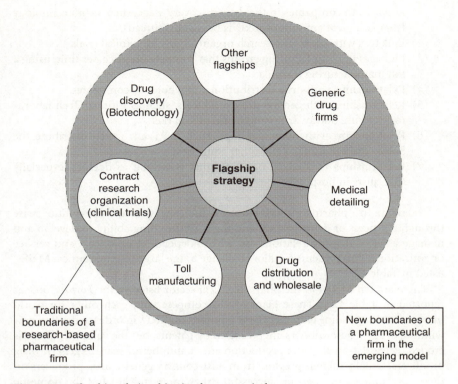

Figure 12.4 Flagship relationships in pharmaceuticals

The consummation of a series of mega mergers (Glaxo with Wellcome, Ciba with Sandoz, Pharmacia with Upjohn, for example) has led to a situation where the diseconomies of scale (in management and operations) have made the vertical integration strategy sub-optimal. Internal rivalry between groups belonging to the pre-merged entities threatened to dissipate the potential gains from synergies across their portfolio of businesses. Of equal concern was the loss of agility which is a critical competence for developing competitive advantage. Hence, the ownership of upstream or downstream activities has come to be seen as a handicap which limits the freedom of choice for top management.

Figure 12.4 illustrates the shift that is taking place in the newly formed pharmaceutical giants. The outer circle illustrates the boundaries of the older style of pharmaceutical giant. This older integrated pharmaceutical multinational firm is being replaced by a new set of independent businesses linked together in a flagship-style tiered network. The attributes of the emerging tiered flagship model feature the following linkages between the pharmaceutical firm and seven partners:

(1) Linkages to companies in the drug discovery stage, such as biotechnology (that is, a great amount of R&D is being outsourced).
(2) Linkages with contract research organizations for clinical trials.
(3) Linkages to manufacturing groups that compete on price per unit, using a toll manufacturing formula.
(4) Relationships with drug distribution and wholesale companies.
(5) Relationships with generic drug producers, such as Altimed/Tech laboratories to use Solvay drugs and be first to market.
(6) Relationships with other flagships, such as Wyatt, which distribute the Solvay drug in Canada and other countries.
(7) Relationships in medical detailing, that is, selling to doctors, especially specialists in hospitals.

Today, in the pharmaceutical industry, the new strategic capabilities arise through a process of deintegration and the corresponding ability to develop and manage a set of flagship relationships with independent producers and service organizations. This presents a major challenge to the large pharmaceutical MNEs, listed in Table 12.2.

There are ten MNEs in the pharmaceutical sector listed in the *Fortune 500*, as reported in Table 12.2. These giant MNEs compete with each other for world market shares, spending extremely large amounts on R&D, in order to develop new winning drugs. These winners are protected by patents, but the value of patents is eroded by legislation allowing production after a number of years to generic drug producers. Usually there is pressure from host-country generic drug producers on their governments to open up successful drugs more quickly and the domestic producers' interest is often tied into the interests of the local consumers in levying lower prices for pharmaceuticals. There is a natural bias by national health authorities in favour of home-grown generic drug producers against MNEs. Indeed the MNEs are subject to a large amount of regulation and, in general, have a strategy of compliance, since large rents are potentially available from the licence to sell drugs in segmented national markets. In principle, there is no significant difference in the strategic behaviour in the face of powerful host-nation governments.

Advances in technology intensify the concentration of economic power in the hands of MNEs. It is not so much the creation of new knowledge that matters (as here smaller, innovating firms can do well) but that in the application for drug registration in major markets that the MNE has an advantage. Most of the manufacturing productivity advances in Japanese MNEs have occurred in incremental process improvements reflecting efficient organizational structures. When there is a perceived shortfall of pure research, the MNEs can buy it from abroad, as the Japanese MNEs have done through their activities in California's Silicon Valley and other US-based research centres.

With a strong national regulatory process still in place, many business opportunities for managers lie in new activities based on the development of therapeutic groups of specialists, as in Figure 12.4. In addition, the R&D no longer needs to be

Table 12.2 World's largest pharmaceutical companies ranked by revenues, 1997 ($US million)

Fortune Global 500 rank	Company	Revenues	Profits	Fortune Global 500 rank by profits	Share of foreign in total assets (%)	Country
144	Merck	23,636.90	4,614.10	14	40	United States
150	Johnson & Johnson	22,629.00	3,303.00	29	52	United States
167	Novartis	21,494.20	3,592.30	23	42	Switzerland
230	Bristol-Myers Squibb	16,701.20	3,204.70	34	46	United States
289	American Home Products	14,196.00	2,043.10	66	34	United States
329	Glaxo Wellcome	13,072.30	3,030.60	41	47	Britain
334	Roche Holding	12,937.20	−1,1400.10	491	n.a.	Switzerland
341	SmithKline Beecham	12,769.30	1,767.60	82	73	Britain
354	Pfizer	12,504.00	2,213.00	58	58	United States
379	Abbott Laboratories	11,883.50	2,094.50	65	31	United States

Source: 'Fortune Global 500', *Fortune Magazine*, 3 August 1998.

Note: Hoechst Marion Roussel (HMR) does not appear in the table although it is a wholly owned subsidiary of Hoechst that specializes in pharmaceuticals. It was formed in 1995 and became a wholly owned subsidiary of Hoechst in 1997. Hoechst is not counted as a pharmaceutical company because HMR only has $7.7 billion in revenues while Hoechst itself has $30 billion in revenues (that is only 26 per cent of Hoechst's business is in pharmaceuticals).

internalized, as patents and drug registrations mean that licences become more valuable than proprietary ownership as sources of ongoing profitability.

The large pharmaceutical MNEs, such as Merck, Novartis, and Glaxo Wellcome face enormous challenges to their traditional strategies of vertical integration (to avoid the dissipation of R&D, patents, and know-how) coupled with world-wide horizontal integration (to spread their firm-specific knowledge advantage on a global basis). Today, the search for flagship linkages is a new business imperative.

The critical strategic management functions which will be retained by the new giants are:

- *Global environmental scanning.* The pharmaceutical firms need to keep themselves constantly informed of medical, scientific, and market developments in all the therapeutical groups in which they have an interest. The expansion of the number of such groups in which the post-merger firms have such a stake makes the scanning task more difficult and complex.
- *Relationships with host governments.* In the past, the principal relationships were with the drug registration authorities. Now, increasingly, these giants have to forge relationships with government bodies concerned with managing other parts of national healthcare programmes. These include: drug delivery, hospitals, and public health, to name just a few. These, and other government agencies, are looking for help from the pharmaceutical giants in coping with the financial problems of escalating healthcare costs, an ageing population, and the spread of new diseases such as AIDS. The new pharmaceutical giants need to position themselves as flagship partners of government bodies, a relationship where the firm has to blend its self-interest with a new capability to help define issues of public interest.
- *Forging and managing flagship relationships with suppliers.* As they attempt to become a preferred partner to smaller firms with specialized skills and competences, the pharmaceutical giants have to learn the skills of collaborative advantage. This is the ability to find ways in which the mutual interest of the partnership replaces the self-interest of each partner. Moreover, they have to be seen as trustworthy in the way they handle commercially sensitive information about cost structures and operational capabilities. Such information is of vital importance to the flagship firm in making decisions about whether and how to proceed with developing relationships, but can be damaging to the other party, if misused.

Implications of the flagship model for managers

Implications for flagship managers

The managers of flagship firms need to develop three capabilities:

(1) *Develop strategic vision.* Managers have to strive continuously to refine and communicate a compelling strategic vision for the business of the network

as a whole. This vision has to be global in scope, sufficiently challenging to motivate employees throughout the network, yet sufficiently realistic to bring forth viable strategies and objectives that can be reached.

(2) *Balance innovation and imitation.* Flagships have to resolve a strategic quandary. On the one hand, managers have to be acutely aware of the strategic positions of their rivals and develop effective responses to their competitors' successes. On the other hand, mere imitation of successful strategies is not a recipe for developing competitive advantage. Imitation has to be balanced with innovation.

(3) *Focus on leadership, not management.* Managers have to learn to allow and encourage managers in their network partners to take full responsibility for managing operations. Flagship managers must avoid micro management of the operations of the alliance partners. This is particularly true when problems surface. Instead of giving directives to address these problems, flagship managers must maintain a leadership posture and delegate the management of devising solutions to their counterparts in the partner firms.

Implications for managers of network partners

The flagship model is not easy to put into practice because of the following seven problems:

(1) Network partners have to accept the reality that they have limited strategic autonomy and must operate within the constraints and directives of the flagship. They have little choice over the products or market they will service, or over the choice of architecture for their information systems. Unless they can achieve mature flagship status, partners have little strategic direction over the network.

(2) Within its assigned domain the partner is expected to be more efficient than the flagship. It should, therefore, aim to produce at lower cost than the flagship or the partners of competing flagships. It needs to keep overheads to a minimum and invest in process technology that reduces costs. It should expect to achieve, or exceed, learning curve targets for cost reduction set by the flagship.

(3) The supplier should meet and eventually exceed the quality expectations of the flagship. Cost competitiveness cannot be used as an excuse for compromising quality standards. Partners must develop an attitude in which cost and quality can be jointly optimized.

(4) Network partners should develop capabilities for meeting the enhanced expectations of the flagship about the pace of new-product development. Flagships have come to rely on the capability of their partner to respond quickly to changes in direction.

(5) Loyalty to the network is a critically important aspect of culture that the

partner is expected to display. Employees must be seen to possess loyalty to the flagship. They may even be expected to use flagship products and display flagship insignia on their workwear.

(6) A major strategic issue for network partners is to keep in contact with the outside competitive environment. When precluded from dealing with other customers, suppliers lose valuable feedback about their relative standing in the market-place. They may have only a sketchy notion about their cost competitiveness, or product developments by their competitors, and little grasp of technological developments in their industry.

(7) Similarly, key customers may be prevented from dealing with flagship rivals. In fact IBM discovered that its exclusive retail dealers had only a poor understanding of the prices and performance of the IBM PC 'clones' and so were not able to counter competition from clone manufacturers. Somewhat like IBM, these dealers failed to recognize the true nature of the threat to their business system that Dell represented when it radically restructured the business system in the PC industry.

References

The 100 Year Almanac and 1996 Market Data Handbook (1996). Crain Communications.

ADAMS, P. (1993). 'The New Face of Automobile Transplants in Canada', *Canadian Economic Observer* (October): 3.1–3.6.

AGUILAR, F. (1979). *Scanning the Business Environment*. New York: Macmillan.

ALLISON, G. T. (1971). *Essence of Decision: Explaining the Cuban Missile Crisis*. Boston: Little Brown.

ARROW, K. (1971). *Essays in the Theory of Risk-Bearing*. Chicago: Markham.

Automotive News (1996). 'Top 50 Global Suppliers' (8 July): 18.

BALIGA, B., and JAEGER, A. (1984). 'Multinational Corporations: Control Systems and Delegation Issues', *Journal of International Business Studies*, 15/2: 25–40.

BALLEW, P., SCHNORBUS, R., and HESSE, H. (1994). 'The automobile industry and monetary policy: An international perspective', *Business Economics*, 29/4: 29–35.

BARREAU, J., and ABDELAZIZ, M. (1987). *L'Industrie éléctronique française: 29 ans de relations Etats-Groupes industriels 1958–1986*. Paris: Libraire générale de droit et de jurisprudence.

—— LE NAY, J., and ABDELAZIZ MOULINE, M. (1986). *La Filière éléctronique française: miracle ou mirage?* Paris: Hatier.

BARTLETT, C., and GHOSHAL, S. (1989). *Managing Across Borders: The Transnational Solution*. Boston: Harvard Business School Press.

—— —— (1991). 'Global Strategic Management: Impact on the New Frontiers of Strategy Research', *Strategic Management Journal*, 12, Special Issue: 5–16.

—— —— (1993). 'Beyond the M-Form Toward a Managerial Theory of the Firm', *Strategic Management Journal*, 14, Special Issue: 23–46.

BESSIÈRES, H. (1989). 'Nouvelle capitale des télécoms', *Télécoms Magasin* (November). Brussels.

—— (1991). 'Où vont les milliards de France Telecom', *Télécoms Magasin* (May).

—— (1993). 'France Telecom franchit la barre des 120 milliards', *Télécoms Magasin* (May).

BLOIS, K. J. (1990). 'Transactions Costs and Networks', *Strategic Management Journal*, 11: 493–9.

BORYS, B., and JEMISON, D. B. (1989). 'Hybrid Organizations as Strategic Alliances', *Academy of Management Review*, 14/2: 234–49.

BOWER, J. D. (1993). 'New Technology Supply Networks in the Global Pharmaceutical Field', *International Business Review*, 2/1: 93–5.

BRUSCO, S. (1982). 'The Emilian Model: Productive Decentralisation and Social Integration', *Cambridge Journal of Economics*, 6: 167–84.

BUCKLEY, P. J., and CASSON, M. (1976). *The Future of the Multinational Enterprise*. London: Macmillan.

—— —— (1980). 'The Optimal Timing of a Foreign Direct Investment', *Economic Journal*, 91/1 (March): 75–81.

—— —— (1985). *The Economic Theory of the Multinational Enterprise*. London and Basingstoke: Macmillan.

BURT, R. S. (1992). *Structural Holes: The Social Structure of Competition*. Cambridge, MA: Harvard University Press.

Business Week (1993). 'The Virtual Corporation' (8 February): 99–103.

Canadian Automobile Dealers Association. Personal communication.

CARPENTIER, M., FARNOUX-TOPORKOFF, S., and GARRIC, C. (1991). *Les Télécommunications en liberté surveillée*. Paris: Technique et Documentation Lavoisier.

CASSON, M. (1979). *Alternatives to the Multinational Enterprise*. London: Macmillan.

—— and COX, H. (1992). 'Firms, Networks and International Business Enterprises'. Paper presented to the annual meeting of the European International Business Association, Reading, UK (December).

CAVES, R. E. (1971). 'International Corporations: The Industrial Economics of Foreign Investment', *Economica*, 38: 1–27.

CAYLA-BOUCHAREL, L., CICERI, M. F., HEITZMANN, R., and PAUTRAT, C. (1990). *Tarification, prix de revient et concurrence*. Paris: France Telecom.

CHANDLER, A. D. JR. (1962). *Strategy and Structure: Chapters in the History of American Industrial Enterprise*. Cambridge, MA: MIT Press.

CHAPPELL, L. (1996). 'Forecast: Fewer Suppliers', *Automotive News* (8 July): 1.

Chrysler Canada (1991). *Report to Shareholders 1991*. Windsor: Chrysler Canada Ltd.

—— (1995). *Annual Report 1995*. Windsor: Chrysler Canada Ltd.

—— University of Windsor, St. Clair College, Industry Canada and Ontario Ministry of Economic Development, Trade and Tourism (1995). *The Windsor Experiment*. Windsor: Ross Roy Communications Canada Limited.

Chrysler Corporation (1994). 'Supplier Relations', *Annual Report 1994* (http://www.chrysler.com).

—— (1995). 'Customer One Initiative', *Chrysler Corporation 1995–96* (http://www.chryslercars.com/CustOnechry/CustOne.htm).

—— (1996*a*). 'Suppliers "SCORE" $1 billion for Chrysler: Long Term Quality Relationships Continue to Pay Off for Automaker', Press Release (31 July).

—— (1996*b*). 'Valve Train Extended Enterprise Spreads Lean Manufacturing Principles', *Supplier Newsletter* (May/June). Chrysler Corporation (http://www.media.chrysler.com/wwwsup/2156.htm).

COASE, R. H. (1937). 'The Nature of the Firm', *Economica*, 4: 386–405.

CONNER, K. R. (1991). 'A Historical Comparison of Resource-based Theory and Five Schools of Thought Within Industrial Organization Economics: Do We Have a New Theory of the Firm?', *Journal of Management*, 17/1: 121–54.

CROSS, B., and GORDON, J. (1995). 'Partnership Strategies for Market Success', *Business Quarterly*, 60/1: 91–6.

D'CRUZ, J. R. (1986). 'Strategic Management of Subsidiaries', in H. Etemad and L. Seguin Dulude (eds.), *Managing the Multinational Subsidiary*. London: Croom Helm, 75–89.

—— (1993). 'Business Networks for Global Competitiveness', *Business Quarterly*, 57/4: 93–8.

—— and RUGMAN, A. M. (1992*a*). 'Business Networks for International Competitiveness', *Business Quarterly*, 56/4: 101–7.

—— —— (1992*b*). *New Compacts for Canadian Competitiveness*. Toronto: Kodak Canada Inc., 25 March 1992.

—— —— (1993). 'Developing International Competitiveness: The Five Partners Model', *Business Quarterly*, 58/2: 60–72.

—— —— (1994*a*). 'Business Network Theory and the Canadian Telecommunications Industry', *International Business Review*, 3/3: 275–88.

—— —— (1994*b*). 'The Five Partners Model: France Telecom, Alcatel, and the Global Telecommunications Industry', *European Management Journal*, 12/1: 59–66.

—— GESTRIN, M., and RUGMAN, A. M. (1995). *Is the Canadian Manager an Endangered Species?* Toronto: Faculty of Management, University of Toronto, mimeo of study prepared for Ontario's Ministerial Advisory Committee on Chemicals.

DOZ, Y., and PRAHALAD, C. K. (1981). 'Headquarters Influence and Strategic Control in MNC's', *Sloan Management Review*, 22/4: 15–29.

—— —— (1984). 'Patterns of Strategic Control Within Multinational Corporations', *Journal of International Business Studies*, 15/2: 55–72.

—— —— (1987). *The Multinational Mission: Balancing Local Demands and Global Vision.* New York: Macmillan.

—— —— (1991). 'Managing DMNCs: A Search for a New Paradigm', *Strategic Management Journal*, 12, Special Issue: 145–64.

DUCH, R. M. (1991). *Privatizing the Economy: Telecommunications Policy in Comparative Perspective.* Manchester: Manchester University Press.

DUNNING, J. H. (1979). 'Explaining Changing Patterns of International Production: In Defence of the Eclectic Theory', *Oxford Bulletin of Economics and Statistics*, 41: 269–96.

—— (1981). *International Production and the Multinational Enterprise.* London: George Allen & Unwin.

—— and RUGMAN, A. M. (1985). 'The Influence of Hymer's Dissertation on the Theory of Foreign Direct Investment', *American Economic Review*, 75/2 (May): 228–32.

DYER, J. H. (1996). 'How Chrysler Created an American *Keiretsu*', *Harvard Business Review*, 74/4: 42–56.

EDEN, L., and MOLOT, M. (1996). 'Made in America? The U.S. Auto Industry, 1955–95', *International Executive*, 38/4: 501–41.

ENGLISH, B. (1996). 'Magna acquires parts unit of Marley PLC for $73.5 million', *Automotive News* (25 March): 42.

ENRIGHT, M. J. (1993*a*). 'The Geographic Scope of Competitive Advantage'. Working paper, Harvard Business School.

—— (1993*b*). 'The Determinants of Geographic Concentration in Industry'. Mimeo.

—— (1993*c*). 'Organization and Coordination in Geographically Concentrated Industries'. Mimeo.

EITEMAN, D. K., and STONEHILL, A. I. (1989). *Multinational Business Finance.* Englewood Cliffs, NJ: Prentice Hall.

ETHIER, W. J. (1986). 'The Multinational Firm', *Quarterly Journal of Economics*, 101: 805–33.

FAMA, E. (1980). 'Agency Problems and the Theory of the Firm', *Journal of Political Economy*, 88: 288–307.

FITES, D. V. (1996). 'Make Your Dealers Your Partners', *Harvard Business Review*, 74/2: 84–95.

FOOT, D., with STOFFMAN, D. (1996). *Boom, Bust & Echo.* Toronto: Macfarlane Walter & Ross.

Ford Motor Company (1995). *Annual Report 1995.* Dearborn, MI: Ford Motor Company.

Ford Motor Company of Canada, Ltd. (1994). *Annual Report 1994.* Oakville, ON: Ford Motor Company of Canada, Ltd.

—— Personal interview (July 1996).

France Telecom (1992). *Rapport d'activité 1991.* Paris: France Telecom.

FRUIN, M. (1992). *The Japanese Enterprise System: Competitive Strategies and Co-operative Structure.* Oxford: Oxford University Press.

General Motors (1995). *Annual Report 1995.* Detroit, MI: General Motors.

—— (1996). 'GM School-to-Work Group Meets', Press Release (11 March).

GERLACH, M. L. (1992). *Alliance Capitalism: The Social Organization of Japanese Business.* Berkeley, CA: University of California Press.

GHERTMAN, M. (1981). *La Prise de decision.* Paris: PUF.

—— (1988). 'Foreign Subsidiary and Parents' Roles During Strategic Investment and Investment Decisions', *Journal of International Business Studies*, 19/1: 47–68.

GLOBERMAN, S. (1986). *Fundamentals of International Business Management.* Englewood Cliffs, NJ: Prentice Hall.

GLUECK, W. (1976). *Business Policy, Strategy Formation and Management Action.* New York: McGraw Hill.

GRANOVETTER, M. (1985). 'Economic Action and Social Structure: The Problem of Embeddedness', *American Journal of Sociology*, 91/3: 481–510.

HAKANSSON, H., and JOHANSON, J. (1988). 'Formal and Informal Cooperation Strategies in International Industrial Networks', in F. J. Contractor and P. Lorange (eds.), *Cooperative Strategies in International Business.* Lexington: D. C. Heath, 369–79.

HAMEL, G. (1991). 'Competition for Competence and Inter-Partner Learning Within International Strategic Alliances', *Strategic Management Journal*, 12, Special Issue: 83–103.

—— and PRAHALAD, C. K. (1989). 'Strategic Intent', *Harvard Business Review*, 89/3 (May–June): 63–76.

HARRIGAN, K. R. (1985). *Strategies for Joint Ventures.* Lexington: D. C. Heath.

—— (1988). 'Strategic Alliances and Partner Asymmetries', in F. J. Contractor and P. Lorange (eds.), *Cooperative Strategies in International Business.* Lexington: D. C. Heath, 205–26.

HARRISON, B. (1992). 'Industrial Districts: Old Wine in New Bottles?', *Regional Studies*, 26/5: 469–83.

Hayes-Dana Inc. (1994). *Annual Report 1994.* St. Catherine's, ON: Hayes-Dana.

HEDLUND, G. (1992). 'Organizational Requirements for Global Knowledge Management— the N-Form Corporation'. Paper presented at the proceedings of the 18th European International Business Association Annual Conference, University of Reading, UK (13–15 December).

HELPER, S. R., and SAKO, M. (1995). 'Supplier Relations in Japan and the United States: Are They Converging?', *Sloan Management Review*, 36/3 (Spring): 77–84.

HENNART, J.-F. (1986). 'What is Internalization?', *Weltwirtschaftliches Archiv*, 122/4.

HILL, C. W. L. (1990). 'Cooperation, Opportunism, and the Invisible Hand: Implications for Transaction Cost Theory', *Academy of Management Review*, 15: 500–13.

—— and KIM, W. CHAN (1988). 'Searching for a Dynamic Theory of the Multinational Enterprise: A Transaction Cost Model', *Strategic Management Journal*, 9, Special Issue: 93–104.

HOOD, N., and YOUNG, S. (1997). 'The United Kingdom', in J. H. Dunning (ed.), *Governments, Competitiveness and International Business.* Oxford: Oxford University Press, 244–82.

—— —— and TRUIJENS, T. (1993). 'European Location Decisions of Japanese Manufacturers: Survey Evidence on the Case of the U.K.', *International Business Review*, 2/1: 39–63.

HOUT, T., PORTER, M. E., and RUDDEN, E. (1982). 'How Global Companies Win Out', *Harvard Business Review*, 82/5 (September–October): 98–108.

HYMER, S. H. (1976). *The International Operations of National Firms: A Study of Direct Investment.* New Haven, CT: Yale University Press.

Industry Canada, Automotive Branch (1995a). *Automotive Strategic Framework.* Ottawa: Department of Industry.

—— (1995*b*). *Statistical Review of the Canadian Automotive Industry.* Strategis: http://www.strategis.ic.gc.ca.

JACKSON, K. (1994). 'Tutor and Pupil: Chrysler adopts Freudenberg-NOK as its lean-manufacturing mentor', *Automotive News* (19 December): 1.

JARILLO, C. J. (1988). 'On Strategic Networks', *Strategic Management Journal*, 9/1: 31–41.

KANEKO I., and IMAI, K. (1987). 'A Network View of the Firm'. Mimeo, Hitotsubashi University—Stanford Conference.

KINDLEBERGER, C. P. (1969). *American Business Abroad: Six Lectures on Direct Investment.* New Haven, CT: Yale University Press.

KISIEL, R. (1996). 'ABS ABSc', *Automotive News* (26 February): 24i.

KOBE, G. (1994). 'Keeping SCORE', *Automotive Industries* (May): 39–41.

KOGUT, B., and ZANDER, U. (1992). 'Knowledge of the Firm, Combinative Capabilities and the Replication of Technology', *Organization Science*, 3/3: 383–97.

—— —— (1993). 'Knowledge of the Firm and the Evolutionary Theory of the Multinational Corporation', *Journal of International Business Studies*, 24/4: 625–45.

KOONTZ, H., and O'DONNELL, C. (1972). *Principles of Management.* New York: McGraw Hill.

KRUGMAN, P. (1991). *Geography and Trade.* London: MIT Press.

LORENZ, E. H. (1988). 'Neither Friends Nor Strangers: Informal Networks of Subcontracting in French Industry', in D. Gambetta (ed.), *Trust: Making and Breaking Cooperative Relations.* New York: Basil Blackwell.

LORENZONI, G. (1982). 'From Vertical Integration to Vertical Disintegration'. Paper presented at the Strategic Management Conference, Montreal.

—— and BADEN-FULLER, C. (1993). 'Creating a Strategic Centre to Manage a Web of Partners'. Working paper, University of Bath.

LUKE, R. D., BEGUN, J. W., and POINTER, D. M. (1989). 'Quasi-Firms: Strategic Interorganizational Forms in the Health Care Industry', *Academy of Management Review*, 14/1: 9–19.

LYONS, T. F., KRACHENBERG, A. R., and HENKE, J. W. JR. (1990). 'Mixed Motive Marriages: What's Next for Buyer–Supplier Relations?', *Sloan Management Review*, 31/3: 29–36.

MCELROY, J. (1992). 'Crusade at Chrysler', *Automotive Industries*, 24.

—— (1995). 'Industry Report Card: Does It Get Any Better Than This?' *Automotive Industries*, 48–58.

MAGEE, S. P. (1977). 'Multinational Corporations, the Industry Technology Cycle and Development', *Journal of World Trade Law*, 11/4 (July–August), 297–321.

—— (1981). 'The Appropriability Theory of the Multinational Corporation', *Annals of the American Academy of Political and Social Science* (November).

Magna International Inc. (1995). *Annual Report 1995.*

MILES, R. E., and SNOW, C. C. (1984). 'Fit, Failure and the Hall of Fame', *California Management Review*, 26: 10–28.

Ministère de l'industrie et du commerce extérieur (1992). *La situation de l'industrie en 1990.* Paris.

MINTZBERG, H. (1979). *The Structuring of Organizations.* Englewood Cliffs, NJ: Prentice Hall.

NOHRIA, N., and GARCIA-PONT, C. (1991). 'Global Strategic Linkages and Industry Structure', *Strategic Management Journal*, 12: 105–24.

—— and ECCLES, R. G. (eds.) (1992). *Networks and Organizations: Structure, Form and Action.* Boston: Harvard Business School Press.

OECD (1993). *Communications Outlook 1993*. Paris: OECD.

Office for the Study of Automotive Transportation, University of Michigan Transportation Research Institute and A. T. Kearney, Inc. (1996). *The 21st Century Supply Chain: The Changing Roles, Responsibilities and Relationships in the Automotive Industry*. Chicago: A. T. Kearney, Inc.

Ontario. Ministry of Economic Development, Trade and Tourism. (1994). 'CIACC: Strategic Action Plan'.

OUCHI, W. G. (1980). 'Markets, Bureaucracies, and Clans', *Administrative Science Quarterly*, 25: 129–42.

—— (1984). 'Political and Economic Teamwork: The Development of the Microelectronics Industry in Japan', *California Management Review*, 26/4: 8–33.

PALMER, M., and TUNSTALL, J. (1990). *Liberating Communications: Policy-Making in France and Britain*. Oxford: Basil Blackwell.

PERROW, C. (1992). 'Small-Firm Networks', in N. Nohria and R. G. Eccles (eds.), *Networks and Organizations: Structure, Form, and Action*. Boston: Harvard Business School Press, 445–70.

PETERS, E. (1995). 'Restructuring of Scotland's Information Technology Industries: Strategic Issues and Responses', in A. Amin and J. Temaney (eds.), *Behind the Myth of European Union: Prospects for Cohesion*. London: Routledge, 263–81.

PORTER, M. E. (1980). *Competitive Strategy: Techniques for Analyzing Industries and Competitors*. New York: Free Press.

—— (1985). *Competitive Advantage: Creating and Sustaining Superior Performance*. New York: Free Press.

—— (1990). *The Competitive Advantage of Nations*. New York: Free Press.

—— and FULLER, M. B. (1986). 'Coalitions and Global Strategy', in M. Porter (ed.), *Competition in Global Strategies*. Boston: Harvard Business School Press, 315–44.

—— and the Monitor Company (1991). *Canada at the Crossroads: The Reality of a New Competitive Government*. Ottawa: Business Council on National Issues and Government of Canada.

POWELL, W. W. (1990). 'Neither Market Nor Hierarchy', *Research in Organizational Behavior*, 12: 295–336.

PRAHALAD, C. K., and HAMEL, G. (1990). 'The Core Competence of the Corporation', *Harvard Business Review*, 90/3: 79–91.

RICHARDSON, G. B. (1972). 'The Organization of Industry', *Economic Journal*, 82: 883–96.

RING, P. S., and VAN DE VEN, A. H. (1992). 'Structuring Cooperative Relationships Between Organizations', *Strategic Management Journal*, 13/7: 483–98.

ROY, F. (1991). 'Recent Trends in the Automotive Industry', *Canadian Economic Observer* (January): 4.1–4.14.

RUGMAN, A. M. (1979). *International Diversification and the Multinational Enterprise*. Lexington: D. C. Heath.

—— (1980a). 'Internalization as a General Theory of Foreign Direct Investment: A Re-appraisal of the Literature', *Weltwirtschaftliches Archiv*, 116: 365–79.

—— (1980b). *Multinationals in Canada: Theory, Performance and Economic Impact*. Boston: Martinus Nijhoff/Kluwer.

—— (1981). *Inside the Multinationals: the Economics of Internal Markets*. New York: Columbia University Press.

—— (1986). 'New Theories of the Multinational Enterprises: An Assessment of Internalization Theory', *Bulletin of Economic Research*, 38/2: 101–18.

—— (1987). 'Multinational and Trade in Services: A Transaction Cost Approach', *Weltwirtschaftliches Archiv*, 123/4: 651–67.

—— (1991). 'Diamond in the Rough', *Business Quarterly*, 55/3: 61–4.

—— (2000). *The End of Globalization*. London: Random House Business Books.

—— (ed.) (1982). *New Theories of the Multinational Enterprise*. New York: St. Martin's Press.

—— (ed.) (1983). 'Multinational Enterprises and World Product Mandates', in A. M. Rugman (ed.), *Multinationals and Technology Transfer: The Canadian Experience*. New York: Praeger, 73–90.

—— (ed.) (1994). *Foreign Investment and NAFTA*. Columbia, SC: University of South Carolina Press.

—— and D'CRUZ, J. R. (1990). *New Visions for Canadian Business*. Toronto, ON: Kodak Canada.

—— —— (1991). *Fast Forward: Improving Canadian Competitiveness*. Toronto, ON: Kodak Canada Inc.

—— —— (1993). 'Partners across borders. Asymmetries in business networks'. Mimeo.

—— —— (1994*a*). 'Partners Across Borders: the Strategic Management of Business Networks'. Mimeo.

—— —— (1994*b*). 'A theory of business networks', in L. Eden (ed.), *Multinationals in North America*. Calgary: University of Calgary Press, 103–16.

—— —— (1996). 'Partners Across Borders: The Five Partners Business Network Model', *International Management*, 1/1: 15–26.

—— —— (1997). 'The Theory of the Flagship Firm', *European Management Journal*, 15/4: 403–12.

—— and DOUGLAS, S. (1986). 'The Strategic Management of Multinationals and World Product Mandating', in H. Etemad and L. Seguin Dulude (eds.), *Managing the Multinational Subsidiary*. London: Croom Helm, 90–101.

—— and MCILVEEN, J. (1985). *Megafirms: Strategies for Canada's Multinationals*. Toronto, ON: Methuen Publications.

—— and VERBEKE, A. (1998). 'Corporate Strategies and Environmental Regulations: An Organizing Framework', *Strategic Management Journal*, 19/4: 363–75.

—— and YEUNG, B. (1989). 'Trade in Services and Returns on Multinational Activity', *Weltwirtschaftliches Archiv*, 125/2: 386–91.

—— D'CRUZ, J. R., and VERBEKE, A. (1995). 'Internalization and Deinternalization: Will Business Networks Replace Multinationals?', in Gavin Boyd (ed.), *Competitive and Cooperative Macromanagement: The Challenge of Structural Interdependences*. Aldershot: Edward Elgar, 107–28.

—— LECRAW, D. J., and BOOTH, L. D. (1985). *International Business: Firm and Environment*. New York: McGraw Hill.

SAFARIAN, A. E. (1993). *Multinational Enterprises and Public Policy*. Aldershot: Edward Elgar.

SIMON, H. A. (1957). *Models of Man*. New York: Wiley.

—— (1961). *Administrative Behaviour* (2nd edn.). New York: Macmillan.

STALK, G., EVANS, P., and SHULMAN, L. (1992). 'Competing on capabilities: The new rules of coporate strategy', *Harvard Business Review*, 92/2 (March–April): 57–69.

Syndicat des industries de télécommunications (1993). *Dossier de presse*. Paris: SIT.

TAYLOR III, A. (1994). 'The Auto Industry Meets the New Economy', *Fortune* (5 September): 52–60.

TEECE, D. J. (1982). 'Towards an Economic Theory of the Multiproduct Firm', *Journal of Economic Behaviour and Organization*, 3 (March): 39–63.

—— (1983). 'Technological and Organizational Factors in the Theory of the Multinational Enterprise', in Mark Casson (ed.), *The Growth of International Business*. London: George Allen, 51–62.

—— (1986). 'Transactions Cost Economics and the Multinational Enterprise: An Assessment', *Journal of Economic Behaviour and Organization*, 7: 21–45.

—— (1993). 'Multinational Enterprise, Internal Governance, and Industrial Organization', *American Economic Review*, 75/2 (May): 233–7.

THORELLI, H. B. (1986). 'Networks: Between Markets and Hierarchies', *Strategic Management Journal*, 7: 37–51.

TSURUMI, Y. (1977). *Multinational Management*. Cambridge: Ballinger.

United States Council for Automotive Research. USCAR/PNGV home page (http://prn.branch.com/uscarhm.htm).

University of Windsor. Faculty of Engineering. Special Projects Office. Telephone interview.

Ward's Automotive Yearbook (1995). Southfield, MI: Ward's Communications.

Ward's Autoworld (December 1995). Entire issue.

WERNERFELT, B. (1984). 'A Resource-based View of the Firm', *Strategic Management Journal*, 5/2: 171–80.

WESTNEY, E. (1995). 'The Japanese "*Keiretsu*" in Perspective', *Perspectives*, 3/2. Toronto, Centre for International Business, University of Toronto.

WILLIAMSON, O. (1975). *Markets and Hierarchies: Analysis and Antitrust Implications*. New York: Free Press.

—— (1981). 'The Modern Corporation; Origins, Evolution, Attributes', *Journal of Economic Literature*, 19: 1537–68.

—— (1985). *The Economic Institutions of Capitalism*. New York: Free Press.

—— (1991). 'Comparative Economic Organization: The Analysis of Discrete Structural Alternatives', *Administrative Science Quarterly*, 36: 269–96.

YANARELLA, E. J., and GREEN, W. C. (1994). 'The UAW and CAW confront lean production at Saturn, CAMI, and the Japanese automobile transplants', *Labor Studies Journal* (1 January): 52.

YOUNG, S., PETERS, E., and HOOD, N. (1993). 'Performance and Employment Change in Overseas-owned Manufacturing Industry in Scotland', *Scottish Economic Bulletin*, 47: 29–38.

ZUCKERMAN, A. (1994). 'Ford, Chrysler, and GM introduce a common quality standard', *Iron Age/New Steel* (November): 22.

Index